The Doulton Burslem Wares

DESMOND EYLES

The Doulton Burslem Wares

BARRIE & JENKINS/ROYAL DOULTON
London Melbourne Sydney Auckland Johannesburg

738.3
EYL

Barrie & Jenkins Ltd

An imprint of the Hutchinson Publishing Group

3 Fitzroy Square, London W1P 6JD

Hutchinson Group (Australia) Pty Ltd
30–32 Cremorne Street, Richmond South, Victoria 3121
PO Box 151, Broadway, New South Wales 2007

Hutchinson Group (NZ) Ltd
32–34 View Road, PO Box 40-086, Glenfield, Auckland 10

Hutchinson Group (SA) (Pty) Ltd
PO Box 337, Bergvlei 2012, South Africa

First published 1980

© Royal Doulton Tableware Limited 1980

Set in Linotron Bembo by Input Typesetting Ltd, London

Printed in Great Britain by Balding & Mansell, Wisbech, Cambs
and bound by William Brendon & Son Ltd, Tiptree, Essex

ISBN 0 09 138260 2

Editorial Consultant: Jocelyn Lukins
Edited by Louise Irvine
Designed by Roger Walker

Contents

Foreword

This book, like its predecessor *The Doulton Lambeth Wares* (Hutchinson, 1975), is intended especially for the collector, the antique dealer, and the student of ceramic history. It contains much hitherto unpublished information about the many different types of pottery and porcelain made during the past hundred years at Doulton's Nile Street Pottery in Burslem, Stoke-on-Trent.

I am greatly indebted to Mr Richard J. Bailey, Managing Director of Royal Doulton Tableware Limited, for the facilities given me to study the Doulton Burslem archives. Fortunately more records have survived at Burslem than at Lambeth, the majority in fair condition and, despite certain gaps and obscurities, they have revealed important new data. One could have wished that more pattern books and other documents had been dated; it has been possible, however, to deduce many missing dates from advertisements, articles and other references in the national and trade press, and in overseas journals, as well as from records kept by former employees and by overseas companies and agents. Mr John Shorter of Sydney, Australia and Mr William J. Carey of New Jersey, U S A, have been particularly helpful in supplying information from old catalogues, invoices and other records which luckily had been preserved in their two countries but were no longer available in Burslem.

After reviewing all the material I had been able to collect over several years, I realized that if this book were to be kept within reasonable bounds of size and cost, and if publication were not to be long delayed, it would be essential to concentrate on those aspects of the Doulton Burslem Wares which were likely to be of the greatest interest to the greatest number of collectors, dealers and students. Before beginning to write it, therefore, I analysed nearly 4,000 historical enquiries received by the Doulton Company and myself during the past few years from collectors in many different countries. Certain questions were found to arise again and again, constituting probably some ninety-five per cent of the total. They concerned the background history of the Doulton enterprise – *particularly the developments in the last century and the early part of this* which led to its rise to fame – the identification of designers and artists, and of trademarks and other backstamps, pattern numbers, etc., and basic information about the many different groups of products. It is questions of these kinds that I have endeavoured to answer as fully as possible.

The early years of the Doulton Company in Lambeth, London, from 1815 to 1877, have already been described at length in *The Doulton Lambeth Wares*. Royal Doulton figures, Toby Jugs and Character Jugs have been described and catalogued in the fullest possible detail in two lavishly illustrated recent publications, *Royal Doulton Figures* by Desmond Eyles and Richard Dennis (Royal Doulton Tableware Limited, 1978) and *Royal Doulton Character and Toby Jugs* by Desmond Eyles (Royal Doulton Tableware Limited, 1979).

Considerable help has been given me, in many different ways, by past and present employees and associates of Doulton and Co. and Royal Doulton Tableware Limited; by museum authorities; by antique dealers and artists; and by the staffs of the Central City Library in Hanley, Staffordshire and the Central Library in Watford, Hertfordshire. Particular thanks are due to the following:

Commemorative Collectors Society
Huntley and Palmer
Moet and Chandon Ltd
Museum of Applied Arts and Sciences, Sydney
Sotheby Parke Bernet and Co.
Victoria and Albert Museum
Margaret Bentley
Bob Bentley
Mr and Mrs Derek Billings
Geoffrey Bridgwood
Douglas Challinor
Denis Clifford

Richard Dennis
Mr and Mrs G. Doulton
David Ehrhard
Jackie Elmer
H. Elsmore
A. John Fiskin
Arthur Foden
Max Henk
Beryl Hoad
Marie Howells
John Jenkins
Sydney Jenman
Robert Koch
W. H. Light
Isobel McGuffie
Stephen Nunn
Richard Parfitt

John Pierpoint
Ed Pry
Bill Saks
Stuart Shrimpton
Anthony Smith
Mr and Mrs Ian Smythe
Stanley Tessel
West Australian Art Gallery
Caroline Wilkinson
Ann Williams
C. Williams Wood
Mr and Mrs Charles York
Mr and Mrs David Zeitlin

I owe also a great debt to the following, now no longer with us: Cuthbert Bailey, Norman Bishell, Eric Hooper, Frank Kerry, Charles Noke, Cecil (Jack) Noke and John Shorter, Senior.

Photography by Bruton Photography, Prudence Cuming Associates and Moira Walters.

I

Royal Doulton and the Collector

Heirlooms of Tomorrow was Royal Doulton's succinct and confident advertising slogan in the 1920s, describing wares such as *rouge flambé*, figures, rack plates and Dickensware. This inspired catchphrase has proved to be a completely accurate prophecy as today all these items are prized collectors' pieces.

Perhaps the slogan was inspired by an article in *The Connoisseur Magazine* for February 1912 by J. F. Blacker, a well-known collector and author of several authoritative books on pottery and porcelain. In this he wrote: 'You may be certain that in the gems of art eagerly bought and treasured by the collector, even among the finest productions of this age, none will take higher rank than the masterly and magnificent creations of the Royal Doulton Potteries, Burslem. . . . When the twentieth century becomes historical, the Doulton ware of today will find its home in the cabinets of the museum and the collector.'

The twentieth century has not yet run its course but Blacker's prediction has long since been fulfilled. The Burslem creations, like the Doulton Lambeth salt-glaze and other art pottery which preceded them, are to be found today in museums and private collections all over the world, and the number of Doulton enthusiasts is continually growing. Even before 1912 discerning collectors had already begun to appreciate the merits and attractions of the varied Doulton ceramics as collectables; there have in fact been Doulton collectors ever since there have been Doulton wares. Professor Sir Arthur Church, FRS, the distinguished scientist and ceramist, recalled in 1900 the very first examples of decorative Doulton stoneware exhibited in Paris in 1867. 'There was,' he said, 'a decided furore on the subject among connoisseurs; every piece exhibited had been eagerly bought.' Church himself was one of the earliest collectors and often sought permission from Henry Doulton to visit the Lambeth works and watch a new batch of vases and other pieces being withdrawn from the kiln, so that he might have first choice. (Imagine the congestion if this precedent were followed today!) Other collectors last century included Queen Victoria, the Prince of Wales (later Edward VII), General Gordon, Sir Herbert Stanley, Marc Solon – himself a brilliant ceramic designer and artist for Sèvres and Minton – inventors James Nasmyth and Thomas Alva Edison, authors George Eliot, John Ruskin and Sir Edmund Gosse, artists G. F. Watts and Gustave Doré, the Liberal leader William Ewart Gladstone, and Sir Philip Cunliffe-Owen, director of what is now the Victoria and Albert Museum in South Kensington, London. Another ardent collector was Sir George Birdwood who was actively concerned with British participation in almost every important International Exhibition between 1871 and 1893. He recalled in 1885: 'I was one of the first [at the International Exhibition, London, 1871] to be attracted to the tall glass case in the art gallery in which the [Doulton] wares were shown, and was charmed by the beauty of forms they presented. . . . I at once purchased half the contents of the case, and I have ever since been extremely proud to know that I was one of the first, if not the very first, to buy a portion of the first batch of Doulton ware ever offered to the public.'

Since those early days the number of collectors of the Lambeth and Burslem productions has grown into hundreds of thousands all over the world. Ever since the important World Exhibitions held in Philadelphia, Chicago and St Louis, in 1876, 1893 and 1904, respectively, tremendous interest has been continuously evinced in the United States. There are enthusiastic collectors too in Australia, Canada, South Africa, New Zealand, and many other lands. It is also very noticeable in recent years how the number of European and Japanese collectors bidding for Doulton pottery and porcelain in London and New York salerooms has steadily increased.

One of the great attractions of the Doulton Burslem Wares for the collector is the unusually wide field of choice they offer both as regards *genre* and price, the latter ranging from a few pounds up to several hundreds per item. They include a great variety of hand-painted vases in many shapes, sizes and decorations from the simplest to the most lavish; hand-painted dinner and dessert services, as well as individual plates, signed by Dewsberry, Hancock, Raby, Curnock and other distinguished artists. Then there are the fascinating *rouge flambé*, Sung, Chang, Chinese Jade and other 'reduction' or 'transmutation glaze' wares; the lovely Titanian and crystalline glaze productions; the mysterious Holbein and Rembrandt chiaroscuro wares; the light-hearted Morrisian and the unusual Brangwyn slip-decorated wares. All of these have their own markedly distinctive characteristics and appeal.

Needless to say, the world-famous Royal Doulton figures and animal models, and the Toby and Character Jugs, offer grand opportunity for forming collections ranging from a modest few examples to many hundreds. Over 2,500 different types have been produced since 1913; of these only some 200 are in current manufacture so that all the obsolete designs provide a fascinating and profitable field for the discriminating collector. And, as it is the practice to withdraw a number of models from time to time from the current range, this means that they, too, soon become valuable collectors' items.

The flagons, jugs, vases and other unusual brown slip-decorated Kingsware items made between c.1899 and 1940 in fairly large quantities are now eminently collectable, as are the hundreds of different and highly decorative rail and rack plates and wall plaques which went out of production during the past few years, and in many cases much earlier. The many coronation and other commemorative wares – ranging from simple printed beakers to lavishly moulded and hand-painted loving cups – attract many collectors, as do the special prestige pieces and the various limited editions.

The various types of nursery ware produced at different times since the 1890s are now much sought after; likewise almost any items from the once highly popular but now discontinued Series Wares – of which one of the best known and largest group is that featuring Dickens characters, but there are many, many others. Since the manufacture of fine earthenware tablewares was discontinued in the 1960s (after the introduction of a new china body) various items from the thousands of different patterns, especially ten-inch plates for use as rack plates, jugs and other hollow-ware, supply great scope for an interesting collection. The same, of course, applies to discontinued china services.

During the past two or three decades there has been a phenomenal increase in the number of collectors specializing in advertising and publicity pottery. The many hundreds of Royal Doulton jugs, flagons, tobacco jars, ash-trays, and containers of various kinds made for distillers, brewers, tobacco manufacturers, biscuit-makers, soft drinks manufacturers and other concerns, offer unusual possibilities in this particular field.

In the following pages useful information will be found about these and other Doulton Burslem Wares. Within several of the broader groups mentioned above, it is possible for the collector to specialize in more limited areas. I know of one collector, for instance, who is building up a unique collection of examples of the work of Percy Curnock at different periods of his long career of almost seventy years with Doulton of Burslem. Another concentrates solely on items featuring hand-painted landscapes by Harry Allen, Joseph Birbeck, Charles Hopkins and other Doulton artists. One collector finds a particular interest in figures of children, another in male figures, and yet another in those depicting flower-sellers and other street-vendors. Figures representing historical characters form another specialized interest, as do the *flambé* animals, fish and birds. Much in demand are the rack and rail plates featuring heads, animals, landscapes, geometrical designs, castles, cathedrals, legendary and literary characters, and numerous other themes. Another rewarding field is the lustre wares; Doulton is perhaps not particularly associated in collectors' minds with lustre but in fact the process was used intermittently from the 1880s into the early 1930s and there is scope here for forming a somewhat unusual collection.

Embracing as they do such an astonishingly wide spectrum of entirely different ceramic *genres* (unparalleled by any other pottery manufacturer, in the opinion of many dealers and collectors), the Doulton Burslem Wares naturally appeal to an equally diverse variety of tastes and predilections. They have ranged over the years from the unashamedly and deservedly popular 'best-sellers', such as the Series Wares of earlier days, to *recherché* and unique individual signed artists' pieces, costing, even in the late 1890s and early 1900s, several hundred pounds each; from the unpretentious but often highly attractive transfer- or block-printed rack plate, to the hand-painted Edward Raby vase in all its dewy, roseate glory, the orchid-adorned and gold-embellished David Dewsberry dessert service, the seemingly diaphanous Titanian Ware painted by Harry Tittensor, Harry Nixon and other brilliant exponents of the ceramic art, or a chaste Chinese Jade offering by Charles Noke. While the taste of one collector will incline him to find his or her greatest satisfaction in non-representational ceramics, such as many of the *flambé* wares and others with reduction and crystalline glaze effects, another will enthuse over a down-to-earth Character Jug of *Sairey Gamp*, a 'dainty lady in crinolines', a realistic representation of a famous steeple-chaser or a championship dog. Taste has been defined – among many other attempted definitions – as 'a sense for what is appropriate'; but what is found inappropriate by one person is often found strikingly appropriate by another. There is a world of difference between a Raoh Schorr study of a calf or a young doe and a whimsical model of three puppies in a basket, but both have found at different times a place in the Doulton range of animals. And for a very good reason. Many now defunct potteries have paved their own rapid route to insolvency by confining their activities to too narrow a field and by taking too narrow and dogmatic a view of design.

In this connection it is interesting to recall the sage advice which Sir Henry Doulton gave to his staff in 1890. 'Manufacturers,' he said, 'may do much to lead public taste in the appreciation of good design but they must to some extent be guided by the diversity of taste that prevails and ever will prevail. There is a great deal of dogmatism on what is and what is not fine art. In art there are many mansions and we should cultivate catholicity of taste.'

Blacker, in the article already quoted from, drew attention to a most important feature of the lower-priced Doulton Burslem Wares. 'Although,' he wrote, the 'fine vases often run into large prices, the same care to turn out a really artistic article is given to the less expensive goods. In many cases – in fact generally – their best artists collaborate in these.' The same policy endures today. Notwithstanding their multifariousness, there is something indefinable yet almost palpable about the various wares that the perspicacious collector soon comes to recognize as signifying *Doulton*. It is indeed remarkable how quickly he or she develops a flair, 'a sixth sense' – call it what you will – for 'spotting', perhaps through a misted-over window, reposing on a distant shelf or in some remote corner, 'a piece of Doulton', whether it be an obsolete figure, a Dickens jug, a commemorative beaker or an artist-signed dish.

A rare, perhaps, but thrilling experience is finding an item which has appropriately been termed an 'escapee'. This is a piece which should never have 'escaped' into circulation – one of a few samples, say, of a figure or Character Jug sent out for market survey and not subsequently put into production; such samples are then supposed to be returned to the factory but on a few occasions this has not happened. Other items become relatively rare fairly quickly because, after having been on the market for some time, they do not develop sufficient sales to warrant their being retained in production and are consequently withdrawn.

Many collections of the Doulton Burslem Wares have begun in quite a small and even haphazard way. A gift of a single figure or rack plate; a legacy of a Queen Victoria Diamond Jubilee beaker from a grandmother; a vase discovered in an out-of-the-way village antique shop – these and other such happenings have kindled the collecting urge and, once kindled, it nearly always goes on and on.

However a collection may begin, it is wise to have some clear ideas as to how it might develop. Generally speaking, it will prove best to concentrate, to begin with, on one definite field or sub-division of a field. It is a great help to cultivate the acquaintance of a number of reputable and knowledgeable dealers; once they know your particular interests they will be in a position to bring pieces to your notice because of their close contacts with other dealers and with what is being offered in the salerooms in various parts of the country. One may, of course, on occasion acquire some very interesting pieces at reasonable prices entirely through one's own efforts but, on the whole, most of the choicest items and the best 'bargains' are found thanks to the efforts of a friendly dealer.

It is becoming more and more difficult in these days to build up a satisfying collection of eighteenth-century (or even early nineteenth-century) pottery and porcelain. Most of it, especially the choicest pieces, has found its way into museums or into private collections which are infrequently dispersed. The total output of Doulton's Burslem Pottery, during the past hundred years of unbroken production, must run into many millions of pieces of ware of many different *genres*. They provide much scope both for the more affluent collectors who can afford to frequent the larger salerooms and the most expensive antique shops in search of unique artist-signed pieces, and also for those of more limited means who find just as great a thrill in the discovery of a *Mark Tapley* plate or a two-handled *Cap'n Cuttle* vase to add to their collection of Dickensiana.

The person who derives most pleasure and satisfaction from his or her hobby is, generally speaking, not primarily concerned with questions of financial gain or a hedge against inflation, important though this will necessarily be for many. All experience goes to show that the collector of the Doulton Burslem Wares will find they bring not only pleasure and satisfaction but also monetary appreciation far out-weighing any inflation up to now. But when all is said and done, 'the excite-ment of the search; the thrill of an unexpected find in some unlikely place; the comparing of notes with other collectors; the correction of some previously widely-held but erroneous assumption – these are among the most rewarding "highlights" of collecting for the ardent and persevering seeker.'

II

The London Background

The Royal Doulton story, unlike that of most of the other well-known English china manufacturers, begins not in Staffordshire – nor even in one of the adjoining counties of Worcestershire, Shropshire and Derbyshire – but in London by Thames-side. It begins, too, not in the eighteenth century but in the early nineteenth. These two differences, as will become apparent as the story develops, were to prove vitally important not only for the Doulton enterprise itself but indirectly for the English ceramic industry as a whole, the greater part of which by 1877, the year of Doulton's arrival in Burslem, was to an unhealthy extent resting on the laurels of its eighteenth-century attainments and was in danger of being enmeshed in memories of past glories.

In 1815 John Doulton invested his life savings of £100 in a small riverside pottery in Lambeth, South London. This pottery, one of many in the area, produced a range of utilitarian salt-glazed stoneware. Aided by Doulton's several years' experience as a thrower at the Fulham Pottery, and his hard work, the pottery thrived and he became a partner.

By 1826 the company was trading as Doulton & Watts, and was already becoming one of the more important potteries in the area. A few years later, Doulton's son Henry joined the company as an apprentice, putting aside any suggestions for other careers. Dedication and personal ambition drove Henry Doulton to acquire quickly a full knowledge of all aspects of the pottery trade, from preparing the clay to selling the wares, and so he was soon able to play a leading role in the running of the pottery. Under his guidance it expanded rapidly, swallowing in the process some of its less efficient neighbours. Henry then began to turn his eyes in other directions. By the late 1830s architectural terracotta and garden ornaments were added to the range, but more significant was Henry's interest in sanitation.

As an intelligent and ambitious Victorian entrepreneur, Henry was probably without equal. It did not take long to appreciate the likely impact of the sanitary revolution that was about to hit London and the new industrial cities.

7

The Lambeth Pottery, as Doulton & Watts was now called, began therefore to turn its attention to the large-scale production of stoneware drainpipes, conduits and related wares. This development was well-timed, and Doulton products were soon disappearing in vast quantities beneath the streets of London and other cities. That many of these sewer and surface-water pipes are still in use today is a fitting tribute to the quality of the Doulton product.

The Lambeth Pottery, and the Doulton family, benefited greatly from Henry's foresight, and it is important to remember that upon the firm foundation of these vital but unromantic objects was built Doulton's future reputation. Without the drains there would have been no Lambeth studio, no Doulton figures, Character Jugs, tableware; indeed, probably no Burslem factory and no Doulton story to tell.

One of the direct results of Doulton's involvement in the sanitary revolution was that the name and reputation of Doulton was spread far and wide. International Exhibition displays increased this still further and the company inevitably began to attract attention outside the ceramic industry.

One area of particular relevance was among the newly-formed art schools which were issuing annually quantities of trained designers keen to gain industrial experience. After a lengthy battle, John Sparkes, the Principal of the Lambeth School of Art, was finally able to persuade an unwilling Henry Doulton to give employment to a few of his students on an experimental basis. Limited to standard clays, glazes and kilns, and buried away in a corner of the factory, the first students produced their rather tentative efforts during the late 1860s, with design and decoration based on well-established historical styles. These early studio wares were enthusiastically received at the Paris Exhibition of 1867 and the International Exhibition in London of 1871.

The most impressive display, however, was sent to the Philadelphia Exhibition, in 1876, an event which marked the beginning of a close and rewarding friendship between the Doulton firm and the North American continent, which still endures.

Henry Doulton, whose success was based on his flexibility and his ability to seize opportunities that offered themselves, immediately gave the Lambeth studio his full support and encouraged it to develop in a dramatic way. By the 1880s this studio was employing over 290 men and girls. Co-operation between art and industry on so great a scale had never been seen before in England and, indeed, has never occurred since. The contemporary press was very enthusiastic; for example, in June 1885 *The Architect* stated: 'One of the artistic developments of the times – little short, indeed, of a revolution – is certainly the one which owes much to the enterprises of Messrs. Doulton & Co.' At first, the quality of the studio products varied greatly, and some eminent critics had understandable reservations. On 4 June 1878 Sir Henry Cole, the Director of the South Kensington Museum, wrote in his diary: 'Drove to Lambeth and went to his [Doulton's] works. Very large. He seems struggling into a sort of untrained style, chiefly done by girls. Every piece passes through 3 or more hands who do what they like. No modelling except a little ornament. One turns and bends. Another scratches ornament, a third paints it according to fancy. There was one Man an untrained genius who could model.'

Fortunately Henry Doulton was not a man (to quote Samuel Johnson) to be 'blown about by every wind of criticism'. By the time of Cole's visit the artists at the Lambeth studios already included Arthur, Florence and Hannah Barlow, John Broad, Frank Butler, Arthur Pearce, George Tinworth and several others destined to win many international awards for their work. It is interesting to recall also that, in that same year, John Ruskin – after viewing the exhibits intended for Philadelphia – 'expressed himself warmly as to the merit of the work', and the *New York Times* wrote: 'The collection of Doulton pottery, about which the critics are wild, is indeed rarely beautiful.' Henry Doulton himself took the sensible attitude: 'One thing that this exhibition has taught me is that *in art criticism there are many mansions*, for equally good judges and authorities had very different opinions as to which were the most excellent specimens.'

However, the real significance of the studio was not only in its products but in its effects on the ceramic industry as a whole. The Lambeth experience encouraged potters, great and small, throughout Britain, to start art departments, and so ultimately brought about the rapprochement between art and industry that Henry Cole and others had dreamt about in the 1840s and 1850s. This new philosophy did much to enhance the prestige of British ceramics abroad, helping Doulton and other great manufacturers of the period, Minton, Copeland, George Jones, etc., to achieve a position of world dominance, the long-term effects of which are the basis for the continued stability of the British ceramic industry today.

The Lambeth studios flourished and encouraged Henry Doulton to cast his eyes and his ambitions further afield. Having already established factories making sanitary, industrial and architectural products in Rowley Regis, St Helens and Smethwick, Henry turned his attention towards North Staffordshire, the traditional home of the English ceramic industry.

III

The Nile Street Pottery

The year 1877 saw the beginning of an important new chapter in the Doulton story. For it was towards the end of that year that Henry Doulton, having seen the Lambeth Art Pottery firmly established, acquired an interest in a medium-sized, medium-grade earthenware factory in Nile Street, Burslem, in the heart of the North Staffordshire Potteries. Before describing this new venture – which was regarded at first with a certain degree of quiet amusement, if not downright scorn, by some of the long-established Staffordshire potters, and even with some scepticism by his own staff in London – let us look briefly at the environment in which it was to develop.

Speed's list of Staffordshire manufacturers in 1625, rather surprisingly, does not mention pottery at all. There had, it is true, been potters in and around Burslem since Roman times, and even earlier, but probably not on a greater scale than in many other parts of the country. Today, on the other hand, the very term 'The Potteries' denotes for buyers of china all over the world a densely concentrated area in North Staffordshire covering some forty square miles, with approaching one-third of a million inhabitants of whom a large proportion still depend for their livelihood on pottery-making and ancillary industries supplying ovens, machinery, colour pigments, lithographs, silk-screen transfers and other essential materials. Is there anywhere else in the world, one wonders, where a district is universally as well known by the name of its main product as by its geographical designation?

In 1616 Thomas Daniel, an 'earth potter', was granted a licence to dig clay at The Hill, Burslem and also on the Withymoor. This record is followed by others of a similar nature in the seventeenth century. Many of the early pot-houses of this time seem to have been basically crofts with one or two small ovens, often only six feet in diameter and eight feet high, adjoining the farmer's cottage. They were to be found where there were beds of suitably plastic clay for making pots; and these beds often lay over easily accessible coal seams which, later on, when wood became scarce, provided fuel for firing the ovens. As pottery-making became more

10

generally established in the area, corn-mills were sometimes converted to water-mills for grinding the raw materials.

Up to the time of the Industrial Revolution there was little reason for potters to congregate in one particular district – except in London where the metropolis with its advantages was a natural magnet. Many small towns and villages had at least one resident potter and there were also itinerant potters who came and went at certain times of the year.

The question is often asked, 'How and why did potting come eventually to be concentrated to such an astonishing extent in and around Burslem and Stoke?' It would seem that several disparate factors may have contributed to this outcome. First there was the presence of satisfactory clays for making red and drab coloured butter pots, slipware chargers, posset-pots and other coarse earthenware products with trailed-on decoration in a lighter colour. Then there were the abundant coal deposits which enabled Staffordshire potters to increase output when this was falling in many other places because of a shortage of wood. Another factor which played a part was the discovery, attributed to the Dutch brothers, David and John Philip Elers, that certain local haematite clays were excellent for making particularly fine red-ware teapots in imitation of the imported Yi-hsing wares from China, so popular with the devotees of the new-fangled fashion of tea-drinking. A certain earlier impetus may have been given too by the Dissolution of the Monasteries which led to monk-potters from Hulton Abbey in Burslem becoming laymen-potters to earn a living. Within easy reach in Derbyshire and Cheshire were deposits of lead ore for one kind of glazing and of salt for another, and with the growing use of steam power and machinery the proximity of the area to Midland foundries and engineering works became advantageous. Also of great importance in the late eighteenth and the nineteenth centuries was easy access to the network of canal waterways which began to be created in the 1760s, leading to a great increase in both inland and export trade; the influence of the canals – in the introduction of which Josiah Wedgwood played a leading part – is still reflected today in local place-names such as Longport, Westport, Middleport and Porthill.

In addition to these factors there was the human element itself – the independent and sometimes stubborn streak in many of the local enfranchised copyhold farmers, used to facing and overcoming difficulties and well fitted to deal with such a refractory medium as clay. And from this native stock were engendered gifted sons to carry on the traditions of their forefathers – men such as John and Thomas Astbury, Thomas Whieldon, Ralph and Thomas Toft, John Turner, Joshua Twyford, Josiah Wedgwood, Josiah Spode, Thomas and Herbert Minton. It is not without significance perhaps that some names have even acquired a kind of dynastic ring; we hear for example of Ralph Wood I, II and III, Josiah Wedgwood I and II; Josiah Spode I, II and III. Bearing in mind the accomplishments and reputations of these and other illustrious Staffordshire potters, it is perhaps not so surprising really that many 'in the trade' were inclined to regard Henry Doulton, despite the exciting happenings in the last few years at Lambeth, as a misguided man for venturing – as an entire newcomer (some even said 'interloper') without any family or local connections – into the stronghold of fine china and fine earthenware production.

Pinder, Bourne & Company

Among the many potteries in Burslem in 1877 was one in Nile Street, near the centre of the town, known as Pinder, Bourne & Company. There had been a pottery on or near the site since the early eighteenth century. During the nineteenth century it had gone through various vicissitudes and changes of ownership before Henry Doulton arrived on the scene and established a firm continuity which has endured to this day. The early history of the works is not too clear but it would seem from old directories and Parish Registers that between about 1802 and 1814 the Nile Street Pottery was being worked by John & Richard Riley who later moved to the Hill Works, also in Burslem, before these were taken over by Samuel Alcock & Co. The Rileys were succeeded at Nile Street by John Cormie, an earthenware potter who in 1827 was Chief Constable of Burslem. Cormie went bankrupt in 1840 and the pottery was taken over by Mellor, Venables & Co. who also had the Hole House Pottery in Burslem and whose printed tablewares were exported to the United States. Cormie's nephew, one Thomas Pinder, who directed the Swan Bank Works, Burslem, for a short period round the mid century, next appears on the scene and from c.1860 to 1862 the pottery was in the hands of a partnership, Pinder, Bourne & Hope. This firm also occupied part of the former Enoch Wood factory at Fountain Place, Burslem, and had acquired some of the Wood moulds from which it continued to produce figures and Toby Jugs. In 1862 the name changed to Pinder, Bourne & Co., and in 1877 a Mr Thomas Shadford Pinder, a great-nephew of the earlier Thomas, was the sole proprietor.

Pinder had managed, despite recurrent financial crises, to build up a trade in medium-class earthenware tablewares – some plain cream, some decorated either with underglaze monochrome landscape and other prints from engraved copper plates (orange, blue and sepia being favourite colours) or with printed outlines of a variety of subjects filled in by hand-painting – a process familiarly known as 'print and tint'. Other Pinder, Bourne products included terracotta and earthenware vases, jugs, bowls and jardinières, many painted with randomly dispersed Japanese sprays, colourful birds, flowers, butterflies and shells against gilded grounds. Greek and Egyptian mythological themes were also featured in which a deep orange colour against a ruby-red background often predominates; some of these bear the signature of W. Gedge, who was associated with a patent granted in 1874 for imitation 'faïence Parisienne'.

Pinder, Bourne also made tea-ware with blue, sepia and olive-green prints and gold finish; cobalt blue vases painted with cupids and flowers and finished with gold stippling; claret cups, jet ware, terracotta garden bases, toilet ware, sanitary ware and telegraph insulators. For a time they continued to produce figures and jugs from the Wood moulds taken over from the previous incumbents. A perusal of a surviving pattern-book reveals an astonishing medley of styles and influences – Japanese, Chinese, Indian, Egyptian, Greek, Gothic, Renaissance, Jacobean, neo-classical – a microcosm indeed of the ceramics of the mid-Victorian era. As W. B. Honey wrote in *English Pottery and Porcelain*, from the mid nineteenth century 'the English potter was caught up by wave after wave of fashion, reacting all too easily and never creating a sincere or original style of his own'. The ceramic designers and artists had gathered around them a multitude of ornamental treasures but this abundance had imprisoned their own original ideas and creative vitality. A new impulse was badly needed.

The Nile Street Pottery in 1877 had 160 employees and eight typical Staffordshire bottle-ovens. It was well-nigh surrounded by public-houses, all of which have long since disappeared, some being absorbed by factory extensions. The Hand and Trumpet, The Quiet Woman, The British Flag, The British Lion, and The British Queen were well patronized by the potters, particularly by those involved in firing and drawing the kilns. It would seem that some child labour was still in use for an old Pinder, Bourne notice discovered during rebuilding in 1948 intimated that *part-time child workers under the age of eight must not work more than ten hours a day on alternate days*! The starting wage for a would-be artist was two shillings (10p) a week as an apprentice. The normal hours were from seven in the morning until six in the evening and wages were not paid earlier than four o'clock on Saturday afternoon. Apprenticeships, usually for seven years, were legally drawn up and the wages for apprentices were gradually increased by small amounts. A course of evening instructions in the Burslem School of Art was usually paid for by the firm. To us today the conditions seem very unenticing but none the less the latter part of the last century, when they largely still prevailed, saw the rise of a wonderful galaxy of designers, artists, modellers and engravers of outstanding ability.

One of the Pinder, Bourne artists in the early 1860s was John Lockwood Kipling, father of the famous writer. He had been one of the first National Scholars at the South Kensington Art School (of which John Sparkes later became Principal) and was employed on some of the designs for the new South Kensington Museum (now the Victoria and Albert) for which work he earned an extra pound a week in addition to his scholarship allowance. Robert Allen, a later Doulton artist, remembered Rudyard (named after the village of that name a few miles from Burslem) being taken to visit the factory.

The new partnership

Thomas Shadford Pinder was an extremely ambitious man, but unfortunately lacked the flair as well as the financial resources to fulfill his great desire – which was to lift his medium-class products into what he called 'the region of higher ceramics', of the kind associated with such famous names as Wedgwood, Derby, Worcester, Minton and Spode. By 1877 his efforts in this direction, though very praiseworthy, had brought him to the verge of bankruptcy. Impressed by the remarkable success Henry Doulton had achieved in the space of a few years, with his new Lambeth Art Pottery, he decided to approach him with the proposition that he should put some money into the Burslem Pottery and help with his knowledge and enterprise to improve its standing.

Fired with enthusiasm by the phenomenal outcome of his recent Lambeth activities and knowing that the work there was now established on a sound basis, Doulton was not averse to the idea of extending his interest in ceramics into this challenging field of fine earthenware. And so, in December 1877, a new partnership was formed to take over the business from January 1878. Henry Doulton invested £8,618, his brother James £4,324, and Pinder's share was entered as £4,324. It was agreed that the firm would continue to trade for the present under its old name and that Pinder, the man on the spot, should continue to manage it. Henry Doulton would provide technical and artistic assistance from Lambeth, visit the factory at regular intervals, and help with further finance if justified.

For the first few months of 1878 the Doulton incursion seems to have caused little stir. Its significance can hardly have been realized by the correspondent of the *Staffordshire Advertiser* who, on 23 March 1878, reported on Doulton's latest success at the Paris Exhibition in these words: 'Doulton Ware is certain to become a lasting name in ceramic annals, and if you in Staffordshire do not bestir yourselves, Lambeth will in truth become *The Potteries* and you will have to choose a subordinate designation!' The editor perhaps had qualms about printing such an outspokenly critical comment and added in parenthesis: 'The which we do not believe!' At that time to question the supremacy of Staffordshire must have seemed well-nigh blasphemy to those of whom Henry Doulton once jokingly remarked: 'In their view we Londoners know very little about God and nothing at all about potting!'

Within the next year or so, however, the Doulton 'invasion', as some called it, had become common knowledge. There were also rumours that things were not going well at Nile Street and that 'the Big Lambeth Potter' (as William de Morgan called him) had 'bitten off more than he could chew'. Rumour for once was right. Doulton had put more money into the venture but it was not producing the hoped-for results. The rate of progress and the quality of production were disappointing, despite the engagement of nearly a hundred new workpeople and the erection of additional kilns and workshops. Serious differences had arisen between Pinder and the Doultons. A brochure published in 1892 recalled the situation in these words:

[The Doultons] had not long taken possession of their new purchase when the numerous difficulties and equally important opportunities to be encountered began to dawn upon

14

them. In the first place they found reason to be greatly disappointed with the material they found at Burslem, so far inferior was it in every possible way to that at the disposal of such eminent firms as Minton, Wedgwood and Copeland, with whom they now found themselves in direct competition. So that during the first two or three years the progress was so disappointing that at the end of the year 1880 a general reorganization was found absolutely necessary. From this time, when the number of hands employed was less than 300 and the class of goods produced consisted chiefly of ordinary earthenware, the progress made was phenomenal.

The threat of failure in his new enterprise, far more than the possible loss of his investment, was the spur needed to make Henry Doulton throw himself whole-heartedly – no longer just a once-a-week visitor – into the task of putting the Nile Street Pottery on a better footing, with a more promising future. He spent the greater part of six months at Burslem, personally investigating every aspect of production and marketing. The more he saw of the way Pinder had been running things the less he liked it. Difficulties between them reached such a stage that they agreed that the matter should be taken to arbitration: the outcome was that Pinder accepted a settlement and retired from the business, the name of which was changed in 1882 to Doulton & Company, Burslem.

Henry Doulton told his grandson Eric Hooper (who later became Chairman of Doulton & Co. Limited) that his advent in Burslem had led to some rather sarcastic comments in the hotels, clubs and taverns where local pottery owners and managers were wont to foregather. 'That stoneware fellow from London who thinks he can teach us to make pots' was one of the milder comments. There was some ribald comment too on the fact that when he visited the painting rooms, where some women were now employed, he invariably doffed his hat – a gesture which confirmed the notion (strengthened by his velvet coat) that he was 'a bit of a fop' and quite out of his depth in down-to-earth Staffordshire. The suggestion that he could repeat there the kind of success he had achieved in Lambeth struck most of his new competitors as highly unlikely.

The aura of the great achievements of the second half of the previous century still hung over The Potteries, giving rise to a certain complacency. In Burslem and the surrounding towns there dwelt a population with, it seemed, an inherited aptitude for pottery-making, the skill which seems almost to be inborn when for generations a community has pursued a specialized craft in a certain measure of isolation. This isolation, by the second half of the nineteenth century – especially the isolation from the cultural and artistic influences of the metropolis and the Continent – had begun to have its dangers as well as its advantages, and many of the wares shown at the Great Exhibition in 1851 and at other exhibitions during the next two decades revealed a great falling-off in standards.

William Owen, writing in 1910 of this period, said: 'The mid-Victorian times were distinguished not merely by a neglect of beauty but by a positive cult of what was ugly. The utilitarianism of the period seemed to preclude not only the endeavours, but the hope, of reconciling use and beauty. . . . And in no art was this poverty of the artistic sense more profound than in that of pottery.' The Great Exhibition was, wrote Gordon Forsyth in *Twentieth Century Ceramics*, 'a colossal Chamber of Horrors, an exhibition of misapplied art'. All the old styles were copied, often quite unimaginatively, including weird mixtures of styles. As long as the cry for 'ornament and more ornament' was met, all was felt to be well. A writer in the *Pottery Gazette* for February 1883 expressed one of the problems thus: 'We are unsettled. We cannot quite make up our minds whether we will found our style on Greek or Gothic, Renaissance or Roman, Japanese or Jacobean, or even on "Queen Anne". '

This uncertainty and this medley of styles is clearly reflected in many of Pinder, Bourne's products. It is also seen in many of the early Doulton Burslem Wares. The most successful of the Pinder, Bourne patterns were continued, with or without modification, under the new Doulton trade-mark for several years, a few into the early twentieth century, for as Henry Doulton remarked in one of his lectures: 'Of course public taste cannot altogether be disregarded; and if a master is to provide for the dependent army of workers the demand must to some extent regulate the supply. Although the intelligent and enterprising manufacturer will always endeavour to lead the public taste, certainly if he leaves it at too great a distance it is at a great cost.'

The evolution of a distinct Doulton school of artists was to take several years. The first step was to gather together, as at Lambeth, a group of genuinely gifted creative designers and to encourage them by every possible means to express freely their individual talents, unhindered by any narrow dogmatic assertions as to what constitutes 'good art' or by the petrified traditions handed down from the past.

IV

Doulton of Burslem

During his investigations at Nile Street, Henry Doulton, a shrewd judge of character and talent, had come to the conclusion that Pinder, Bourne's young decorating manager, John Slater, given the right encouragement and opportunities – such as visits abroad to widen his horizons, and, most important, a team of talented artists to support him – could prove to be the right man for the task of transforming the artistic side of the enterprise. Slater came of an old stock of ceramic artists. His grandfather, William Slater, had been apprenticed to painting and gilding at Pinxton and Derby, later working in Randall and Robins' enamelling studio at Spa Fields in London, where he decorated much English china for the London dealers before returning to Derby as decorating manager. John's father, Joseph (William's second son) was at different times designer, gilder and armorial crest painter at Derby, Alcock's Hill Pottery in Burslem and Minton's in Stoke. He then became head of the majolica section of Brown, Westhead, Moore and Co. at Cauldon Place, Hanley.

John's brother, Albert, had been a flower painter at Minton's and then designer and manager of Pinder, Bourne's Art Department; when he left in 1867 or thereabouts to go to Minton, Hollins & Co. of Stoke, the famous tile firm, John succeeded him. John had previously studied at the Stoke-on-Trent School of Design under Silas Price from whom he always said he had 'derived inestimable benefit'; while there he had won the first prize for two years running at the Hanley Exhibition for students. Before joining Pinder, Bourne he had served an apprenticeship at Minton's under their distinguished French Art Director, Léon Arnoux. In 1871 he gained the first of many exhibition honours, an Honourable Mention at the London International Exhibition.

The really pressing need at Nile Street, Henry Doulton soon realized, was for a competent General Manager who would be able to act wisely on his own initiative, who could be entrusted with a considerable measure of authority without it going to his head, and who could be relied upon to act upon Doulton's dictum to Slater:

'Forget, for heaven's sake, most of what was done here in the past. We are going to make a new beginning and I intend, come what may, to bring the products here up to the standards we have set ourselves at Lambeth.'

John Cuthbert Bailey

The astonishing news that a young man of twenty-three, John Cuthbert Bailey, was to become General Manager of the Nile Street Pottery caused a great deal of comment in The Potteries, where it was felt that a much older and more experienced man was needed for such a responsible position. The local wiseacres were now more than ever convinced that it was only a matter of time before Doulton would have to abandon the whole Burslem venture.

Bailey, at the age of fourteen, had worked for a short while at Henry Meir's pottery at Greengates, Tunstall. He then served an apprenticeship with Bates, Elliott & Co. of the Dale Hall Pottery, Burslem, whose successors, Bates, Walker & Co. he represented in London before joining Pinder, Bourne in a similar capacity. Referring at his retirement nearly fifty years later to Henry Doulton's quite staggering choice, Bailey said: 'Mr Doulton purchased the works out of bankruptcy; they simply had to make progress. He had extraordinary courage and enthusiasm, and had a unique power of inspiring others with some of this enthusiasm. The best evidence of his courage is the fact that he put a young man of twenty-three as manager over a works that had been a financial failure.' This confirms what Gosse tells us in his biography: '[Doulton's] boldness in choosing out for responsible positions young men, of whose capacity and character he had satisfied himself, was remarkable. To such a man, if he gave his confidence at all he gave it fully. He made no suspicious reserves. His managers, if once he put his trust in them, were absolutely certain of his support. "Whatever you do on the Works," he used to say, "I shall support you in public, no matter what words we may have about it in private." '

Bailey recalled in 1929 some of the advice Henry Doulton had given him. 'There are three things,' he said, 'that go to make a success of a firm. These are – first, quality of output; secondly, prompt execution of orders; and thirdly, price. And always in that order. You can get a good price for a fine thing more easily than you can get a poor price for a bad thing. Besides, the one does you good, the other does you a lot of harm.'

One of the first things Bailey set out to do was to reduce the fantastic variety of products, many quite unprofitable, which Pinder, Bourne had been trying to keep going in what was after all a comparatively small factory. Slater and Bailey formed an admirable team. They both proved to be men who could appreciate Henry Doulton's aims and put them into effect. It was well said of Bailey at the time of his retirement that he 'typified essentially the evolution of the pottery industry from the restricted craftsmanship and conservative business methods of Victorian times to the scientific means of production and highly developed business organisation of the twentieth century'. Slater had the faculty of selecting and training young artists and encouraging them to develop their own particular gifts, however different these might be from his own. He was the ideal man to help Doulton to follow out in Burslem the policy, already proved so fruitful at Lambeth, of drawing upon the best native British talent available, both locally and further afield. Speaking in 1889 of art education, Sir Henry (as he had then become) remarked that he had never so far found it necessary to import talent from abroad. 'The nation,' he said, 'only needed to develop a proper system of art education to encourage artists and designers in abundance.'

Slater was able to attract not only several of the most promising young artists and craftsmen from the local Schools of Art and Design; he found that when the changes being made under the new management were voiced abroad, gifted designers, artists, modellers and engravers, with years of experience at old-established potteries in Staffordshire and adjoining counties were interested to participate in the new venture. They could see, as one of them afterwards put it, that 'Henry Doulton was determined to make a go of it'. They realized too the encouragement given to the Lambeth artists to develop their creativity, and this was a great inducement to any artist who might feel that his abilities were not being given enough scope by a less progressive management. Thus, within a few years, there was gathered together one of the most distinguished staffs that any earthenware pottery in the country could boast.

By encouraging his design staff to express freely their own individual ideas and talents, Slater was able to avoid keeping solely to traditional pottery. Tradition, however, was by no means ignored. Indeed, one of Slater's own earliest personal successes, while he still had only an earthenware body at his disposal, was a revival of the centuries-old Near Eastern and Hispano-Moresque technique of lustre-painting. Here his study of chemistry as well as of art enabled him to develop the beautiful iridescent effects which characterized the earlier wares while exploiting them in an original style. Slater also developed an unusual new style of decoration to which the name 'Spanish' was given. A feature of this was exceedingly-fine raised gold outline traceries of flowers, leaves, arabesques and other motifs, combined with on-glaze enamel painting and raised paste, often on a vellum or ivory ground. Some of the vases and ewers in this style have gilded dragon handles or embossed and moulded dragons crawling up the sides. This style, regarded as a novel Doulton 'speciality' had a great vogue in the 1890s and early 1900s, keeping several departments busy for a long time and doing much to add to Doulton's fame overseas. Much of it is over-elaborate for present-day tastes. In years to come Slater was to win numerous awards for his work at exhibitions in Paris, Brussels, Chicago, St Louis, Turin, Ghent, Milan, Sydney and other places.

Slater, besides being an artist, was an inventor. As early as 1883 he had been experimenting with a photographic process to transfer designs to pottery, and in 1889 he took out a patent for 'Improvements in Decorating China and the like by means of which paintings and designs are reproduced on a photographic plate to obtain a negative, and from the negative a gelatine printing surface produced, from which the design can then be printed on a transfer paper in any of the colours commonly employed for china painting'. Further patents for improvements on this method were taken out in 1894 and 1896. It was used particularly as an alternative to engraving for transferring faint outlines of designs which were then gone over in fine raised gold traceries or filled in by hand-painting, and also for reproducing photographs for transfer to commemorative wares and rack plates.

Another Slater patent was for a process he began to develop about 1884, in which fine lace, linen and other fabrics were used to form background patterns on clay for subsequent decoration with ceramic pigments and often gilding. This process was used not only at Burslem but, on a much bigger scale, at Lambeth for the so-called *chiné* and *chiné-gilt* decorations. Slater did a great deal of research also on parian-type bodies, vellum grounds, shaded grounds, on *Rose du Barry*, turquoise and topaz groundlays, and reduction glazes.

It is not generally known that, between c.1885 and the early 1900s, Doulton of Burslem made stained glass. A special kiln for firing this was still in existence recently as well as an interesting stained glass window, on the staircase of the Nile Street offices. At Slater's former residence at Rock Cottage, Brown Edge, looking out over the Derbyshire hills, are several other windows which he designed. In a publication entitled *A Descriptive Account of the Potteries* printed in 1893, it is stated that Doulton could supply stained glass 'suitable to any situation or class of architecture', and I am told by a former employee now in his eighties that many churches, chapels, public buildings and houses in the Midlands still have examples of this glass. Some may be identified as Doulton by the symbol of the four interlaced Ds which form part of the usual Doulton trade-mark.

'One thing at a time'

Up to 1884 only earthenware was made at Nile Street and, helped by the artistic and technical experience available in Lambeth – particularly in decorating the faïence, impasto and silicon wares – a superior range of products began to make some impact. Esther and Florence Lewis, Ada Dennis (later Mrs Gandy), Linnie Watt, Walter Gandy and Arthur Pearce were among the Lambeth artists who collaborated with Slater from time to time in producing new designs. The limited range of colours available for underglaze decoration on earthenware precluded any attempt to rival the more striking effects that could be obtained with the on-glaze enamel painting of the English and Continental china factories. However finely potted, however good the shapes and decorations, an output restricted to earthenware was no longer enough if one wished to build up a reputation to equal that of Minton, Spode and Derby: even Wedgwood, after an unsuccessful attempt in 1812, had had to re-introduce bone china in 1878.

Slater and Bailey both hankered after a bone china body to show what could be accomplished in that medium by the new group of artists they had assembled. They made several attempts to persuade Henry Doulton to agree to build a china-works – which it was estimated would cost some £25,000 (a goodly sum in those days) but which they promised would be the most up-to-date in Staffordshire. Doulton, however, faithful as ever to his policy of 'one thing at a time' refused to hear of such a thing until fully satisfied that the fine earthenware production was on a firm foundation. Between 1877 and 1880 the number of workers at Nile Street had already increased from 160 to 300; during the next four years it rose to over 500. The insulator and sanitaryware sections were doing well, but the decorated earthenware had hardly begun to pay its way; in fact, between 1877 and 1880 the loss written off for the Burslem works was £21,029. Between 1881 and 1884 the result of the four years' trading was 5 per cent on the capital invested and nothing more. At the Lambeth headquarters, Bailey and Slater were looked on as something of a danger to the whole Doulton concern, and one of the managers there scathingly described the Nile Street venture as 'a bung hole without a barrel'. Fortunately Henry Doulton himself was not too discouraged; 'it needs time' he would say. Meanwhile strenuous efforts were being made to build up an export trade. The Burslem products were exhibited in Paris, Calcutta, Sydney and Melbourne between 1878 and 1884; representatives were sent on regular journeys to the Continent, Australia, India and the United States of America.

Bailey and Slater persisted in their efforts to persuade Doulton to sanction the making of bone china, without which their travellers were having to turn down valuable overseas business. He agreed eventually to their buying in some undecorated china from another Burslem pottery, Bodley & Son, to be specially painted by Doulton artists for his inspection. He stipulated, however, that none of this was to be sold under Doulton's name, and he reminded them that Josiah Wedgwood III's brief dalliance with bone china, between 1811 and 1815, had been a failure.

A visit to France

A galling problem arose for Bailey and Slater when Doulton's principal overseas traveller, Sam Mawdsley, returned from the United States with a valuable order for new tableware designs by Fred Hancock – one of Slater's most gifted artists – provided they could be supplied on a translucent body instead of on earthenware.

It happened that, shortly before this, Slater had been sent to France by Henry Doulton to study the ceramics in the famous collection there, and to visit the Sèvres, Haviland and other china factories. 'You must not grow so practical,'

Doulton said, 'as to forget the theoretical. The moment a man ceases to be a student, he begins to be rusty as a teacher. Go to France and see for yourself what it is they have which we have not in Staffordshire.' (One wonders if Slater was tempted to say he already knew very well what they did not have in Nile Street – namely china!)

During this visit, as Slater afterwards recounted to his friend, John Shorter, Doulton's Australian agent, he met many French artists, ceramic and otherwise, and one night was invited to a party which went on into the small hours, and at which the wine and cognac flowed abundantly. He awoke the next afternoon in a hut on the outskirts of Barbizon, in the Forest of Fontainebleau, having, as he confessed, 'no recollection whatever' of why he was there. What had happened was that a French ceramic painter, Georges Léonce, noted especially for his life-like bird studies, had taken him to his studio and looked after him until the effects of the heady French wines, to which he was unaccustomed, had worn off.

A discussion arose between the two artists as to whether or not Léonce could produce on English bone china the same brilliant colours and delicate nuances as on hard-paste feldspathic French porcelain. The outcome was a wager. When Slater returned to Burslem, he was to send over an undecorated glazed bone china dessert set, made by Bodley, and if Léonce could equal on it his painting on porcelain, Slater would pay him £50 for his work. Léonce's results were in fact superb. Slater's only criticism was that Léonce had not signed a single piece. Back came the the terse reply: 'They are signed all over. There is no man can paint birds like Léonce.' This unique dessert service, or part of it, eventually found its way to Australia and some pieces from it are now in the Museum of Arts and Sciences in Sydney. (At a later date, when Doulton had begun to make bone china, Slater reproduced Léonce's birds on other services by a combination of his photographic transfer method and hand-painting. These items are now exceedingly rare.)

When Slater returned to Burslem there was still the question of the potential American order to settle. Slater, no doubt under the influence of his recent visit to France, decided to obtain a supply of glazed white porcelain from Limoges. Samples were then painted by Hancock to be sent to America for approval; if approved they could then be shown to Henry Doulton to see if he would sanction the use of further Limoges porcelain which Slater preferred to the Bodley china.

By some mischance the Doulton trade-mark was printed on these samples and, to make matters worse, the day they were to be packed, Henry Doulton arrived from London and decided to go on a 'grand tour' of the factory, ending up in the warehouse. With his uncanny flair for finding weak spots he noticed the samples and saw at once by their somewhat greyish tinge that they were not bone china. On turning over a saucer he was horrified to see the Doulton Burslem trade-mark. 'And where did this come from?' he demanded.

Slater recalled many years later that it was a wet and stormy day and, as the works were rather scattered, Henry Doulton was carrying a large umbrella. When he heard the ware came from Limoges he would listen to no excuse that it was intended to tell him all about it later; he went into a fury such as nobody at Burslem would ever have thought him capable of – for ordinarily he had remarkable control over his feelings. The storm raged inside as well as out, as he brought his umbrella down again and again on the samples, smashing some to smithereens. (Slater rescued a few packed pieces which he kept for years in his private collection. He much later presented some to John Shorter who in turn presented them to the Sydney Museum.)

The unfortunate Mawdsley, who was least to blame, was called in and dismissed on the spot; Bailey and Slater were suspended and told they would hear more. Doulton then called for his hansom which had been waiting for some time, and when he arrived at Stoke station he found the train to London had already left so that he had to stay the night at the North Stafford Hotel. The following morning, to everyone's amazement – not to say consternation – he was back at Nile Street. Bailey and Slater had good reason to fear that this meant the end of the Burslem venture or that, at best, the whole place would be turned over to making only the more profitable sanitaryware and insulators. 'Good-morning, Bailey; good morn- ing, Slater,' said Doulton. 'Will you be so kind as to send for our architect. I have decided to build a china-works.'

In the midst of his rage he had still taken in the superiority of Hancock's artistry on a translucent porcelain body; he had already far more money than he would ever need; he could well afford to patronize a laudable enterprise even if a profitable outcome was not assured. And think of the glory if it did succeed! He had thought the whole matter over and over during the night and, fair-minded employer that he was, had decided that he too was not free from blame for having so long frustrated Bailey's and Slater's aspirations which arose, after all, from a sincere desire to enhance the name of Doulton. Mawdsley was reinstated forthwith and for many years afterwards played a valuable part in extending Doulton's export markets; Bailey and Slater were forgiven and Henry Doulton never again referred to their temporary fall from grace. And so it was that on 1 December 1883, there appeared in the 'Buyers Notes' in the *Pottery Gazette* the brief but pregnant announcement: 'Messrs. Doulton of Nile Street Works, Burslem, are commencing the Manufacture of china.' Of all the readers of this notice none but a handful knew what a drama lay behind it.

The factory was enlarged in 1884, 1887 and 1889 – partly by new building, partly by the acquisition of other premises in and off Nile Street on the old Kilncroft and Silvester sites. In 1907, such was the growth of the china side of the business, that it became necessary to build a new and larger works for its production.

V

The Doulton School

From 1884 onwards the fine earthenware body tended to be reserved for good-quality tableware for everyday use and for the less expensive types of ornamental pottery. China was developed for the more expensive tablewares; a wide range of tea services; richly decorated service plates and fish and game plates; dessert services; and the hand-painted and often lavishly gilded vases and the like, so popular in that era. A superb bone china body – strong, white and notably translucent – was perfected by Slater. A much larger group of designers, artists, gilders, etchers, engravers and modellers was assembled. Some, already at Nile Street, had been trained earlier in the art of china decoration, either at local Art Schools or at Minton, Derby, Coalport and other china-works. These included Robert Allen, William Allen, Edward Birks, Wilmot Brown, Fred Hancock, Charles Holloway Hart, William Hodkinson, Leonard Langley, Walter Slater (a nephew of John), Edward Tipping, Samuel Wilson, Albert Wright and Charles Yeomans. To their ranks were added over the next few years other artists already well known and destined to become still better known in the field of English ceramics – men such as Edward Raby, Fred Sutton and Thomas D. Bott from Worcester; David Dewsberry from the Hill Pottery, Burslem; John Hugh Plant and Enoch Piper from Coalport; Joseph Birbeck from Cauldon; Charles Brough from Copeland; Louis Swettenham and Louis Bilton from Minton; William Skinner from Davenport; and Edwin Wood from Wedgwood. Most important of all for future developments, came Charles J. Noke, who had been trained as a modeller at the Royal Worcester Porcelain Works and had worked there for sixteen years; he was destined to succeed Slater in 1914.

Under the guidance of men such as these, promising young students and apprentices like Jospeh Hancock, Percy Curnock and Harry Tittensor grew to maturity. (Brief biographical details of all the above-mentioned and many other designers and artists will be found in Appendix 1.)

Never before in Staffordshire had such a large and gifted group of ceramic artists come together in one centre. Never before had a ceramic studio been so little tied

View of the Nile Street pottery, c.1925

Earthenware plate with printed sepia decoration from a dessert service which was in production before and after Doulton took over Pinder Bourne, c.1880
9 in.(22.5 cm.) in diam

Right: Earthenware plates with printed and hand-coloured decorations. These were in production before and after Doulton took over Pinder Bourne, 1876 9¼ in.(23.5 cm.) in diam

Earthenware plaque painted by a Pinder Bourne artist, c.1878 12¼ in.(31 cm.)

View of bottle ovens at the Burslem factory, c.1910

The Pinder Bourne stand at the Paris Exhibition, 1878

Portrait of John Slater, c.1910

Right: Page from the *Art Journal* of 1878
illustrating some Pinder Bourne pieces
shown at the Paris Exhibition, 1878

Earthenware plaque and presentation vase
with ornate relief decoration. Both items
date from the early years of Doulton's take-
over of Pinder Bourne
Vase, 16 in.(41 cm.) high

Earthenware vase painted in the Spanish Ware technique by David Dewsberry, and shown at the International Health Exhibition, 1884
12 in.(30 cm.) high

Portrait of J. C. Bailey, c.1920

Below right: Earthenware jug decorated in the Spanish Ware technique on a Slater patent ground, c.1890
13 in.(33 cm.) high

Earthenware plaque decorated with mermaid design in lustrous glazes, c.1890
16 in.(40 cm.) in diam

Earthenware vase decorated in the Spanish Ware technique with gilded dragon modelled in relief by John Slater, 1890
13 in. (33 cm.) high

Bone china plate printed in sepia with a photographic image of Kaiser Wilhelm II. This process was patented by Doulton and Slater in 1893
8¾ in. (22 cm.) in diam

Earthenware jug printed with *Spray* pattern on a Slater patent ground, c.1885
12 in. (30 cm.) high

Right: Earthenware plate painted by Lambeth artist Frances Linnell on a Pinder Bourne blank, c.1885
19¾ in. (50 cm.) in diam

Bone china plate painted in on-glaze colours by the French artist Georges Léonce, 1883
8¾ in.(22.3 cm.) in diam

Coffee cup and saucer painted in on-glaze colours by Fred Hancock on French Limoges hard porcelain body, 1883
2½ in.(6 cm.) high

Earthenware vase and cover,
with incised and gilded *Art Nouveau* design, c.1905
7¼ in.(18.5 cm.) high

Right: Earthenware plate with decoration of fruit and gilt detail, c.1885
10 in.(25 cm.) in diam

Bone china cabaret set with printed and hand coloured decoration on a matt glaze, 1896 4¾ in.(12 cm.) high

Below right: A selection of bone china plates with richly gilded and painted decoration, c.1905–30. From left to right, (top row) J. Birbeck and D. Dewsberry, (centre) P. Curnock, (bottom row) G. H. Evans and J. Birbeck. 10½ in.(27 cm.) largest diam

Above: Earthenware vase with raised gold decoration by Callowhill, c.1888 10½ in.(26 cm.) high

Two views of decorating workshops, c.1910

Catalogue page, c.1926, showing a range of richly gilded and painted dessert plates and services

Three photographs from a Doulton brochure showing the casting, throwing and decorating of ware in the early twentieth century

Portraits of David Dewsberry (left) and Percy Curnock (right) taken from a Doulton brochure, c.1910

Portrait of Percy Curnock, 84 years old and still painting, 1952

Below: Bone china vase with raised gold floral decoration, supported on dolphin tripod, attributed to David Dewsberry, c.1890 6½ in.(16 cm.) high

Above centre: Bone china vase painted with a snow scene by C. Beresford Hopkins, c.1900 8½ in.(21 cm.) high

Right: Bone china urn painted with classical scenes and motifs by Jack Hewitt, c.1889 13 in.(32 cm.) high

Bone china tea service with raised gold and rose painting
by Percy Curnock, c.1910
5 in.(12.5 cm.) high

Far left: Bone china vase
with roses in gilded
cartouches painted by
Percy Curnock,
Burslem, c.1920
12 in.(30 cm.) high

Left: Bone china vase
with reserve panels
painted with pastoral
scenes by Joseph
Hancock, 1906
13½ in.(33.5 cm.) high

Illustration from the *Art Journal*, 1908, showing a range of vases, including pieces by C. Beresford Hopkins, G. White, S. Wilson, G. Buttle and E. Raby

Below right: Bone china vase gilded and painted with a portrait by F. Sutton, c.1910 5½ in.(14 cm.) high

Bone china vase with raised gold Florentine designs, attributed to F. Hodkinson, c.1910 10¾ in.(27 cm.) high

Bone china vase, with gilded handles, painted with a farming scene by Harry Allen, 1911
8 in.(20 cm.) high

Below left: Bone china vase with raised gold decoration and view of Dunvegan Castle painted by Arthur Perry, 1920
10 in.(25 cm.) high

Bone china ewer modelled with mask terminals by C. J. Noke and with unfinished floral decoration by Fred Hancock, c.1893
18 in.(45 cm.) high

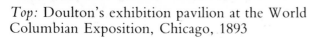

Top: Doulton's exhibition pavilion at the World Columbian Exposition, Chicago, 1893

Centre: Parian vase with pierced decoration and painted floral design by C. J. Noke, c.1893 2½ in.(6 cm.) high

Right: Photograph of C. J. Noke, c.1910

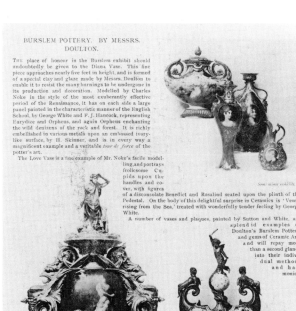

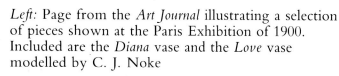

Left: Page from the *Art Journal* illustrating a selection of pieces shown at the Paris Exhibition of 1900. Included are the *Diana* vase and the *Love* vase modelled by C. J. Noke

Below left: Page from a pattern book showing a mermaid centrepiece similar to C. J. Noke's bone china centrepiece exhibited at the World Columbian Exposition (see colour section)

Below right: Bone china vase with gilded decoration and painting of the *Sleeping Beauty* by G. White, c.1910 14½ in.(36.7 cm.) high

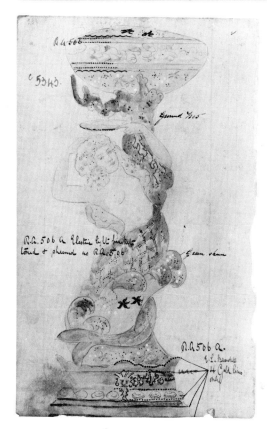

Right: Bone china tea service, including self-pouring teapot patented by a Manchester engineer, J. J. Royle. The decoration of Australian wild flowers was painted by Louis Bilton, 1892
Teapot, 7½ in. (19 cm.) high

Above left: Catalogue page illustrating a range of designs available on the Royle's Toilet Aquarius which was patented c.1891
12¼ in. (31 cm.) high

Above right: Catalogue page showing a range of toilet sets, c.1910

to a particular tradition for, among the array of talent assembled by Slater and Bailey, with Henry Doulton's now enthusiastic blessing, were artists who were able not only to draw upon the inspiration of earlier styles, such as the baroque, rococo, neo-classical and oriental, but who could open up new paths of their own, bringing for example original approaches to landscape, floral and figure painting, a chaster use of gilded embellishments and new conceptions of figure modelling.

The Doulton artists from the 1890s onwards began to create a school of their own, the originality of which was expressed by a writer in the *Pottery Gazette* in these words: 'The artistic quality, though easy to recognize, is not readily definable; and though with some wares a means of expression may be found by reference to this, that, or the other country or period, this is *not* the case with Doulton art, which is distinctly original, and is not to be regarded as derived from any country or century. It is just "Doulton", and to the *cognoscenti* that implies a very high degree of artistic conception and accomplishment.'

Obviously one cannot take such enthusiastic praise too literally. Many of the Doulton Burslem creations do certainly evince considerable originality, some are entirely new expressions of ceramic art; in others, however, the influence of earlier art movements and especially of the taste of the Victorians is evident, just as in the products of other famous potteries during this period, but one often finds that it had been absorbed and transmuted in a creative way. A good example of originality is the approach to floral painting. This was referred to by W. Turner in an article in *The Connoisseur Magazine* for March 1913, from which the following is an extract:

I trace the development [of floral painting] on porcelain in four stages from the first half of the eighteenth century to the present time. At our early English factories of Bow, Chelsea, Derby and Worcester, we see the influence of foreign artists. It is conspicuous in the so-called 'Imari' style so much patronised at Derby. Then there was the underglaze blue hand-painting at Bow and Worcester which is clearly an imitation of Nankin. After these and *pari passu* we have the raised flowers of Dresden imitated at Chelsea and Derby, and the wreaths and academic roses of France largely adopted at Chelsea. This first stage is from 1745 to 1785.

The second or naturalistic style is illustrated by Billingsley's and Evans' work, 1785 to 1825. The third period is shown in the paintings of such men as Cook of Coalport. The style is naturalistic and effective but cheaply turned out. It has not that elaborate retouching and re-firing of the Derby-school and hence was called by the potters 'the flat style'.

We now come to the fourth stage which may be called the triumphant one of British ceramic art. Some fourteen years ago I became acquainted with this new development and in order to get at its initial stage I wrote to the Art Director of Doulton's [John Slater]. He replied thus: 'The style was first produced at this factory, and was started on the work for the Paris Exhibition of 1889. As you are aware, pottery painters at all the classic factories worship the god *stipple*. The brush with the finest point was the only one used for finish. In this [new] style, however, the richness, the breadth, the atmosphere and the colours are all obtained with the broad flat wash. The colours are all transparent and can only be obtained by continued re-firings of one thin glaze over the other.'

At the Paris Exhibition of 1889, at which Doulton again won the *Grand Prix*, the number of exhibits was small compared with those from Lambeth. This was because Henry Doulton felt the time was not ripe to make a big feature of what had quietly been evolving at Nile Street since china began to be made there. The fact that he allowed some vases with the new style of flower painting to be included is an example of his uncanny flair for choosing *la chose juste*. It was just an indication of greater things to come.

Edward Raby was one of the leading exponents of this new style. J. F. Blacker, connoisseur and author, wrote after visiting him in his studio at Burslem: 'What struck me was the wonderful grace in grouping the flowers all round the vase, the masterly quality of broad expression, free from stippling and niggling, and the general softness and richness of colouring.' By 1913, Turner said this new kind of floral painting had 'spread itself to all the other leading factories'. This is but one example of the influence Doulton had on the industry as a whole. In the technical sphere too the Doulton factory was ever to the fore, experimenting with new types of oil- gas- and electrically-fired ovens, improved bodies, new methods of glazing, new machinery which would cut out much arduous and repetitive work without adversely affecting quality – often, indeed, improving it. It was openly admitted in The Potteries that before installing new ovens themselves other firms would often wait to see if they had been a success at Doulton's.

Notable honours

In 1885, Henry Doulton received what he regarded – apart from his knighthood two years later – as the crowning honour of his whole career. This was the award of the distinguished Albert Medal of the Society of Arts. This had been instituted in 1863 as a memorial to the Prince Consort; among previous famous recipients had been Professor Louis Pasteur, Sir Joseph Hooker, Lord Kelvin and James Prescott Joule.

The medal was awarded to Doulton, to quote the official record, 'in recognition of the impulse given by him to the production of artistic pottery in this country'. The Council of the Society also had in view 'the other services rendered by Mr Doulton to the cause of technical education, especially the technical education of women; to sanitary science and, though in a lesser degree, to other branches of science'.

Doulton was deeply moved by the honour – he was the first potter to receive the Albert Medal – and even more by the fact that the Prince of Wales (afterwards King Edward VII), as President of the Society, had agreed to confer the medal, not at Marlborough House, as was the custom, but at the Lambeth headquarters in the presence of Doulton's own workpeople who, Doulton wished, should share in the distinction. The ceremony took place in the large showrooms on the Albert

Embankment, which was crowded to the doors with representatives from all sections of the offices and works, members of the Doulton family, friends of Henry Doulton, and members of the Society of Arts. The choir from Westminster Abbey came across the river to grace the occasion and, after the presentation, the Prince of Wales visited the Lambeth studios and factory, and signed a loving cup which he watched being made on the potter's wheel.

In presenting the medal the Prince said: 'This medal has been awarded only to those who, for distinguished merit in promoting arts, manufactures and commerce, were worthy of receiving it. From all *you* have done, Mr Doulton, for art – not only in this country but throughout the world – I do not think there is anyone more deserving of the high compliment we are about to pay you.'

Two years later, in 1887, Queen Victoria celebrated the completion of fifty years of her great reign. As part of the festivities thousands of children were entertained in Hyde Park, each receiving a Jubilee beaker, of which 45,000 were made to the special order of the Prince of Wales who gave Henry Doulton a rough sketch of what he wanted, based on a commemorative piece he had seen in Russia.

So far as the Doulton Potteries were concerned the crowning event of the Jubilee Year was when the Queen conferred a knighthood on their employer, who thus became the first potter ever to receive such an honour. An American writer in the *China Decorator* expressed the New World's opinion thus: 'Sir Henry Doulton has done more for the advancement of ceramic art in his country than any other potter, not even excepting Josiah Wedgwood.' In 1895, on the occasion of his seventy-fifth birthday, Sir Henry Doulton, referring to the Albert Medal and his Knighthood, told an assembly of his workpeople: 'My friends, I owe these honours in great measure to you. I could not have done without you. Some of you, perhaps, could not have done without me. I feel that you have been associated with every honour that has fallen to my lot.'

Royal Doulton

From Queen Victoria onwards the British monarchy has shown a marked interest in the progress and achievements of the Doulton Potteries. A year after the death of Sir Henry Doulton, his son and heir Henry Louis Doulton converted the business into a limited company which came into being on 1 January 1899 under the name of Doulton & Co., Limited and superseded the earlier Lambeth and Burslem companies, although Burslem always retained a considerable degree of autonomy.

In 1901 King Edward VII conferred an almost unprecedented honour upon the company by not only presenting its Chairman with his Royal Warrant but by specifically authorizing it to use the word 'Royal' to describe its products – a rarely granted privilege quite distinct from the bestowal of the Warrant. As several manufacturers have since 1901 assumed the designation 'Royal' it must be emphasized that Doulton is one of a very few who use this distinguished prefix by a specific right conferred by the Sovereign.

Charles J. Noke

Charles J. Noke was once asked how it was that he and so many others had been willing to give up assured futures with famous firms to throw in their lot with the, at first, somewhat suspect and speculative venture in Burslem. His reply was significant: 'Not for the money, which was much the same as elsewhere, but for the freedom and the promise. Henry Doulton was like a fresh sea-breeze. We had seen what he had done with salt-glaze in a few years – more new inspiration, more real *originality* than other potteries had produced for the past sixty years. It is impossible for anyone of the younger generation [this was in 1937] to begin to conceive just what an impact Doulton made on Staffordshire. To talk to him was invigorating, challenging, demanding the best one could give. He was just what the industry needed. The others had "to pull their socks up". Imagine their feelings, when at the Chicago Exhibition (1893) an American critic wrote: "*Doultons have completely outstripped their rivals and are today the leaders in English potting.*" What the Elers, Whieldon, Wedgwood and Spode had done for the industry in the eighteenth century, this man – by his tremendous vitality, his irrepressible enthusiasm, and his genius for inspiring others – did in the nineteenth. Strange, isn't it, that he too came to Burslem from Vauxhall, like the Elers? Why did we throw our lot in with him? I suppose in some way we sensed all this and felt he was the man we had been waiting for.'

Bertrand Rhead reported in 1912 that Noke had told him he 'had been fortunate to fall in with a management so broad and sympathetic as to afford him the opportunity, not too common, to give of his best and most sincere work, and while at times it goes against the grain to carry out ideas that do not command themselves entirely to his personal judgment, he regards it as a plain duty and privilege to meet the demands of the firm's clients, making the work as good and artistic as will be acceptable to the public that pays for and uses them'.

Charles Noke was born and bred in Worcester within a short distance of the famous porcelain factory. His father, a connoisseur, collector and dealer in antiques, had one of the largest collections of old china in the Midlands – including Chelsea, Bow, Derby, Sèvres and Meissen figures. From his earliest years Charles was brought into touch with the ceramic art, not only through his father's personal collection and the wares constantly passing in and out of the antique shop but also by direct experience in the fascinating china-works near the Cathedral. Thanks to his father's friendship with the heads of the firm he was often allowed to roam around the factory; of all the departments it was that devoted to modelling and ceramic sculpture which fascinated him most. Here he loved to watch the famous

James Hadley creating from the plastic clay elaborate vases, centre-pieces for table settings, figures and animal models. He was allowed to take home some modelling clay from which he would shape pieces for Hadley's comments. They showed promise and in 1874, when still not quite sixteen, he persuaded his father to allow him to start work as an apprentice modeller and designer; at the same time he began a long course of study at the Worcester School of Design. After Hadley left in 1875, to set up as an independent designer, Noke came under the direction of George Evans, George Owen and other well-known Worcester modellers.

Noke remained with Worcester for some sixteen years until 1889. In that year, John Slater, who had seen some of his work at exhibitions, invited him to join Doulton & Company of Burslem. This he did, and his special talents soon began to make themselves felt there. By this time the decoration of china and earthenware at the now much enlarged Nile Street Pottery was of a very high order and, as Bertrand Rhead wrote in the American journal *Pottery and Glass*, in December 1912, 'it was in the combination of this fine decoration and [Noke's] experience of shape and line that a special field was opened for his efforts. Full advantage was taken of this opportunity to co-ordinate the two factors of artistic production.'

The first-fruits of Noke's first few years as Doulton's chief modeller were revealed and acclaimed at the great Chicago Exhibition of 1893, officially known as the World's Columbian Exhibition. His particular gifts as a modeller were evident in many of the tablewares, centre-pieces and ornamental wares, and most notably in a series of large vases, specially created as 'prestige pieces' for the occasion.

The Chicago Exhibition 1893

By 1891 Sir Henry Doulton was satisfied that, now such immense strides had been made at Nile Street, the time had come to show the world what his once scorned Burslem Pottery 'could really do'. The Chicago Exhibition, at which the first large prominent display of Burslem Wares was staged, gave the opportunity. During the preparations he visited Nile Street many times, and often when a china oven was being emptied or 'drawn' as the potters call it, he would rush in while the pots were still hot, seize a piece on which he had set great hopes, and carry it off in ecstasy to the showrooms – calling out to everybody he met on the way, from the youngest apprentice to the oldest artist; 'Come and look at this.' When all the exhibits were ready, he assembled a meeting of everybody in the works, thanked them warmly for their help and said: 'We have endeavoured to produce an exhibit worthy of the firm and worthy of England.' His use of the word '*we*' was typical.

The Doulton display was described by Sir Philip Cunliffe-Owen, Director of the South Kensington Museum, as 'Henry Doulton's greatest triumph'. The twin arcaded pavilions, linked by a central domed hall, all built of Doulton terracotta, had been designed by Arthur E. Pearce of the Lambeth Art Department. In the hall, a magnificent coloured tile frieze, in twelve sections, portrayed the basic processes of pottery-making. George Tinworth's great *History of England* vase, over four feet high, was a notable item, as was the American group previously shown at Philadelphia.

The large vases, all modelled by Noke, were in a general Renaissance style and richly painted by Mitchell, Hancock, White, Wilson, Piper and Labarre. (Charles Labarre was brought over from France especially because of his excellence in painting cupids and classical figures.) The *Columbus* vase, painted by Labarre, standing nearly six feet high, was surmounted by a bold and picturesque figure of the great navigator; above the handles were two other finely executed figures – one symbolizing 'Emancipation' and the other 'Sleep'. The American *Trenton Sunday Advertiser* wrote that this 'suggested rather the *atelier* of the sculptor and painter than the workshop of a pottery . . . elevated as it is to the highest pinnacle of art'. *The Staffordshire Sentinel* described it as 'a triumph of pottery . . . the whole composition a marvel and a delight'.

Another outstanding exhibit was the five-feet-high *Diana* vase with a figure of the huntress goddess at the summit, her hound at her feet; four different copies were made, each painted by a different artist. Surmounting the *Dante* vase was a figure of Jupiter, while on the pedestal sat Dante, Beatrice, 'Poetry' holding a lyre, and 'Fame', a male figure with a laurel wreath. The boldly modelled *Chicago* vase, the romantic *Love* vase, many other smaller vases and pots, the free-standing figures – these all demonstrated Noke's versatility as a modeller combined with the artistry of the Doulton painters. The large vases were the most spectacular exhibits but the dessert plates created no less an impression. Of these there were two hundred different designs on several shapes, painted by ten of the leading artists. The game plates and fish sets also attracted great attention.

It was at this exhibition that the first Doulton figures were shown. In addition to those incorporated in the modelling of the large vases, in centre-pieces for fruit and flowers, and in lamps, candelabra and electric light brackets, there were a few large independent figures including *Jack Point, Moorish Minstrel, Lady Jester, A Jester* (seated) and, most unusual of all, a duplex figure of another jester, standing by a column with one face joyful and the other sad. These figures were larger than most of those produced later on in the well-known HN-series; they, as well as several others made during the next few years, ranged generally from about nine to twenty inches in height, and – instead of being in either a china or earthenware body – were made in parian. This was tinted an ivory or vellum shade and had only a slight 'smear' of surface glaze. The usual decoration was with pink and green sheens and gilding. Occasionally these figures were left unglazed; the *Jester*, for example, has been noted in a white parian body.

It is recorded that a *Jack Point* figure, some sixteen inches high, was sold at the exhibition to an American collector for $400 and one of the large vases for £1,500.

The early Noke figures apparently did not have a great appeal, and were probably made in limited numbers. Although the modelling was of a high order, the style of decoration was considered drab compared with the gay modelling of the popular small French and German figurines.

Other exhibits from the Burslem Pottery included an extensive range of tea, dinner, coffee, and dessert services, biscuit boxes, chocolate pots, bon-bon trays and lamps. The 'Royle's Patent Self-Pouring Teapot, as used by Queen Victoria, Princess Alexandra and other members of the Royal Family', had a great success. This was worked on the hydraulic principle: the lid was first raised and a small hole in the knob closed by the finger; when the lid was lowered the tea ran from the spout without any need to lift the large teapot from its stand – 'a boon for mothers of large families'. (This teapot was the invention of a Mr J. J. Royle of Manchester and although made in quantities between c. 1886 and 1900 is a fairly rare collector's piece nowadays.) 'Royle's Patent Aquarius' was also shown; this was a horizontally elongated toilet jug in a metal frame allowing it to be tilted to pour without lifting. A large selection of other toilet sets was also shown. Another unusual item was the 'Gibbon's Party Plate', made by Doulton for an American inventor. It comprised a tray, saucer and cup for use at garden-parties, the point being that, thus equipped, 'the least resourceful and most bashful of men can not only attend to his own requirements but has an arm free to offer a lady'. One wonders if any of these 'party plates' are in existence or whether the bashful swains managed to drop even them.

Versatility and Originality

Any remaining doubts as to whether Doulton's Burslem Pottery was going to repeat the phenomenal success Sir Henry had achieved at Lambeth were silenced once and for all by the Doulton exhibits at Chicago. The *Art Journal* in April 1893 described the rise of both the Lambeth and the Burslem Potteries very succinctly:

Seldom has it happened in the experience of a single generation to see the birth and complete development of an entirely new Art Industry. Yet in the short space of some twenty years there has been originated and perfected at the Lambeth Potteries, without the aid of previous tradition, a wealth of ceramic method that seems likely to become a conspicuous feature of that Renaissance of English Art which dates from the Victorian era. . . . At Burslem on the contrary, the whole available skill and tradition of several generations has been brought to bear. The most typical productions of these two Art Potteries form a striking and unique collection which, for range of material and versatility of design, cannot fail to help greatly the great reputation of this country for skill in ceramic decoration.

The originality of the Doulton productions was stressed by the *Staffordshire Advertiser*: 'Every piece in the fine collection is new in shape, design and decoration, and unlike anything hitherto sent to America.' *The Staffordshire Post* made the same point: 'Originality is again to the fore . . . exquisitely charming pieces of workmanship. . . . Throwing and turning to perfection; only potters can appreciate the difficulties overcome in those large pieces.' One of America's leading ceramic artists wrote: 'The most interesting place to me was the Doulton Pavilion. The most interesting because it represented the most progression and had the greatest variety.'

Of all the hundreds of appreciations in the British and American press, perhaps the one which gave Sir Henry Doulton the greatest joy was that from Sir Henry J. Wood, one of the Royal Commissioners for the Exhibition and a Member of the Council of the Society of Arts. He wrote: 'The finest collection of pottery I have ever known to be forwarded by an individual exhibitor to any international exposition. In saying that I do not except even the magnificent collection sent from Sèvres, the French government factory. Taken altogether this collection of Doulton's is the finest ever seen.'

Doulton took seven of the highest awards at the exhibition – the largest number granted to any pottery firm. The ceramic historian, J. F. Blacker, gave one reason for their success when he commented: 'Essentially their genius was modern with no records or triumphs dating from the eighteenth century and, *fortunately*, no hidebound traditions to be followed.' Under the triumvirate of Doulton, Bailey and Slater, and with the collaboration of Noke and all the other designers and artists, the Nile Street Pottery had been raised by the end of the nineteenth century to one of the greatest in the world – all this within only twenty years of Henry Doulton taking over full control. To quote William Turner's *Connoisseur Magazine* article once again: 'The Doulton ware of today will assuredly be sought after as examples of the best ceramic types of a remarkable period in the history of this industry, when the decoration of even commerical pottery had become one of the fine arts. Some of the Doulton ware of this period will certainly take rank as gems of art in years to come. Never before have enamel colours used by the potter been so well understood and applied, whether for the imitation of natural colours in floral decorations and landscapes or for conventional ornamentation.'

Art and utility

Turner's reference to the commercial wares – what the potters called their 'bread and butter wares' – is a reminder of all the many other activities at Nile Street besides those which captured the headlines at times of great exhibitions and high awards. While Doulton was ready to subsidize the Burslem enterprise for a long time out of the profits on the more prosaic utilitarian wares made at the other factories in Lambeth, Rowley Regis, Smethwick and St Helens, it was his aim, and that of Bailey and Slater, that it should eventually be able to stand on its own feet. To this end, great attention was paid to the development – alongside the *tours de force* for exhibitions and the exquisitely hand-painted, gold-embellished china service plates and game plates for the wealthy American market – of a wide range of more simply decorated and comparatively inexpensive, yet well-designed, fine earthenware tablewares and bone china tea services. He always insisted that everything which went out from the Doulton ovens, whether it were a plain cream-glazed ink-bottle, a moderately-priced dinner-service or an elaborately moulded, hand-painted and gilded vase, should be the best of its kind in its particular range, well-potted from the best clays, glazes and other ceramic materials. He was positively pained by scimped, slipshod or meretricious workmanship.

Apart from the tablewares and art pottery, a large department was developed for making china and earthenware lamps, of which by 1893 Doulton of Burslem had become possibly the largest, certainly one of the largest, manufacturers in England. Another profitable branch of the business was the many different designs of toilet-ware. Before bathrooms and, in the more expensive types of houses, wash-basins in bedrooms, became more general after the First World War, toilet-sets, usually comprising basin, jug, soap-dishes and chamber-pot, were a basic necessity both in castle and cottage. An 1894 catalogue shows seventy-two different designs including the 'Royle's Patent Aquarius' already mentioned. The designs are so attractive that collectors are today prepared to pay quite highly for a lithograph decorated jug and basin and much more for one of the wholly or partly hand-painted specimens. The jugs are often used now for floral arrangements and the humble chamber-pots are also much sought after. Some of the most expensive toilet-sets for Royal and wealthy households were hand-painted by Charles Hart and other artists and had coats-of-arms and heraldic devices in raised gold by Enoch Piper.

Among other products in the late nineteenth and early twentieth centuries were flower pots and pedestals, aspidistra pots, scent bottles, biscuit jars, trinket sets, cuspidors (spittoons), kitchen pans, baking dishes, churn jugs, tobacco jars, milk pans, pudding bowls, candlesticks, footwarmers, umbrella stands, jardinières, ice-jugs and pails, bulb bowls, and a range of hospital and laboratory equipment. The manufacture of sanitary earthenware and electrical insulators was also continued at Burslem until transferred to other works in the 1930s.

In striving always for a sound balance between the purely decorative art wares and expensive tablewares, on the one hand, and the utilitarian on the other, John Bailey doubtless had well in mind the following sage advice by Sir Henry:

In our own country we have several examples of schools of pottery which have existed but are now extinct. Chelsea, Bow, Lowestoft, Liverpool, Bristol and Swansea have all become names of the past, notwithstanding their high excellence and the extensive patronage which they once received. Most of these have succumbed before the introduction of cheaper methods of decoration and more economical modes of manufacture. Indeed, it is a striking fact that, with scarcely an exception, only those potteries have been able to maintain a long-lived career which have relied for their staple manufacture on utilitarian rather than decorative wares. This principle is true even of artistic pottery. A proportion of the useful seems to be an essential condition of any degree of permanence. A school of decorative pottery only is short-lived – firstly because it is dependent on individual taste and culture and, secondly, because it is not by itself remunerative. Wedgwood, Worcester and Minton have, undoubtedly, maintained their continuous production through so long a period by as careful attention to domestic requirements as to original art wares.

The close of an era

In 1895, on the occasion of his seventy-fifth birthday when a presentation was made to Sir Henry by his employees, he said: 'They have a custom in Japan that when a man is past the age of sixty he is recognized by his family as "the honourable retired one" and is not expected to do any more work. But I have deeply felt the responsibility of employing 4,000 people and circumstances have not, in my judgment, admitted of my retirement. I have done my best to maintain the position of our firm, and I may add for your encouragement – and perhaps for my comfort – that our business was never in a healthier condition.'

Commenting on the presentation, the *British Clay Worker* described Sir Henry as 'a Prince of Clayworkers . . . he has swelled a mere handful of workers into a standing army. It is given to few men of seventy-five to combine, in so marked a degree, sterling business capacity with literary and artistic tastes, and a wide knowledge of men and things.'

A year after this presentation Sir Henry had to undergo a serious operation which he bore with great courage, and although he knew that the surgeon's skill had only prolonged his life for a short while he felt it his duty to continue his work. By the summer of 1897 he had finally to give up and on 17 November of that year he died at his house in Kensington.

In a speech which he made in 1929, looking back on his early days at Burslem, when he constantly came into intimate touch with Sir Henry Doulton, Charles J. Noke described him as, 'A man who, when the history of this industry is seen in its proper perspective, will be recognised as one of the greatest potters of last century. He not only talked pottery but accomplished fine results in it, and left a notable mark in his day and generation.'

It would be wrong however to imply that Sir Henry Doulton had been a 'one-man band'. Nobody was more insistent than he on how much he relied on his loyal co-adjutors. Certainly the continuing success of the Burslem factory owed much to the fertile mind of C. J. Noke and successive Art Directors.

Cecil J. Noke

From 1920 until his nominal retirement in 1936, Charles J. Noke had the collaboration of his son, Cecil, who played an important part in new developments.

Cecil J. Noke, before coming to Doulton, had been apprenticed to an architect and then served as an officer in the First World War. His father first put him to study both underglaze and on-glaze painting under Leonard Bentley and Robert Allen, so that he could learn to understand fully the processes for which he would be called upon to design after completing his studies at the Stoke and Burslem Art Schools. He then worked with his father and Harry Nixon in producing *flambé*, Sung and Chang Wares. Unlike his father, he had no special talent for modelling although he suggested and sketched many ideas for figures and Character Jugs which others developed. One of his special hobbies was etching, and for several years before he succeeded his father as Art Director in 1936 he was in charge of all engraving at the factory. He was also responsible for many well-known tableware designs and was much involved in the launching of the Brangwyn Wares, the *Championship Dogs* and Raoh Schorr animal models. During the greater part of his independent art directorship he had to contend with all the problems connected with the Second World War and its aftermath.

His death in 1954 shocked his colleagues and his many friends all over the world by its utter unexpectedness. Modest, friendly and unassuming, he was a much-loved leader and inspirer of the Burslem team of designers and artists.

The Burslem Pottery today

In 1955 Joseph W. Ledger, ARCA, a designer with wide experience in ceramics, glass, murals and other fields, became Art Director at the Burslem pottery. Under his guidance a new generation of designers, artists and modellers drawn from the Royal College of Art and other centres is continuing and enhancing the Royal Doulton traditions.

VI

Holbein, Rembrandt, Kingswares, Morrisian and Allied Wares

Up to this point it has been possible to follow developments at Doulton's Burslem factory, and to describe its productions, in more or less the order in which they arose. But during the last decade of the nineteenth and the first third of the twentieth century, many new fields of ceramic design, decoration and technique were opened up, the subsequent evolution of which sometimes extended over several decades – in certain circumstances right down to the present day. To attempt to deal with these often overlapping developments in strict chronological order, flitting constantly from one product to another, would inevitably prove confusing; therefore, to facilitate reference, the various *genres* of Doulton ceramics will from now onwards be discussed, either singly or in appropriate groups, in separate chapters.

The 1890s saw the introduction of several unusual styles of decoration in the creation of which Slater and Noke collaborated closely – the former in developing new bodies, glazes and colours, the latter in exploiting these to produce altogether novel types of treatment. By this time it was not just in his original field of ceramic sculpture that Noke's gifts had become apparent; Slater, whom he was eventually to succeed, had now begun to regard him as what he called his 'coadjutor' in the whole field of design.

An artist of uncomplicated but certain vision, Charles Noke had no time for debating esoteric profundities about the nature and function of art. His task, as he saw it, was to *practise* ceramic design, not to theorize about it, and to this – except for his golf and his reading, especially of Shakespeare, Dickens and Burns – he devoted all his waking hours. Bertrand Rhead, after visiting him both in his studio in Nile Street and his home in Stoke, described him as constantly 'experimenting and hatching plots for new themes in pottery of which I saw a remarkable store'. William Owen, who interviewed him in 1910, was struck by his 'remarkable versatility as a pottery artist', his special flair for combining modelling with fine

36

decoration, and his development of many new types of pottery and porcelain. 'In Noke,' wrote Owen, 'Mr Slater has a colleague, and Doulton's have a keenly intelligent worker, who keeps the firm in front in all modern development of artistic pottery production.' One cannot but be amazed at Noke's versatility, vigour and inventiveness, manifested in one new development after another, each one representing a different way of exploiting the art and craft of the potter.

The Holbein Wares

In 1895, after a year or two of preliminary trials, Noke introduced an unusual style of ware, slip-painted underglaze, to which he gave the name *Holbein*. This was made from a hard-fired porcelain body devised by Slater, composed chiefly of kaolin (china clay) and feldspar. A special transparent ivory glaze was evolved to 'fit' the body; this sometimes produced an unusual surface effect which has been described as resembling 'droplets of rain'. (Like the early Chinese crackle effects this may have come about by accident rather than intention.) Many examples of the Holbein Wares combine painting with low relief modelling and/or inlaid decoration with clays of different colours. Reproductions of heads after Holbein, Rembrandt, Van Dyck and other artists, combined with *Art Nouveau* decoration, are frequent features, as are numerous gradations of light and shade and the uses of dark masses as a foil to the decoration.

In developing the Holbein Wares, the artists particularly associated with Noke were William G. Hodkinson, Harry Tittensor and Walter Nunn. Pieces signed by J. Hollinshead, J. Hindley and W. Slater have also been noted. Commenting on what he called 'this latest of numerous Doulton Wares', J. M. O'Fallon wrote in the *Art Journal* of February 1896: 'Holbein may have impressed [Noke] at first with the *heads'* idea but now he multiplies his own variety of heads on plaques, curious vases and other uncommon things, and his quaint figures and ornaments are somewhat original. The patterns are well-studied and modelled in low or in high relief; or cut out and inlaid with various coloured clays, after the fashion of the *Henri Deux* or *Orion* wares. His work, when glazed, takes on a decidedly Rembrandtish chiaroscuro in parts, fastens the attention, and keeps the imagination busy at play through its endless lights and shades of burnt sienna, the prevailing colour; but yellow, orange, cream, red and several other colours are brought out in it with equal success.'

The name given to this ware is rather misleading. As Mr O'Fallon remarked, Noke may well have got the idea of reproducing portrait heads from Holbein, for whom he had a great admiration – especially for his subtle use of light areas silhouetted against a dark background, as exemplified for instance in the portrait of Christina of Denmark. There are, however, vases, loving cups, candlesticks, chargers and other pots marked Holbein Ware – and made apparently from the same hard-fired body – which depict no heads at all. Some too have heads presumably emanating from the Doulton studios – not from 'old masters'; others again are decorated entirely with sinuous motifs, foliate scrolls and stylized plant-like forms in typical *Art Nouveau* style. Particularly inappropriate seems the use of the description 'Holbein decoration' in a 1908 Doulton catalogue for a series of vases, bowls and other pots decorated with rural scenes in a very English style.

The *Pottery Gazette* for June 1901 mentioned that Holbein Ware was then still in demand. Production continued until 1915, but not on a large scale, because of the time-consuming and expensive nature of the decorating methods. The ware is currently proving of considerable interest to collectors.

Some pieces are dated. Between 1895 and c. 1903 a special mark (No. B5, page 178) was used: this is also found on some later specimens in combination with No. B7, page 178, but Holbein Ware is not always specifically marked as such.

The Rembrandt Wares

Introduced about 1898, the Rembrandt Wares, as the name was probably chosen to suggest, are mostly characterized by the interplay of light and dark pigments in dramatic contrast. At a distance, some of the pieces – mostly vases – might even be mistaken for Holbein Ware. Not only the portraits and chiaroscuro effects, but also the colour schemes, are repeated, the hues of the slips and pigments running through warm browns, subdued reds and rich yellows to hints of blue and green. Closer examination at once shows, however, a fundamental difference. Instead of the hard porcellaneous Holbein body, the robust Rembrandt Wares are made from local unrefined marls similar to those used for the rough saggars (fireproof containers) in which pottery used to be fired to protect it from the heat of the kilns. The larger items were supplied on metal stands and with metal covers showing marked *Art Nouveau* influence – as did much of the decoration, apart from the portraits.

The *Art Journal* for January 1908 described these wares as 'a serious and successful attempt to produce, in a simple, direct and artistic manner, decorative pottery . . . the materials used are of almost primitive simplicity . . . the decoration all being done in the plastic clay, relying only on the interest of the design and the rugged certainty of the treatment'.

Each piece (unless not circular in shape) was thrown by hand on the potter's wheel. The painting was done mainly in coloured slips – semi-liquid clays – stained with metallic oxides and covered by a rich glaze. The portraits which are a special feature of this ware are based on paintings not only by Rembrandt but by Frans Hals, Holbein, Van Dyck, Velasquez and other famous artists. It was possibly the great and widely publicized exhibition of Rembrandt paintings in 1898 in Amsterdam (to celebrate the coronation of the young Queen Wilhelmena) which led to the choice of that name by Noke. The artists mainly associated with him in the development of these wares were Harry Tittensor, Arthur Eaton and Walter Nunn.

Most of the Rembrandt Wares have, in addition to the portrait an appropriate motto or proverb. For the *Gay Cavalier*, for instance, it is 'Laugh and the world laughs with you.' For *A Man in Armour* we find 'In days of old when knights were bold.'

The manufacture of Rembrandt Wares was discontinued during the First World War and quantity production was not resumed. Although believed to have been made in larger quantities than the Holbein Wares, examples do not often appear in the salerooms and when they do are commanding rapidly increasing prices.

The superficial resemblance between some Rembrandt and Holbein pieces has led, on at least one occasion, to the Holbein mark being stamped on a Rembrandt item which was obviously made of the coarse marl already mentioned. It seems there was no special mark for Rembrandt Wares.

Other slip or barbotine wares

Besides the Holbein and Rembrandt a number of other designs, hand-painted with coloured slips in what is sometimes called the barbotine technique, were produced between c. 1890 and 1915 and, on a more limited scale, between c. 1920 and 1939. These have generally much lighter backgrounds against which are painted impressionistic birds, stylized cypresses and other trees, pomegranates, sprays and twirls of fuschia, clematis, convolvulus, wistaria and other flowers, grapes, sailing ships etc. Tones of blue, green, orange and ivory – sometimes intermingling and mottled – predominate in many of the backgrounds.

Considerable freedom was accorded to the painters so that many of the hand-painted designs may be termed unique, in the sense of being variations of a basic theme. Some of them have something of the flavour of the work of contemporary illustrators such as Edmund Dulac. They are well worth looking out for and could form a very interesting field for the discriminating collector who is seeking something different.

The Kingswares

By far the most popular (and nowadays most often seen) of the slip-decorated Doulton Burslem productions were the Kingswares (or King's wares as they are described in early records). These were produced in large quantities between c. 1898 and 1939 for sale in Great Britain and overseas and, being less expensive to produce than the wares previously mentioned in this chapter, could be sold at much lower prices.

The Kingswares were not formed on the wheel but were shaped from semi-liquid clay (slip) in plaster moulds. Those parts of the moulds bearing the impressed designs of figures and other details (which produced the so-called 'embossed' effect characteristic of these wares) were coated with slips of the required colours; the moulds were assembled and the dark brown slip generally used to form the body was then poured in, whereupon the different slips united by adhesion without intermingling. When a sufficient layer of clay had adhered to the inside of the porous absorbent mould the remaining slip was poured away, the mould was left to dry and then the shape removed.

A transparent ivory glaze fired over the variously coloured slips produced a most attractive finish. The low-relief figures of the 'characters' which are a usual feature of the Kingswares are mostly in subdued greens, yellows, reddish and lighter browns. Occasionally a yellow glaze was used. Some plain jugs and other items were also made in the Kingsware body, glaze and shapes.

There is a tremendous variety of both shapes and decorations. To take shapes first of all, the collector will come across several designs of match-stands, tobacco jars and ashtrays, mugs and beakers, at least ten different sizes of variously shaped jugs, tea and coffee pots, cups and saucers, sugars and creams, clock-cases, candle-sticks, variously shaped flagons, loving cups, plaques, shaving mugs, scent bottles, tankards and some twenty differently shaped and decorated vases, including at least two with two handles. The most collectable of Kingsware items however are the whisky flagons, some of which were used for advertising purposes by firms such as John Dewar.

The range of characters depicted is extensive. On the regular Doulton flagons alone one can find: *The Alchemist, The Artful Dodger, Bacchus, Bardolph, Bill Sykes, Chadband, Churchwarden, The Coachman* (with fixed head and loose head), *The Connoisseur, Don Quixote, Fagin, The Fisherman, The Forty Thieves, Golfers, Hunting Scenes, The Huntsman Fox, John Barleycorn, Jolly Good Fellow, Memories, Mendoza, Mr Micawber, The Monk, The Night Watchman, The Old Watchman, Mr Pickwick, Pickwick's Toast, The Pied Piper, The Pipe Major, Sailor's Story, Sam Weller, Sporting Squire, Stiggins, Tony Weller* and a figure-shaped flask of this character, *Virginia, The Wizard.* Miniature versions of some of these flagons, now very rare, were also produced.

The flagons made for the Dewar company are usually inscribed 'Dewar's' or 'Dewar's Scotch Whisky'. An order of at least 1,000 flagons was stipulated but in some cases 2,000 or 3,000 are believed to have been ordered. Many of the early designs were registered in Doulton's name and then assigned to Dewar upon the understanding that they would order from Doulton all they required of each design, 'provided there be no increase in price'. The dates of registration, where known, are given below in brackets. The other flagons were all pre-1936.

The following is a list of characters, etc. found on the special Dewar flagons (some of these, it will be noticed from the previous list, are found *also* on flagons not bearing the Dewar name): *Admiral of the Fleet, The Alchemist, The Arkwright Club* (1905), *The Beefeater* (1908), *Ben Johnson* (1909), *Bonnie Prince Charlie* (1913), *Captain*

Earthenware spittoon and plate printed with
aeronautical subjects to commemorate the first
International Air Race, 1909
7¼ in.(18 cm.) high

Below left: Catalogue page, 1894, illustrating a
range of domestic wares. As these items were
often catalogued as 'Sunderland ware', it is likely
that they were sold by Doulton, but were made
on commission elsewhere

Earthenware umbrella stand with Art Nouveau
style decoration, c.1905
25 in.(62 cm.) high

Above: Holbein Ware vase painted with raised flowers, c.1890
5½ in.(13.5 cm.) high

Above right: Holbein Ware vase painted with a group of men drinking and smoking, c.1900
14½ in.(36 cm.) high

Right: Illustration from the *Art Journal*, 1896, showing some Holbein Ware

A selection of Rembrandt Ware from a Doulton catalogue showing the original metal stands and covers, few of which now survive

Left: Morrisian Ware jardiniere printed with a design based on illustrations by the American artist Will Bradley, c.1910
10¾ in.(27 cm.) high

Below: A selection of Kingsware made between 1900–1939. Similar flasks were used to advertise Dewar's Scotch Whisky
10¾ in.(27 cm.) maximum height

Right: Two bone china vases with raised floral decoration, the one on the left by William Hodkinson, the one on the right by Kelsall. Both c.1895
Largest vase, 7½ in.(19 cm.) high

Below: Bone china vase with a *pâte sur pâte* figure on a chocolate ground by J. Hindley, c.1900
6½ in.(16.5 cm.) high

Bone china boxes and covers with printed patterns under lustre glazes, c.1920
Taller box, 7¼ in.(18 cm.) high

Right: Bone china vase decorated in the Luscian technique with raised gold design on the neck, by Walter Nunn, c.1895
10½ in.(26.5 cm.) high

Above: Bone china vase decorated in the Lactolian technique by W. Slater, gilded by R. Ridgway, c.1903
10¾ in.(27 cm.) high

Top left: Bone china vase decorated in the Lactolian technique by Robert Allen, c.1900 3 in.(7.5 cm.) high

Centre left: Bone china vase painted with stylized foliage in pastel colours, 1912 8¼ in.(21 cm.) high

Bone china vase with Egyptian landscape scene under *flambé* glazes, c.1912 12½ in.(31 cm.) high

Bone china coffee and tea service with silver mounts and *flambé* glazes, 1906 7½ in.(19 cm.) maximum height

Above left: Bone china vase with prunus decoration
under Sung glazes by H. Nixon, 1923. 7 in. (18 cm.)
high

Above right: Bone china vases decorated with crystalline
glazes, c.1910. Largest vase, 13¼ in. (34 cm.) high

Two bone china elephants with *flambé* glazes
modelled by C. J. Noke, c.1930
13 in. (33 cm.) high

NOT in a spirit of mere imitation, but rather as a modern homage to the glorious craftsmanship of the old Chinese potters, these pieces were produced by Doulton after a lengthy and costly search for long-lost secrets.

The masterpieces of the early Chinese potters of the Sung Dynasty, which lasted from 954 to 1279 A.D., owed their rare beauty to mysterious glazes which have baffled European potters for generations. How the body and glazes were prepared, and how the glaze was applied, were secrets apparently lost for all time. And now, after well-nigh one thousand years, wares have been produced at the Royal Doulton

Pages from a Doulton brochure publicizing Sung and Chang Wares, c.1925

Bone china vase with painted decoration of a peacock under Sung glazes designed by A. Eaton and C. J. Noke, c.1925
15¼ in.(38 cm.) high

CHANG the Elder, one of the greatest master potters of all time, lived during the Southern Sung Dynasty (1127 - 1279 A.D.). He was especially famed for his crackled ware and brilliantly coloured glazes which, like those of others of the same period, European potters have sought for centuries to evoke anew, but in vain. Here again, after countless experiments, Doulton's have bridged the centuries, and in the words of a connoisseur " have produced a ware which, from every point of view, both technical and artistic, is the equal

Bone china vases with painted decoration of birds and Titanian glazes. Left and centre, by Harry Allen; right, by F. Henri, c.1918
Tallest vase, 10 in.(25.5 cm.) high

Below right: Bone china lamp and vase with Chang glazes, designed by C. J. Noke and Harry Nixon, 1930
Lamp, 12 in.(30 cm.) high

Below: Vase with Chang glazes over painted Japanese flowers designed by C. J. Noke and Harry Nixon, c.1930
5¾ in.(14.5 cm.) high

Above: A group of Titanian Wares showing a range of designs available in this glaze effect, c.1925
Jug, 6 in.(15.5 cm.) high

Far left: Bone china vase with Titanian glazes and decoration of a peacock painted by Harry Allen, c.1915
10¼ in.(26 cm.)

Left: Bone china flask with Titanian glazes and decoration of a polar bear painted by Harry Allen, c.1920
7 in.(13 cm.) high

Photograph from
a Doulton
brochure showing
the Queen's
reception at the
Burslem factory,
1913

Right: The Royal
visit to the Nile
Street factory,
1913

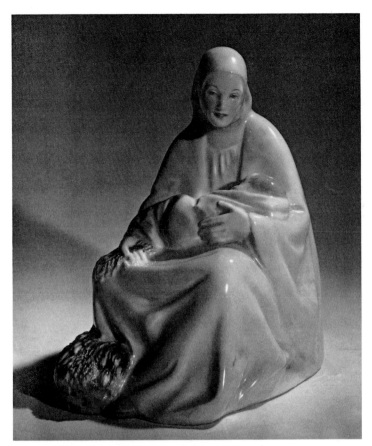

Madonna of the Square designed by Phoebe Stabler and introduced in 1913
7 in.(18 cm.) high

Below left: Henry Irving as Cardinal Wolsey and Ellen Terry as Queen Catherine with vellum glazes designed by C. J. Noke in the early 1890s. Coloured versions of these figures were introduced in 1919 and 1920 as part of the HN range
12¾ in.(32 cm.) high

Below: Return of Persephone designed by Charles Vyse, 1913
16 in.(40 cm.) high

Below and right: Photographs from a publicity brochure showing a figure maker and decorator, 1913

Right: Bone china menu holder in the form of mouse musicians with vellum glaze designed by George Tinworth. Similar models were produced in stoneware at the Lambeth factory c.1900
3 in.(7.5 cm.) high

Right: Darling, first version. The original model was designed by Charles Vyse, and a modified version has been in continuous production since 1913
7½ in.(19 cm.) high

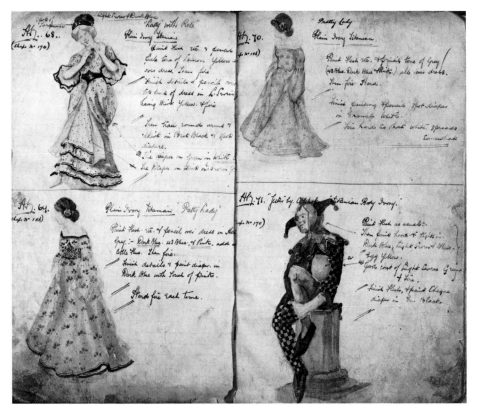

Pages from a figure design book showing drawings of *Pretty Lady, Lady with Rose* and *Jester*, 1916

A group of characters from history and fiction, introduced in 1918 and spanning 50 years of figure production
Tallest figure, 11½ in. (29 cm.)

Right and below right:
Catalogue pages illustrating a range of figures designed by Leslie Harradine, c.1926

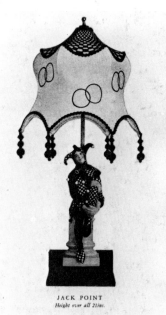

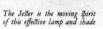

JACK POINT
Height over all 21ins.

The Jester is the moving spirit of this effective lamp and shade

THE MASQUERADERS
Height over all 16ins.

Beautiful modelling adds the finishing touches to an original idea in lighting effects

Above: Catalogue pages showing two figure lamps; *Jack Point* designed by C. J. Noke and *The Masqueraders* by Leslie Harradine. c.1925

Harlequinade.

The Bather.

Pierrette.

Lytton as "Jack Point" and Elsie Maynard.

Butterfly Girl.

Shepherdess.

Shepherd.

The Mask.

The Dandy.

The Belle.

Chelsea Pair.

Chelsea Pensioner.

Victorian Lady.

Yeoman of the Guard.

"Old London Cries" "Strawberries."

The Proposal.

Polly Peachum— "Curtsey."

"Old London Cries" "Carrots and Turnips."

Parson's Daughter.

The Masqueraders.

Balloon Woman.

Diana, designed by David Evans and introduced in 1928. This figure was adapted from a smaller bronze of the same subject which was exhibited at the Royal Academy
14 in.(36 cm.) high

Left: The Cloud, designed by Richard Garbe for limited production in 1937
23 in.(58.5 cm.) high

Advertisement for Royal Doulton figures and limited edition jugs; from the *Pottery Gazette*, 1935

Far right: Masks moulded as stylish girls' faces introduced in 1933 and 1934 8 in. (20.5 cm.) high

Wall mask representing *Saint Agnes* designed by Richard Garbe and introduced in 1934 11½ in. (29 cm.) high

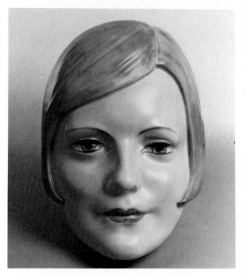

Phillips (1938), *The Churchwarden, The Connoisseur, The Crier* (1909), *Crown Flagon* (1937 – edition of 950 only), *Dr Johnson* (1905), *Don Quixote, Fagin, Falstaff* (1907), *George the Guard* (1909), *Golfers, Haymarket, Here's a Health unto His Majesty* (1936 – edition of 900 only), *Hogarth* (1906), *John Barleycorn, Jolly Good Fellow, Jovial Monk, The MacNab, Memories, Micawber, Mississipi Steam Paddle, Nelson, Mr Pickwick, Pipe Major* (1916), *Sam Weller, Sma' Scotch* (1905), *Sporting Squire* (c.1909), *The Spirit of the Empire* (1915), *Spirit of Friendship* (1906), *Stiggins* (1936), *Tony Weller, The Town Crier* (1909), *Uncle Sam* (1907), *The Watchman, The Whisky of his Forefathers, Ye Weary Pilgrim.*

A Kingsware flagon featuring *Mr Micawber*, inscribed 'The ever expectant' and 'Federal Law forbids sale or re-use of this bottle', was made for the Hudson Bay Company, c. 1946. The edition was probably 3,000. Kingsware flagons featuring *The Crusader, Rob Roy, The Pirates, The Governor*, and *The Tavern Scene* were made for Greenlees Claymore Scotch whisky.

Several of the characters in the foregoing lists are also found on flagons and vases with a white body instead of the usual brown. These are often confused with Kingsware.

Many characters were also to reappear years later in the form of figures, Toby Jugs and Character Jugs. Charles Noke himself played a major part in the inspiration and design of many of the flagons and other items. Some of the prototypes were also designed by Harry Tittensor, Arthur Eaton, Leonard Langley and Harry Fenton. Other artists were probably involved but their names have not been recorded.

The following are some of the wholesale prices in 1932: *Coachman* flagon with loose head, 42.5p; *Tony Weller* figure, 42.5p; Coffee pot (*Huntsman* design), 32.5p; ½lb tobacco jar, 35p; loving cup (*Here's a Health* etc.), 95p – apparently the most expensive item then in production; *John Barleycorn* flagon, 35p.

Many of the characters depicted on the flagons appear also on jugs, teapots, tobacco jars and other items. In addition, the following characters or subjects have been noted on items other than flagons: *The Cup that Cheers, Dame, Darby and Joan, Duke of York, Dutch Children, Essex, The Fat Boy, Fireside, Friar, Jester-in-Stocks, Judge, Lynton Witch, Man on Barrel, Mephisto, Mississippi Steam Paddle, Parson Brown, Quince, Toby, Smoker.* Tea and coffee services were supplied in several different designs: *Dame, Darby and Joan, Dickens, Dr Johnson, Don Quixote, Fireside, Huntsman, Lynton Witch* and *Pied Piper.*

These lists are not complete owing to insufficient documentation. Finding unrecorded items and subjects can be a further challenge to the Kingsware collector.

Morrisian and allied wares

The unusual name Morrisian was given to a type of decorated earthenware introduced about 1900 and produced in fairly limited quantities (judging by its comparative scarceness nowadays) until about 1924. Unfortunately the records are not specific about the nature of the ware, the quantities made or particular patterns. However, generally, pieces bearing the distinctive Morrisian mark are decorated with a yellow and sometimes also a red coloured glaze over a black transfer printed design.

The name has been thought to have been derived from Morris dancing, but it seems more likely that Noke chose the name in acknowledgement of the influence of William Morris. Several of the border motifs on Morrisian Ware are reminiscent of those found in Morris's illuminated books produced at the Kelmscott Press and also his textile designs. Most Morrisian Ware designs reflect the influence of the Arts and Crafts Movement which was inspired by Morris.

Several patterns appear with the special Morrisian backstamp. The most striking range was closely based on the American artist Will Bradley's series of illustrations for 'Beauty and the Beast' which appeared in *Bradley His Book*, published in America in 1896. Another popular range includes at least twenty-five designs of dancing girls in pairs and groups, some holding cymbals, tambourines and garlands. In the records the description Morrisian is also applied to twelve different altar vases with prints depicting angels but these do not always bear the special backstamp. Another design classed as Morrisian but without the distinctive mark depicts golfers in the seventeenth-century dress set into the typical tapestry-type borders and rims. This pattern is similar to the *Jacobean* Series Ware design which also features golfers with Jacobean-style borders.

Patterns normally associated with Morrisian Ware such as dancing girls are also found in other colourways, particularly blue and white. Similarly, patterns not usually considered as Morrisian appear in comparable yellow and red colour schemes such as the oriental-style *Oyama* design of dragons and *The Dukeries* design which depicts a formal garden.

Morrisian Ware designs are found on vases, teapots, jugs, salad bowls, tobacco and biscuit jars, chamber-pots and other items.

The designs for some, if not all, of the Morrisian and allied wares have been ascribed to a Miss A. Pearce (or Pierce) who is described in a catalogue published in 1936 (by the Sydney, New South Wales, Technological Museum) as 'a leading artist in the Modern Art styles who worked both at Lambeth and Burslem'. There is no trace of a Miss Pearce (or Pierce) in any of the Doulton records and it may be that the attribution should be to Arthur Pearce, a gifted all-round artist who was at the Lambeth studios from 1873 to 1934.

He studied at the South Kensington School of Art and at Julien's atelier in Paris. Harry Barnard, a Lambeth colleague, who later became curator of the Wedgwood Museum in Etruria, Stoke-on-Trent, wrote of Pearce: 'He had a vast knowledge of historical styles and ornaments, was a gifted etcher, water colour painter and illuminator, and was constantly consulted by, and collaborating with, other Lambeth artists.' It is known that in the early days of the Burslem enterprise, Pearce,

Ada Dennis, Florence E. Lewis and Walter Gandy sometimes helped John Slater on the design side. Some of the Morrisian designs are certainly similar to others found on illuminated manuscripts by Pearce.

VII

Enamelled Pottery:
Hyperion, Luscian, Lactolian and Lustre Wares

Among the rarest of all the Doulton Burslem ceramics are some panels, plaques, chargers and tiles designed by Charles J. Noke intermittently over a period of a decade or so from about the turn of the century. It is thought that not more than one hundred of these unique pieces, most of them in *Art Nouveau* style, were made.

These ceramics are unusual examples of enamelling on *pottery* instead of on *metal*. The technique (not to be confused with the ordinary on-glaze enamel painting of china) was the outcome of many patient experiments by Noke. Production was expensive and hazardous, and this no doubt accounts for the paucity of examples; it seems that many pieces to which he had devoted much time were destroyed by Noke for not reaching the desired standard.

The parian-like feldspathic body had to undergo at least three and often up to five or six firings, increasing greatly the risk of kiln losses. Relief modelling, combined with glowing transparent enamels, was built up in successive layers somewhat in the manner of *pâte-sur-pâte* (see page 47). An unusually rich effect was produced such as is not often seen in enamelled metalwork. The enamelled pottery resembled to some extent *champlevé* in the way colours were applied, and *cloisonné* in the manner in which the broad masses of enamel were filled in. Gold, applied in a final firing, was used extensively in some of the designs.

Among the subjects depicted were *Love's Messenger*, *Vanity*, *Cupid Chained*, *Cupid Robbed*, *A Reflection*, *A Golden Morn*, *The Sybil*, *The Pot of Basil* and *Flowers for Jewels*.

In the execution of these enamelled pieces Noke was particularly assisted by William G. Hodkinson.

44

Hyperion Wares

Hyperion was the name given early this century to a style of painting, particularly floral, done entirely by hand on bone china in a very delicate manner – no use, it seems, being made of outline prints from engraved copper plates. Outlines, where needed for gold traceries and the like, were finely pencilled freehand by the artist. Mostly associated with Noke in this kind of decoration were Edward Raby, Walter Slater, J. Kelsall and Fred Walklate.

A note in the catalogue of the John Slater Collection in the former Sydney Technological Museum, New South Wales (now the Museum of Applied Arts and Sciences) stated that this class of decoration was introduced by Mr C. J. Noke about 1900 and was a very popular style on the English and American markets. Its use was in fact continued for several years and was sometimes combined with *pâte-sur-pâte*.

Freehand painting was of course a regular feature of many of the artist-signed Doulton Burslem Wares; the distinctive attribute of the Hyperion appears to have been its marked delicacy of colours and the free modern style in which poppies, lilies, vine and other blossoms were depicted on both white and coloured grounds, especially a tender *Rose Pompadour*.

John Keats was one of Noke's favourite poets. The name Hyperion was suggested by Keats's *Dream of Hyperion* and indeed some of the ware in this style has something of a subdued dream-like quality. *The Pot of Basil*, another of Keats's poems, inspired one of the enamelled panels mentioned earlier in this chapter.

Luscian Wares

The Luscian Wares, utilizing a new bone china recipe and a new matching glaze, both devised by John Slater, were also introduced around the turn of the century – an extraordinarily active time for both Slater and Noke. This ware was described in the *Art Journal* of January 1896 as being 'painted underglaze with flowers, birds, hill and woodland scenes and the like, in appropriate hues with all the softness of the Sèvres *couleur changeant*'. In the *Pottery Gazette* for May 1898 it was referred to as producing 'a rich soft effect by the skilful blending of various colours painted on the glaze – orchids and other flowers by Dewsberry, cattle and birds by Sam Wilson'.

It is interesting to note that while the two descriptions agree about *the soft effect* of the painting, they disagree as to whether this is on-glaze or underglaze. The reason probably is that although (as on most porcelain and china with a wide range of colours) the decoration was technically on-glaze, in the Luscian Wares, by skilful glazing and firing methods, the colours sank *into* the velvety glaze, producing a singularly soft and delicate almost underglaze effect.

Mr J. M. O'Fallon, in the *Art Journal* article already quoted, went on to comment on the careful and exquisite finish of the vases, dessert plates and other plates in the Luscian range: 'Sky and hill,' he wrote, 'and hedgerow and stream, and field and covert, animate with bird and beast, and insect and butterfly [are] now softened with soft greys and blues or enlivened with tender greens and chromes, and reds and siennas combined, to have us thinking very pleasant things; and that, if it be simple art, is truthfully happy art, and has a quality that high art seldom attains to – and that is – you feel you could live with it and have no misunderstanding.'

The reference to simple and happy art that one could live with must surely have pleased Charles Noke. This was an ideal he sought after in all his later work – whether in the Holbein, Rembrandt and other wares already described, or in the reduction-glaze wares, the figures and Toby and Character Jugs, loving cups and presentation jugs described in later chapters. In these he broke away from the strong nineteenth-century Worcester influence that still pervaded much of his work at the time of the Chicago Exhibition. Sometimes, but not often, considering the vast range of his creations, the simplicity perhaps verged on the banal, the happiness on the over-ornate and flamboyant, but taking it all in all, his achievement, both as Slater's assistant and then as his successor, played an inestimably important part in the rise to fame of the Burslem Pottery.

In developing the Luscian Wares, Noke was assisted by several of the leading Burslem artists. David Dewsberry and Sam Wilson have already been mentioned. others were Henry Mitchell, Edward Raby, Louis Bilton, Joseph Hancock, Walter Slater, Harry Piper and George White. Robert Allen and Leonard Langley, at that time assistant art directors, also played an important part in the development of these and other beautifully decorated wares of the period. Langley had been Slater's first apprentice and Allen had studied design under Slater since 1870.

Pieces are rarely seen bearing the actual description 'Luscian' and the name soon dropped out of use although the style it had represented went on for many years. It was probably china in the Luscian tradition which an American expert described in 1924 in the words: 'The charm of Royal Doulton Bone China rests in the liquidity of its translucence, the purity of its body texture, and the lustrousness and richness of its wonderful velvety glaze, which afford a background for refined decorative ornament unapproached by any other fabric. Colours take on brilliancy as if by magic, *sinking into the glaze* and becoming incorporated with it.'

Lactolian Wares

The Doulton variety of feldspathic parian body which Slater had developed for Noke's figures and other models shown at Chicago in 1893 was adapted for yet another turn-of-the-century innovation to which the odd name Lactolian was given. It was presumably derived from the Latin for 'milky' and was used to describe the

Burslem type of *pâte-sur-pâte* decoration. This was first shown at the Paris Exhibition of 1900 at which Doulton, because of past success in Paris, was *hors concours*. Doulton's participation with a magnificent display of ceramics none the less brought immense prestige. The *Journal of Decorative Art*, commenting on the exhibits, describes the firm as 'pre-eminent among English manufacturers of decorated pottery and china'.

PÂTE-SUR-PÂTE

'Paste-upon-paste' ('paste' being the French term for 'body') was a decorative process combining painting and modelling to provide a cameo-like effect. It was first evolved by the Sèvres factory about 1859 and further developed by Marc Louis Solon who took it to Minton in Stoke-on-Trent in 1870, subsequently designing and decorating many vases and plaques in this technique. The process, which was lengthy, difficult and expensive, has never been better described than in Solon's own words, taken from an article in the *Art Journal* for March 1901:

The piece it is intended to decorate must be in the clay state, that is to say, just as it leaves the hand of the potter, and before it has been submitted to any firing. Upon the still pulverulent and porous surface the artist sketches freely the main lines of his subject. Then with a painting brush dipped in 'slip' – a term used in the trade for clay diluted with water to the consistency of a batter – he proceeds to lay on the foundations of his relief work. Coat after coat the slip is carefully applied; no fresh coat is to be added before the preceding one is perfectly dry. . . . With the preliminary brushwork a rough sketch is produced, in which care has to be taken to give to each part comparatively its right degree of relief; but the surface is rough and rugged and no attempt has been made to introduce any detail. The work has now to be treated in the same way as a sculptor would treat a bas-relief of plaster of Paris or of fine grained stone. By means of sharp iron tools the substance is scraped, smoothed, incised; forms are softly modelled, details neatly defined, outlines made rigorously precise. As long as the artist is not satisfied he may take the brush again and use it alternatively with the tool, raising one part, effacing another, as he may think it expedient. The last finishing touches, which shall preserve to the details a sharpness that glazing and firing would otherwise obliterate, are painted on with the thicker slip in a style quite peculiar to the treatment of *pâte-sur-pâte*. Although the clever management and clever graduations of the transparencies are only developed by vitrification, the operator has no other guide in that respect but his experience and judgement. Great disappointment may follow the firing of a piece, all miscalculations first being made manifest when it comes out of the oven. At that moment, unfortunately, it is too late to make any alteration; the work once fired can no longer be touched up; errors and misfortunes must stand as they are.

The foregoing description clearly shows the exacting and hazardous task the Burslem artists were undertaking in launching the Lactolian Wares. Was it perhaps a pardonable desire on Slater's part to show the world that even the Sèvres and Minton speciality of *pâte-sur-pâte* was not beyond the capacities of his team of artists – that the disparaged 'interloper' of 1877 had in just over two decades become a leading light in the industry?

A type of *pâte-sur-pâte* decoration by Doulton artists had in fact already been seen in Paris at an earlier exhibition in 1878, but this was on Lambeth Stoneware, not on bone china. This had been made on a very small scale and differed considerably from the Sèvres and Minton varieties. It had been discontinued about 1887. Nevertheless Slater was able to learn something from the experience of Florence Barlow, one of the few Lambeth artists who had practised the technique and was still at Lambeth in the late 1890s when he began serious research. He was also helped considerably by William Hodkinson, a fine all-round artist, who had learned some of the secrets of *pâte-sur-pâte* while apprenticed at Minton under Monsieur Léon Arnoux.

Doulton Lactolian Ware is rare. It was made for only a few years and then only in small quantities; it was probably discontinued for economic reasons. A single medium-sized vase sometimes took nearly a month to complete and even in 1900 could cost £100 to £200, so demand was limited to a few connoisseurs. A present-day collector who has, or is fortunate enough to acquire, a specimen of Lactolian has something to treasure for the work was of a high standard.

The artists mainly involved were Robert Allen, who was responsible for most of the designs, William Hodkinson, George White, Walter Slater, David Dewsberry and J. Hindley, an artist of obviously considerable ability but about whom the records give little information. William Skinner, one of Doulton's leading gilders, was responsible for most of the raised gold work.

Lustre Wares

It is strange that one hears or reads very little about Doulton Burslem Lustre Wares for they were made at one time in quite appreciable quantities. They should offer an interesting field for a specialized collection.

Lustre pieces were, as has already been mentioned in Chapter IV, among John Slater's earliest successes and their manufacture was continued under the subsequent art directorship of Charles and Cecil (Jack) Noke until the early 1950s, though on a limited scale.

Lustre painting was introduced into Staffordshire towards the end of the eighteenth century. In the first half of the nineteenth century it had a great vogue, then declined, but was revived in London in a very attractive form by William de Morgan in the 1880s. Its history is an ancient one, dating back to pre-Islamic Egypt, and it was made by Persian, Arabian and Hispano-Moresque potters.

The metallic sheen and glittering reflections which characterize Lustre Wares when held up to the light are produced by painting over a special glaze with pigments containing finely divided particles of metal, especially gold, silver, platinum and copper. When the pots are fired a second time in a reducing atmosphere (that is to say, in an oven to which, at a certain temperature, the ingress of air is restricted) their surfaces become covered with a thin, even, metallic film.

Doulton records show the production of many lustre pieces, especially vases and bowls of small and medium size, between the 1890s and 1930. After 1930 manufacture was continued (except during the war years) on a small scale until about 1952. In 1917, according to the *Pottery Gazette*, a great variety of Doulton Lustre Wares could be seen in the firm's 'new Holborn Viaduct Showrooms' in London, including some notable pieces with a deep ruby glow, peacock hues and the silvery sheen of mother-of-pearl. At the British Industries Fair in 1919, Queen Mary was greatly interested in the latest examples shown there and bought a particularly lovely 'peach blow lustre piece'.

John Slater had always a great affection for the lustre technique and was constantly experimenting to produce new monochrome and polychrome effects. The range of Doulton lustre colours was said by the *Pottery Gazette* to be unsurpassed in the industry. It included lemon yellow, greenish yellow, yellowish grey, bluish silver, chartreuse green, olive green, greenish gold, golden brown and several other shades of brown, pink, purple and orange.

In some rare examples lustre effects are combined with *flambé* and Titanian glazes. Some of the lustred pots have attractive and intricate geometrical decorations, arabesques, scrolls, palmettes, *fleurs-de-lis* and other stylized floral and foliate designs; others are decorated with birds, mermaids, dragons and other figures. Some more intricate designs were developed by what is known in the trade as 'the resist process'. In this the decoration is painted or printed on the glazed surface of the ware with a resist such as clay mixed with honey; the surface is then covered with the metallic solution and the pot is refired. The resist disappears during the firing, leaving the decoration 'reserved' against a lustrous background.

It should be noted that in some of the Doulton Lustre Wares, especially those involving also *flambé* effects, the trademark may be very difficult to discern, only becoming visible when light strikes it at one particular angle. Sometimes a considerable portion of the trademark has been obliterated altogether. It may be that some collectors of lustre have fine examples of Doulton without realizing it.

VIII

Flambé, Crystalline Glazed, Sung, Chinese Jade, Chang and Titanian Wares

In the late 1890s John Slater and Charles Noke, encouraged by John Bailey, embarked on a quest which had for many years been firing the imagination and inspiring the researches of several other ceramists in France, Denmark, Germany and the United States. Their ambition was to rediscover the secret of, and to reproduce with consistent success, the vivid lustrous red glaze – often splashed, streaked or mottled with blue, turquoise, yellow, green and grey – to which French collectors of Chinese pottery and porcelain had given the generic title *flambé*.

The origins of these glaze effects were already largely lost in legend when the French Jesuit missionary-priest, Père d'Entrecolles, wrote to Europe about them, in the early 1700s, in his *Lettres Edifiantes et Curieuses*. The old Chinese master-potters had at first worked by methods of trial and error. When a hitherto unknown glaze, or colour effect, appeared they had to try to recall and repeat the whole sequence of procedure which had resulted in its first manifestation. In this they at times succeeded but at others were frustrated when, for reasons they could not fathom, the desired results failed to arise. An unusual effect might be ascribed to the work of spirits or to peculiar astrological conditions. One twelfth-century Chinese writer, for instance, attributed the appearance of a red *flambé* underglaze colour to the influence of Mars, saying that when this planet 'approaches its greatest brightness, things happen magically and contrary to the usual order'.

Facts and legends

During the glorious Sung period (960–1279), some Chinese potters had in fact already acquired considerable skill and mastery over their materials and processes.

They experimented with different clays, glazes and other basic materials, built new types of kilns, and – most important for the successful production of *flambé* wares – learned how to vary the amount of air entering the kilns at different stages of the firing process.

By the twelfth century some of the Sung potters had developed what are now known to the connoisseur as the Chün wares, characterized by a wide range of luminous, opalescent glaze effects from a pale 'moonlight' greyish-blue through lavender and violet to near purple. These glazes were sometimes splashed with purple and crimson by the addition of an oxide of copper. When thickly applied, these Chün glazes accumulated in characteristic thick drops and rolls near the base of the pot. Another unusual effect developed during this period was the 'crackle' or 'broken ice' glaze. This probably first arose accidentally but was later produced deliberately with varying widths of fissures. During the fourteenth and fifteenth centuries *sang de boeuf* and other fine copper-red glazes were perfected; these ranged from a soft restrained hue to a rich, brilliant colour. After this the secret seems to have been lost until rediscovered in the reign of K'ang Hsi (1662–1722). In the nineteenth century, even in China, the art of producing good *flambé* effects was largely forgotten.

Père d'Entrecolles knew that some form of granulated copper was an essential factor in obtaining the special red glaze. It was said to have been mixed with a kind of stone, probably alum, as well as with youths' urine. It was difficult at first for European ceramists to separate facts from legendary accretions. In the latter part of the nineteenth century it had nevertheless been established that the colouring medium used by the Chinese potters had included some form of oxide of copper and that the actual colours obtained during firing depended on the use of a 'reducing' instead of an 'oxidizing' atmosphere at some stage of the operation. W. B. Honey in his *Art of the Potter* explains this by saying that the colours 'vary with the atmosphere of the kiln, whether "oxidising" on account of the free admission of air, or "reducing" when the supply of air is limited and smoke is produced; this imperfect combustion of the fuel gives rise to carbon monoxide, which takes up oxygen from (or "reduces") whatever oxygen is exposed to it in the hot kiln'. The copper oxide when thus reduced to cuprous oxide produces the glorious red colour. By varying the phases of oxidizing and reducing, vivid reds streaked with blues and greens were attained, and other fascinating transmutations could arise by the use of small admixtures of other metallic compounds, certain wood ashes and organic substances.

Cuthbert Bailey takes a hand

Slater and Noke had by 1900 succeeded in producing the occasional good specimen of *flambé* but at great cost. The proportion of failures was very high indeed and they were still very far from discovering and mastering the conditions which would enable them to produce the desired effects consistently and satisfactorily enough to make the exercise a viable commercial proposition. Things were still at this stage when in 1900 John Bailey's son, Cuthbert, joined Doulton of Burslem.

During his school holidays young Cuthbert Bailey, it is recounted, used to haunt the factory of which his father had long been the general manager. After coming first in all England in the science examinations at South Kensington, he was offered a scholarship to Cambridge University, but he elected instead to enter the Doulton Burslem Pottery and devote himself to the scientific and technical aspects of pottery-making, continuing his studies part-time at Stoke Technical College. The physical and chemical properties and behaviour of ceramic materials, and the design and construction of improved types of kilns, especially with a view to fuel economy, became his special fields of study and in these he later pioneered important developments of great benefit, not only to Doulton, but to the whole British pottery industry.

Cuthbert Bailey had not long been at Nile Street before he became irresistibly fascinated by the work on the *flambé* glazes which Noke and Slater had been conducting. To discover *exactly* the conditions under which these beautiful colour effects could be obtained on a sustained scale, and not just occasionally, was the task which he soon set himself as a particular objective. In the whole complex of ceramic problems at that time it would have been difficult to find one more challenging. Although well understood in Europe by this date, few potters in England had so far mastered the *flambé* process. Experiments by W. Howson Taylor at the Ruskin Pottery, and by the Burton Brothers at Clifton Junction, had resulted in occasional first-rate examples of *flambé*, but a scientifically controlled consistency was hard to achieve.

At the time Bailey began his investigations, another young Staffordshire potter named Bernard Moore had already attained an appreciable measure of success, on a small scale, in his experiments with *flambé*, lustre, crystalline and other out-of-the-ordinary glaze effects. The son of a pottery manufacturer in Longton, Moore, according to one of his contemporaries, had 'an instinctive almost uncanny' understanding of ceramic processes. William Burton wrote that 'to him alone belongs the credit of being the first Englishman to successfully reproduce the old Chinese effects'. Besides helping his brother, Samuel, to run the family business in Longton, Bernard Moore began to work as a consultant for other pottery firms. At John Slater's suggestion he was asked to collaborate in Bailey's researches, and so in 1902 he was appointed as a consultant by Royal Doulton for a fee of £2,000.

The co-operation of the two young enthusiasts proved of great mutual benefit. The practical facilities which Doulton could offer, backed by their financial resources, far exceeded those at Moore's own disposal; on the other hand, his copious records of, and deductions from, his earlier researches prevented much waste of time on false paths.

For many years after the Doulton *flambé* wares had become world famous, Moore continued to produce his own signed pieces on a restricted scale at his studio in Wolfe Street, Stoke-on-Trent, using porcelain blanks bought from a great number of manufacturers including Doulton and Minton.

Many of his choicest pieces were unfortunately destroyed by a fire at the Brussels Exhibition of 1910. In the course of the first three decades of this century Doulton went on to produce a range of transmutation and reduction glaze effects which in variety, richness and novelty, far surpassed the results of the early 1900s, but there is no question that in the early stages of production Moore's collaboration was of great help.

Charles Noke's long experience of glaze and colour reactions and, above all, his great flair for marrying form and colour, also contributed to the successful development of the new range. Once the basic principles of the special glaze effects had been established, he proved an adept, not merely in achieving results that vied with those of the old Chinese master potters but some, indeed, which went far beyond any that they or their successors in China and Europe had ever attained. John Slater's knowledge of chemistry was also called upon when difficult problems arose. In the early stages, however, the successful outcome of the researches at Nile Street was due above all to Moore and Cuthbert Bailey's infectious enthusiasm and to their incredible patience which many failures and disappointments never seemed to daunt. The lion's share, not only of the practical as distinct from the theoretical research work, but of the translation of the results into controlled factory procedures, fell upon Bailey. Fortunately he was endowed with great physical endurance and resistance to fatigue. His contemporaries at Burslem in the early 1900s recalled that, during certain critical phases of the investigation, he never left the factory by day or night for weeks on end, snatching only brief periods of sleep on a camp-bed in his office. He built and rebuilt many of the experimental kilns with his own hands and fired them himself.

The Doulton organization was fortunate in having at this time recruited an enthusiastic young man whose devotion to the ceramic art reminds one, to some extent, of one of Sir Henry Doulton's great heroes, the French potter, Bernard Palissy. But Bailey was more fortunate than Palissy in that his education had given him a good scientific and technical grounding, and that he had behind him a firm with the faith and resources to enable him to pursue his work on the special glazes over a long period during which the likelihood of achieving the desired goal – consistently good results on a viable commercial scale – seemed at times very doubtful.

One of the most difficult problems to overcome was precisely how to manage the firing between the two phases of oxidation and reduction so that the characteristic red and, where desired, subtle graduations of other colours could be captured and fixed permanently for the future delight of connoisseurs and collectors. Only after three years of sustained effort, involving the repeated building and rebuilding of special kilns, innumerable experiments with different compositions of bodies and glazes, and the analysis of many hundreds of trial-pieces, were the conditions established under which the transmutation effects could be repeated with reasonable certainty.

'Everything but antiquity'

The first public display of the new Doulton *flambé* wares was at the St Louis Exhibition in the United States in 1904. Perhaps never before in the history of ceramics had any product created such a world-wide interest. The transmutation colours, including some never before seen, even in Chinese ceramics, caused a great stir among collectors, connoisseurs and museum experts, who competed to secure specimens for their collections. For the *flambé* and other exhibits (including some from Lambeth) Doulton received no fewer than thirty awards, including two *Grands Prix* and four gold medals – a success so unprecedented in ceramic exhibition records that when a cable arrived at Doulton's head office in Lambeth, announcing the news, Lewis Doulton felt there must be some mistake and hesitated to make it public until written confirmation was received. Royal patronage followed within a few months when Doulton were asked to supply special collections of the new wares to both Queen Alexandra and the King of Sweden.

It must, too, have been a proud day for Cuthbert Bailey and his colleagues when Arthur V. Rose, Tiffany's famous pottery expert, with an unrivalled knowledge of oriental art treasures in the museums and private collections of Europe and America, gave the following assessment of the Doulton achievement:

It has been my good fortune to examine many of these Doulton specimens, and I can safely say that for perfection of glaze, as well as for exquisite colouring and purity of form, they rival the finest of the Chinese. As collectors have already given up in despair searching for choice specimens of the early Chinese red glazes, they have at least the satisfaction of knowing that they can now acquire superb examples of Doulton porcelain, made in the same manner, coloured, streaked or mottled, which are their equal chemically and artistically; in fact have everything that the most enthusiastic collector could desire but *antiquity*. From the complicated nature of the process, every piece is practically an individual specimen, bearing upon it the marks of the master, and worthy, therefore, of its place in the finest collections of ancient or modern pottery.

Rose's opinion was endorsed by other experts in America and Europe. The *Art Journal* for April 1905 wrote that the Doulton glaze effects 'vie with the best examples of the East' and made the important observation that, although some might regard these beautiful glazes merely as revivals of the lost art of the Chinese, 'there is added to the rediscovery that element of control which is the best guarantee of progress'.

Among the Doulton artists who worked with Noke in developing *flambé* effects as a design medium were Harry Nixon, NRD, Wilmot Brown, William G. Hodkinson, Charles Yeomans, Frederick Moore, Arthur Eaton and Fred Allen. Nixon, a most versatile artist who joined the staff of the Art Department in 1900, later became Charles Noke's chief collaborator in exploiting the artistic possibilities afforded by the transmutation effects, and his signature or monogram, as well as Noke's will be found on many fine pieces. Moore, Eaton and Hodkinson also decorated many pots that are now much sought after. Brown and Yeomans were more particularly associated with the development of what are known as the 'landscape *flambés*', an original Doulton idea, in which beautifully engraved and painted pastoral and woodland scenes, and English, Italian, Egyptian and other landscapes, in a dark tone, merge mysteriously and contrastingly into the lustrous red background. During the 1920s and 1930s Charles Noke's son, Jack, also designed several new shapes and decorations for the *flambé* and other reduction glaze wares. Fred Allen, about whom little is recorded, appears to have been active during part of the same period. Between 1916 and the early 1920s a number of *flambé* and other pieces were designed by Reco Capey, an industrial designer who later became Professor of Design at the Royal College of Art in South Kensington.

Records survive of over three hundred different shapes and sizes of vases alone and, of course, each was decorated in many different ways. Apart from vases, there were bowls, flower-pots, ashtrays, figures, animals, 'grotesques' and, somewhat surprisingly, coffee-sets and tea-sets. Concerning the tea-sets, an Australian journal commented in 1912: 'Purchasers who can only sigh in longing for a splendid Chinese *rouge flambé* jar at £450 will find consolation in a beautiful Royal Doulton *rouge flambé* tea-set at £6/17/7 – destined to be some happy woman's imperishable pride.' However, production of *flambé* tablewares was limited by the difficulties in producing a red consistent enough for matching pieces.

Writing also in 1912 in the *Connoisseur Magazine*, J. F. Blacker made a similar comment concerning the Doulton *flambé*:

The millionaire collector, whose money purchases the gems of ancient art, possibly reaps less pleasure from his treasures than the man whose home embodies the results of his feelings, expressed by a careful choice of such wares as he can afford and which he delights in. I would endorse what was said by W. Owen: 'The last thirty years, which covers the Doulton regime in Burslem, has seen the development of one of those great art potteries of the world which have done so much to make the fictile art one of the most enduring records of human achievement.'

In the same article Blacker referred to the great beauty of some of the mottled *flambés*, the wonderful shades and tones of colour, having 'a delicacy, richness and refinement beyond description'. By this time the range of transmutation colour effects embraced mushroom greys, fluorescent yellows and purples; many beautiful reds from the muted to the most vivid, and an extensive range of blue, green, turquoise, haricot and peach-bloom effects.

Ranges of *flambé* animals were introduced during the early 1900s; some of these early models are still produced today. Figures in *flambé* are comparatively rare; they include some of Tittensor's well-known series of spooks, some Buddhas and other oriental-style figures, and some 'grotesques'. The early models are well worth looking out for and include at least ten elephants, eleven foxes, seven penguins, four tigers and four lions of different shapes and sizes, besides a number of other creatures – bulls, bison, camels, llamas, pigs, monkeys, cats, mice, pigeons, owls, drakes, ducks, mallards, kingfishers, guinea fowl, parrots and leaping salmon.

The following are a few wholesale prices in a list for February 1938:

5 in. (13 cm.)	mottled vase	:	37½p
10 in. (26 cm.)	mottled vase	:	£1.25
4½ in. (11 cm.)	landscape vase	:	37½p
11 in. (28 cm.)	landscape vase	:	£1.25
Large tiger	HN 1082	:	£1.75
Penguin	HN 946	:	£1.00

These prices were for more or less standardized shapes and fairly simple decorations, but even for the finest individually decorated large vases, some of which could be described as *tours de force*, prices rarely exceeded £20. One of the great attractions of the *flambé* and allied wares is that even in the less expensive range each piece had slight variations and each of the more costly pots was definitely a unique piece because control was exercised within certain limits only, the rest being left to the alchemy of the kiln. And although results could be largely predicted with reasonable certainty, the 'trial by fire' could still bring about, sometimes disappointments, sometimes effects of a richness and beauty surpassing all expectations.

About 1915 a new much thinner and much lighter body was perfected for the *flambé* wares. On this some new lustred 'opaline' effects, combined with the *flambé* treatments, were introduced, which inspired a writer in the *Pottery Gazette* to enthuse about their 'irridescent shimmer of prismatic reflections' and their 'kaleidoscopic scintillation of all the hues of the rainbow'.

From the early 1930s onwards there appears to have been a falling off in demand. Tastes had changed and no doubt by this time the *flambé* effects had lost their novelty. The restrictions imposed on decorated wares during the Second World War brought manufacture virtually to an end. Since then production of animals has been successfully revived, while other wares have been produced on a more limited scale.

The crystalline glazes

During their experiments with glaze effects, Bailey and Noke, perhaps at Moore's suggestion, spent some time discovering how to produce what are called 'crystalline' glazes. These are characterized by random groups of starry and radiating

Stained glass window in
John Slater's house,
c. 1890

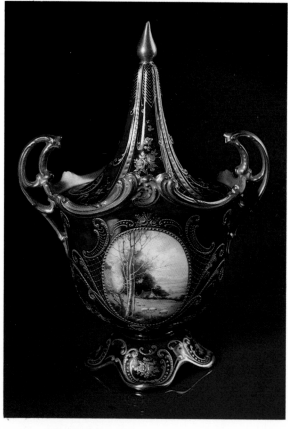

Above: Bone china covered vase with elaborate gilding and country scenes painted by William Hodkinson, c. 1898
8¼ in. (20.5 cm.) high

Above left: Earthenware vase painted with Australian wild flowers from sketches by Louis Bilton, c. 1890. This piece was made for the Art Union of London
8 in. (20 cm.) high

Left: Bone china teapot with gilt decoration, painted by Albert Wright, c. 1885
11½ in. (29 cm.) high

OPPOSITE:
Above left: Bone china vase with gilt details, painted by Edward Raby, c. 1898
11 in. (27.5 cm) high

Above right: Bone china vase modelled with gilded scroll and fruit handles by C.J. Noke and painted by Louis Bilton, 1893
16 in. (40 cm.) high

Right: Bone china centrepiece modelled by C.J. Noke, 1893. This and the piece above (right) were shown at the World Columbian Exposition, Chicago, 1893
14 in. (35 cm.) high

Right: Bone china vase painted
with peonies by Edward Raby.
This monumental piece was made
for the World Columbian
Exposition, Chicago, 1893
48 in. (120 cm.) high

Holbein Ware vase
painted with cattle by
William Hodkinson,
c. 1908
6½ in. (16.5 cm.) high

Rembrandt Ware vase
painted with a portrait
after Van Dyck and the
inscription *A merry heart
goes all the day*, c. 1900
12 in. (30 cm.) high

Above: Coarse
earthenware vase
decorated with stylized
trees in the *Barbotine*
technique, c. 1910
8½ in. (21.5 cm.) high

Left: Earthenware teapot,
jug and vase printed in
the Morrisian style,
c. 1900
Teapot, 8¾ in.
(22 cm.) high

Right: Bone china vase
decorated in the Luscian
Ware technique by Walter
Nunn, c. 1900
13 in. (32.5 cm.) high

Bone china bowls
decorated with lustre
glazes, c. 1920
6¼ in. (15.5 cm.)
largest diam.

Two bone china vases
decorated in the
Hyperion style, the one
on the left by William
Hodkinson, the one on
the right by Fred
Walklate. Both c. 1910
Tallest vase, 8½ in.
(21.5 cm.) high

Below: Bone china vase with Sung glazes designed and decorated by C.J. Noke and Fred Moore, c. 1920. 7 in. (18 cm.) high

Bone china vase with painted decoration of deer and stylized trees under Sung glazes, designed by C.J. Noke, c. 1920
11 in. (28 cm.) high

Bone china vase decorated with green crackle glazes mingling with *flambé* glazes, probably made as an experiment by Cuthbert Bailey, c. 1902
9½ in. (24 cm.) high

Bone china animals
and Buddha
decorated with
flambé glazes,
c. 1920
4¾ in. (12 cm.)
maximum height

Bone china powder
bowl, lamp base
and handled cup
with Chinese Jade
glazes, designed by
C.J. Noke and
Harry Nixon,
c. 1930
Lamp base, 11¾ in.
(30 cm.) high

Above: Vase with Chang glazes designed by C.J. Noke, c. 1925
8 in. (20.5 cm.) high

Left: Bone china vase with Titanian glazes freely painted with a Japanese lady by Harry Tittensor, 1919
14 in. (35 cm.) high

A group of flower sellers designed by Leslie Harradine and introduced in the early 1930s
Tallest figure, 6¾ in. (17 cm.) high

Bone china *Double Jester* or *Mirth and Melancholy*, designed by C.J. Noke in the early 1890s
21 in. (53 cm.) high

A group of nude figures designed by Leslie Harradine and introduced in the 1920s
Tallest figure, 10¼ in. (26 cm.) high

Above: *Clown* and *'Arry*, designed by Harry Fenton, both showing rare variations. This *Clown*, introduced in 1937, has red hair instead of the normal white, and this *'Arry*, produced c. 1947, has additional moulded pearl buttons, hence his nickname, *Pearly Boy* Tallest jug, 6½ in. (16.5 cm.) high

Left: A group of distinctive figures designed by Peggy Davies in the 1950s 7½ in. (19 cm.) high

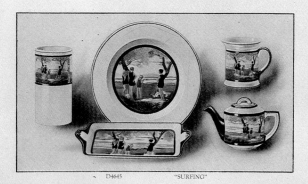

Above: *Golfers* series, introduced in 1911. In the background is a simulated canvas golf bag made at the Lambeth factory Plate, 10½ in. (26.5 cm.) in diam.

Left: Catalogue page showing the *Gnomes* and the *Surfing* series, introduced in 1927 and 1926

Right: Bone china tureen with floral decoration in the Lactolian technique by Robert Allen, c. 1900. This piece was made for the Paris Exhibition of 1900 12 in. (30 cm.) long

Left: Bone china chocolate jug with painted panels of roses by Percy Curnock, 1893
8½ in. (21.6 cm.) high

Below: Bone china cup and saucer with roses painted by Percy Curnock, 1899. Saucer, 5¾ in. (14.5 cm.) in diam.

Simple and stylish
in effect, decorative
in treatment and
modern in conception

BY APPOINTMENT

the EDEN pattern
on LINCOLN shape
makes an immediate
and irresistible appeal

 ROYAL DOULTON

BURSLEM   ENGLAND

PROGRESS BUILT ON QUALITY

Advertisement from the *Pottery Gazette*, 1930,
showing the *Eden* tableware pattern

"GAYLEE"

THE Gaylee is in brilliant colours on attractive modern shapes. The four examples shown on this page are typical of a long range of articles for all purposes and of striking form, which can be grouped into sets suitable for many occasions.

Royal DOULTON

DOULTON & CO., LIMITED,
ROYAL DOULTON POTTERIES,
BURSLEM, STOKE-ON-TRENT.

Advertisement from the *Pottery Gazette*, 1934,
showing the *Gaylee* tableware design

A group of limited edition jugs and loving cups. From left to right: George V Silver Jubilee loving cup, 1935; the Apothecary loving cup, 1934; the George Washington jug, 1932; and the Treasure Island jug, 1934
Tallest jug, 10 in. (25.5 cm.) high

Bone china figures: the *Tibetan Girl*, advertising Grossmith's *Tsang I Hang* perfume, 1924; the *Sketch Girl*, c. 1923; and the group *London Cry*, advertising Yardley's *Olde English Lavender*, c. 1925. All were designed by Leslie Harradine

crystals of various sizes and conformations embodied in the smooth transparent glaze.

There was nothing new in itself in the development of crystals in certain glazes; this was in fact a defect which had long plagued pottery manufacturers, especially tile-makers, leading to many rejects. To induce crystals in a glaze *deliberately* for their future decorative effect was an entirely different matter but it had a definite appeal in a period when European potters were beginning to realize the inherent attractiveness of glaze effects as a sole method of decoration. To produce these glazes was an extremely difficult technique of which the Royal Copenhagen ceramist Clement had been a pioneer in 1886, as far as Europe was concerned, although two years earlier a variety known as 'tiger-eye' glaze had been produced in the United States at the Rookwood Pottery in Cincinnati. In the early twentieth century they were also made successfully by several other pottery factories, including Meissen.

In the firing of ceramic glazes there is a critical range of temperatures during which devitrification takes place; if the rate of cooling is retarded through this particular range, crystals are apt to develop, especially in a glaze with a certain content of zinc oxide. (By rapid cooling over the critical period crystals have no time to form.) Just as certain Chinese potters had learned how to produce their beautiful 'crackle' or 'broken ice' glazes by inducing, and even intensifying, what is normally regarded as the serious fault of 'crazing' (the appearance of hair-like cracks) so Bailey and Noke, like Clement and others, learned how to take advantage of the crystalizing phenomenon for artistic ends. Noke found it an altogether absorbing labour to combine glazes of different colours, crystals of various sizes and formations, with suitably-shaped pots. A special body, somewhat akin to Chinese feldspathic porcelain, had to be evolved to take the appropriate glaze; the heat during the '*grand feu*' firing had to be maintained at a steady temperature of some 1,400° Centigrade for some hours – not an easy condition to comply with in the days when coal-fired kilns were still being used. Unfortunately, even slight variations in the degree of heat could ruin hopelessly the special effects being aimed at, and as the crystalline glazes could not be fired with other wares output was limited.

The results of Bailey's and Noke's efforts were described by J. F. Blacker as 'ceramic gems with entirely unexpected and largely unpredictable characteristics which cannot be produced at will'. The American *Pottery Gazette* said of them in September 1907: 'Comparison may fearlessly be claimed for these pieces with the productions of any European factory. In some cases indeed they have outclassed all rivals in this particular effect.' When they were shown at the Brussels Exhibition in 1910 it was reported that collectors and connoisseurs queued to obtain them, and within a few hours from the opening almost every piece had been sold. Much the same thing happened at Turin in 1911 and Ghent in 1913.

Among the specimens produced all-white and ivory-coloured pots predominated with a myriad crystals sparkling like frost on a window-pane. Vases, designed by Hodkinson, on the surface of which sinuous glittering goldfish moved as it were through a pool of crystals, are very attractive. Rare varieties are the pots with crystalline glaze in a light colour merging with *rouge flambé* below. Red, blue, turquoise, yellow and brown glazes are also found. Realistic-looking crabs with the tops of their shells scintillating with large crystals are unusual examples of this technique.

The crystalline glazes were undoubtedly an artistic and technical triumph but the results were too 'chancy' to make the continuance of their production an economic proposition, especially after the First World War when the firm was going through a period of serious financial difficulties and was unable to pay any dividends to its shareholders. Production, which had already been on a limited scale for some years, appears to have been discontinued altogether about 1918.

In some ways Cuthbert Bailey apparently found that being 'the son of the boss' had its disadvantages and in 1907, once the production of the *flambé* wares had been established on a sound basis, he left Doulton of Burslem to prove his independence and broaden his experience in other branches of the ceramic industry. In 1925, however, he returned to Nile Street to succeed his father as General Manager.

John Slater retired in 1914 and was succeeded by Charles Noke who had been already acting as joint Art Director for two or three years. The following fine tribute was paid by Noke to his predecessor for whom he had always had a great affection:

To the true potter the all-importance of pots is an inspiring ideal. In that ideal he lives and breathes and has his being; he is impelled to express it visibly in form or colour, or to break his heart in impotent endeavour. . . . And so, amid the smother and smoke of the potters' ovens, John Slater worked and strove for his ideal. But always the free hand, the readiness to give another's ideas a run, his sole anxiety that the best that could be done should be done, so that the finished pot should approach that ideal for which he constantly and persistently strove. This breadth of outlook assured the development of original minds, and gave each man when signing his work the chance to feel a real personal interest in every piece made. . . . John Slater, art director and artist, has left an impress upon the character and quality of Doulton pottery that will not soon be forgotten.

These words reveal a good deal not only about the artist of whom they were written but equally about the artist who wrote them. Noke was to carry on and enhance the tradition of craftsmanship and artistry which has been established under Slater's aegis over nearly four decades.

The Sung Wares

It seems that after Cuthbert Bailey resigned in 1907 Charles Noke was asked by Slater to take over the major responsibility not only for the artistic development of the transmutation and crystalline glaze wares but also for their further technical evolution. Noke continued to experiment with the reduction glazes, striving to perfect and extend some of the unusual effects, such as the flocculated blue and violet markings which had arisen during the development of the *rouge flambé*.

During the First World War, when ordinary trade was seriously curtailed, and normal demands on his time as a modeller were not so pressing, he intensified his researches into special bodies and glazes, the result being not only the development of the Titanian Wares but also of a new family of transmutation glazes to which he gave the name Sung. His aim, in which he clearly succeeded, had been to extend the range of colours and to obtain greater control over the mottled, feathered, flocculated and veined effects which are to be seen on some of the earlier *flambé* wares. Indeed, although the name Sung does not appear to have been used on the wares until 1919 there exist numerous pots made several years earlier, and merely marked *flambé*, to which the new description could equally apply.

In giving his new production the name Sung, Noke paid homage to the old Chinese masters who had inspired his and Bailey's first achievements in this esoteric field of ceramics. In one way, however, the name is misleading, for although *some* of Noke's pots recall effects seen in the old Chinese wares many display a far wider mastery over the reduction glaze effects. Among the experts who at once realized this was *The Times* art critic who, when the Sung Wares were first shown at the British Industries Fair in the Crystal Palace, Sydenham, in 1920, commented: 'Doulton's Sung glaze surpasses in transmutation colouring anything produced during the Sung period by the Chinese.' Writing a little later that year, J. F. Blacker went so far as to say: 'Regarding the name "Sung" glaze applied to this ware, I can safely assert that the Sung dynasty, which lasted from 954 to 1279 A.D., never saw any porcelain as wondrous as this, and that the King-te-chin manufactories in their best periods produced nothing like it . . . however, *faute de mieux* the appellation is sufficiently distinct. You will remember "Sung" and thus the name will fulfill its mission.'

The *Pottery Gazette* for April 1920 described the Doulton stand at the Crystal Palace as 'probably the *pièce de luxe* of the entire Fair'. During their visit to the Exhibition, King George V and Queen Mary were greatly interested in the new ware and the King, who had a long discussion with Noke, surprised him with his grasp of the problems involved in producing it. Their Majesties had in 1913 visited the Burslem works and recalled having seen some of the processes the earlier *flambé* pots had to undergo. Noke later remarked smilingly that the only man beside himself who knew the full secret of the Sung glaze was King George V, and he was certain it would be safe with him!

The response of the experts to Noke's new achievement must have given him great satisfaction. Gordon Forsyth, himself a distinguished potter, wrote to Lewis Doulton:

I consider it to be the very finest effort that has yet been made in the history of English pottery to produce wares of high artistic value. Undoubtedly great credit is due to your firm, to your art director and to your artist for the appreciation of fine clay shapes and for the glorious colour effects obtained that can only result from a right appreciation of the artistic possibilities of the craft. That a large firm like yours should have tackled this problem so successfully has given me the greatest pleasure, and confidence in the fact that we are really beginning to get a living tradition in the artistic side of English pottery.

Overseas, the reception of the Sung Wares was equally favourable. Among the many American tributes was this from Professor S. Parkes Cadman, the famous art historian:

While the World War devastated Europe, Doulton's persisted in their efforts to build up color schemes on classic shapes such as modern pottery had never known. The results defy description and must be seen to be appreciated. Every piece of this precious ware has its own individuality, speaking in tones all its own, and entitling it to a place in the finest collections. . . . New ranges of color shading off into harmonies of greens, greys, iridescent blues and a Persian violet – which seems to be the ultimate and perfect gain – fascinate the most critical taste. Films of transparent plum color and masses of blues and greens are sprayed over the glaze like the delicate fronds traced by the frosts on a window pane. Any title for these creations is of necessity generic and affords one but the merest clue to these opulent varieties of colours, named or nameless, which indicate that chemical wizardry, guided by competent brains, yet has new realms of loveliness and grace to explore.

J. F. Blacker, in the article already quoted from wrote: 'There scarcely seems to be any limit to the range of colours applied to this most interesting ware, with its marvels of lustre colouring, varying from the tint of hoary lichen of old thorn trees to the rainbow tints of a soap-bubble, glowing and glimmery with coloured fire.' To obtain some of these colours mentioned by Professor Cadman and Mr Blacker, double oxidizations and double reductions were involved. The new combinations of *flambé* and lustre effects, including new purple, heliotrope and pearl grey, and the superimposition of a *flambé* glaze over pots which already had a Titanian glaze resulted in many unique pieces. Apart from the pots which depended entirely for their aesthetic appeal on shape and coloured glaze and lustre effects, many were also designed in which underglaze hand-painting or printing from engraved plates in black or colours – a process already seen in some of the earlier *flambe* wares – was used with strikingly effective results to portray a host of subjects: peacocks, eagles, pheasants, birds of paradise and wondrous exotic imaginary birds with outstretched wings; dragons, deer, stags, bears and other animals; foliage, prunus blossom and other flowers; intricate geometrical patterns. Sometimes these designs were highlighted with splashes of white enamel and outlined with delicate gold traceries. Attractive examples of the latter technique are the paintings of quaint tropical fish moving sinuously among seaweeds and other marine plants on a delicate blue ground, and what was described by a collector as 'an ancient pike or jack darting from the reeds to chase a school of minnows, painted in lustrous greens and purples on a lovely ground of red, splashed with blotches of yellow'.

Some of the smaller vases and bowls are in a delicate china body of egg-shell thickness. In addition to the pots a number of figures – men, women, animals and birds – appeared in the new glazes. Some of these are similar to those already produced in *rouge flambé* but are painted with the new glazes. The treatment was broad and massive, the effect depending not so much on detailed modelling as on general form and colour. One of the most unusual (and apparently most popular, for Blacker wrote of it as being 'in great demand') was the figure entitled *The Smiling Buddha*, depicting the oriental teacher seated, with his head inclined to one side, contemplating a tiny figure of a man perched on his knee.

Prices given in a 1927 or 1928 catalogue for some of the Sung Wares ranged from 54p for a 3 in. (8 cm.) diameter bowl to £3.60 for one 10 in. (25 cm.) in diameter, and from £2.15 for a vase 5½ in. (14 cm.) high to £45 for a covered vase, 22 in. (56 cm.) high, beautifully decorated in many colours with an exotic bird. A vase 13 in. (34 cm.) high, similarly decorated, was priced at £11.

The artists already mentioned in connection with the earlier *rouge flambé* were also those principally involved in the decoration of the Sung. Production ceased in the early 1940s and, except for some examples of 'Veined Sung', has not been resumed.

It was a standing order in the Doulton studios and factory that every single piece of Sung, down to the tiniest, had to pass through Mr Noke's hands before being released for sale. Nearly all the finest pieces are signed underneath by him as Art Director. This signature is a sign of approval of quality; it does not necessarily mean that Noke himself was responsible for the decoration.

Chinese Jade

Chinese Jade is the unusual name which Noke gave to an equally unusual type of ceramic introduced in the same year, 1920, as the Sung, after experiments dating back to 1913. There is a record of fifteen samples having been sent in February 1921 to Doulton's agent in New York, William Pitcairn. These included vases, bowls, two figures, an elephant and a leaping salmon. The range had increased very little by 1936 when an internal price record listed the items then in production as a Chinese woman with tree support, a seated Buddha, a leaping salmon, two other fishes, an elephant, a llama, a horse, a chalice, two lily bowls, a powder bowl and five vases.

The natural material jade was venerated by the Chinese for its coolness, hardness and almost magical translucency. There is mention in early T'ang literature of a ceramic material – probably a porcellaneous stoneware – described as 'false jade'. It may have been this which gave Noke the idea of trying to imitate jade. Be this as it may, the Doulton so-called Chinese Jade represents a remarkable technical achievement -- what was described at the time as 'a veritable *tour de force*'. The ware, which was difficult to produce and was apparently never made in large quantities, is a rarity today. It has usually a white glaze of remarkable purity, revealing in places subtle graduations and veins of green and turquoise. Some of the vases and other shapes were based on early Chinese bronze and pottery prototypes.

For a ware of such unique character and not at all easy to produce, the wholesale prices quoted in the record mentioned above are incredibly low. They range from 20p for the smallest vase to £1.37½ each for both the female figures and the leaping salmons. Apart from Noke the artist mainly involved was Harry Nixon. Production ceased in the early 1940s and has not been resumed.

The Chang Wares

Noke, in collaboration with Harry Nixon, went on exploring those 'new realms of loveliness and grace' of which Professor Cadman had spoken. They were joined by Noke's son, Jack, and in 1925 they were able to announce yet a further development in the transmutation glaze effects. This was an entirely new ware to which they gave the name Chang because of a certain supposed resemblance in some of the early examples to the thickly glazed Chinese wares which had been attributed to a possibly mythical Sung dynasty potter, Chang the Elder. Here again, as with the Sung Wares, one cannot help feeling the choice of name was not really a happy one, for the fact was that never, in China or elsewhere, had anything like the great majority of these new Doulton pots been produced. They really merited an entirely new name for an entirely new *genre*.

The so-called Chang Wares are distinguished from Doulton's earlier *rouge flambé* and Sung productions by the much heavier type of refractory body needed to carry the thick suety, opalescent and brilliantly coloured glazes which were its outstanding feature. Some pieces were coated with three or more superimposed glazes of different colours and thicknesses, the top one usually beautifully crackled and often running down in tongues of various shapes and densities towards, and sometimes over, the base. The crackle effect was a characteristic feature of almost all the Chang Wares, however else they varied, and was used to great artistic effect. The way in which the glazes combined a soft velvety lustre with glorious colours was without parallel in either ancient or modern pottery. The *Pottery Gazette* well described these wares as 'one of the most startling ranges of new ornamental pottery that has seen the light of day for half a century'. A well-known connoisseur of the period, W. G. Menzies, declared:

In the history of ceramics the British potter has much of which to be proud, and the two hundred and fifty years since that old Fulham potter, John Dwight, took out his first patent for the manufacture of porcelain contains nothing which surpasses in brilliancy this, the latest crowning effort of the Royal Doulton Potteries. In any phase of artistic effort tradition is bound to play a big part. The first Doulton to become a potter learned his craft under the aegis of Dwight's successor, William White, and in the century and more that has elapsed since then his successors have never called a halt. Year after year by improvements and discoveries they have placed the artistic products of their potteries on a plane which has seldom been equalled and never surpassed in modern times, and the patronage of Royalty is an endorsement of the permanent success of their efforts. The masterpieces of the early Chinese potters were destined for Imperial use. A similar appreciation is merited by some of the more imposing pieces of 'Chang' ware.

The two foregoing quotations are typical of the response on the part of collectors and connoisseurs to the new range.

The extensive gamut of Chang glazes included a wide range of reds, yellows and purples, blues and greens and browns. White, ivory, grey and black were also used in novel ways. The glazes were often mottled, clouded, splashed or veined with boldly contrasting colours. Some appeared opalescent, others lava-like. Besides simple and beautifully proportioned vases, the pots in the range included dishes, snuff-bottles, lamps and flower bowls modelled by Noke with sinuous dragons on them. Other small bowls modelled with lotus buds are singularly attractive.

Nearly all Chang pieces bear the signature of either Charles Noke or his son Cecil (Jack). This does not necessarily mean that either of these modelled and/or decorated the item. It does indicate, however, that the pot had passed through their hands for approval. Harry Nixon was also involved in the design of many pieces on which his name or monogram will be found. Production of the Chang Wares ceased in the early 1940s and has not been resumed.

Although Noke and his colleagues succeeded in establishing the essential measure of control over the transmutation effects without which consistent production of the *rouge flambé*, Sung, Chinese Jade, Chang and crystalline glaze wares would have been impossible, within these broad limits many surprising things could still happen in the kilns through the mingling and spreading of colours in ways that could never be *wholly* predicted. No two pieces, therefore, are ever exactly alike and this gives these wares an added attraction in the eyes of the discerning present-day collector. As W. G. Menzies remarked over fifty years ago:

It is a human weakness to want something no one else possesses and purchasers of even the smallest piece of this remarkable ware can feel a satisfaction that they own something which, if similar to others as regards shape, is entirely dissimilar as regards the colourings, splash-ings and fleckings of the glaze. To possess one of these pieces is a permanent joy. Every minute new beauties become apparent and the slightest movement reveals effects of light and color of unexpected brilliance.

These words were written particularly about the Chang but they can be applied to the great majority of the other reduction glaze wares as well.

The Titanian Wares

As a designer and modeller, and later on as Art Director, Charles Noke had an extraordinary dual flair which was to bring great success to Doulton. On the one hand, he had a sound commercial sense for what would have immense popular appeal – such as the *Dickens, Jackdaw of Rheims, Coaching Days* and other Series Wares; the many rack plates; the limited editions of loving cups and presentation jugs; and the figures, Character Jugs and other expressions of popular art described elsewhere in this book. On the other hand, he would suddenly astonish and enchant the *cognoscenti* with such *récherché* offerings as the Sung and Chang Wares.

The Titanian Wares, introduced in 1915, on the evolution of which he had been quietly working for three or four years, are another example of his unusual talents. As with the Sung and Chang Wares, it is impossible to do justice to the beauty of the Titanian in words, and even the finest colour illustrations fall short of conveying their unique delicacy and distinctive quality. Like the old Chinese wares engraved 'For the Imperial fondling of Ch'ien Lung' many of them appeal to the sense of touch as much as that of sight. They cry out to be handled. They show a superb mastery of materials, glazes and pigments, and a rare sensitivity for form and colour as aesthetic influences. Although Noke was their primary inspirer, a whole team of chemists, craftsmen-potters and artists co-operated to transform his ideas into ceramic reality.

Before the Titanian Wares could be perfected, a particularly translucent yet strong body had to be evolved. In the smaller pots this recalls the finest egg-shell porcelain of China; if a small bowl, for example, is held against a strong light the outside decoration can be seen inside. To wed with this special body, a new glaze and new blends of ceramic pigments based on metallic compounds had to be evolved.

The new ware was favourably received by the press. The correspondent for the *British Architect*, May 1915, remarked 'Another charming ware of great refinement is, we think, called the "Titanian". It largely resembles the ware from the Royal Porcelain Works at Copenhagen. The delicate colouring in its soft gradations of tone, and beautiful renderings of figures and landscapes, will command the interest of a large public.'

Another connoisseur described the atmosphere created by the Titanian Wares as one 'which would make a painter on canvas sigh with envy'. With their tender pastel colours and mottled and clouded effects, their greenish-greys merging with shadowy, smoky blues and mellow greens in many subtle graduations, there is something about many of the Titanian pots that is almost ethereal, evocative of the realms of poetic fancy, opening 'magic casements' into a world with no more substantiality than the morning mist.

The name Titanian, given apparently because a compound of the metallic element titanium was an essential component of the special glaze, was a happy choice, for many of the pieces conjure up visions of the fairy kingdom of Oberon and Titania. Some of the pots have no formal decoration at all but achieve their effects solely by the tender veils of colour enveloping the simple shapes. Others reveal, through a haze of hues in which a characteristic smoky blue generally predominates, such subjects as bees hovering over flowering thistles; spiders spinning their webs over fronds of bracken with a robin as an interested spectator; gnomes on toadstools; fairy revels; rabbits peering out of the mist; barn owls perched on moonlit branches; a field mouse delicately poised on an ear of corn; a polar bear in a setting of snow and ice; gulls skimming the waves.

Charles Noke was an admirer of the American poet, Henry Wadsworth Long-fellow. One wonders if the type of themes for the Titanian Wares was suggested by the following lines. Whether this was so or not, they are, as J. F. Blacker pointed out, singularly apposite:

> The leaves that rustle, the reeds that make
> A whisper by each stream and lake,
> The saffron dawn, the sunset red,
> Are painted on these lovely jars;
> Again the skylark sings, again
> The stork, the heron and the crane
> Float through the azure overhead,
> The counterfeit and counterpart
> Of nature reproduced in Art.

The artists mainly associated with the development of the Titanian Wares were Robert Allen, Harry Allen, Harry Tittensor, Harry Nixon and F. Henri. Percy Curnock decorated many pieces in the early days: examples by Charles Nixon and A. Leach are also found. Some of the bowls painted by these artists have an inside glaze of such depth and clarity as to give the impression of being filled with water. Among the large vases, Allen's paintings of owls, night herons, swans, storks and other birds, and Tittensor's studies of oriental ladies, *Omar Khayyam's Potter*, *Night in the Lagoon*, *Fisherfolk*, and *The Old, Old Story* are much admired.

The varieties of Titanian include pots in which this treatment is combined with *flambé* and Chang effects; others with acid gold rims and raised gold rims and raised gold, silver and enamel embellishments designed by Robert Allen and carried out by Thomas Morton, William Skinner and William Massey – three of Doulton's finest craftsmen-gilders; and vases in Japanese style with outlines of flying birds, wistaria and insects outlines in raised gold. Combinations of Titanian decoration with orange, lemon, green and silver pearl lustre effects are also found. A number of figures – among them a mandarin, a seated Buddha, spooks, gnomes and some of the Forty Thieves – were produced in Titanian body and glaze.

An unusual application of the Titanian style was for tea and coffee sets and other items of tableware, with partly printed and partly painted patterns depicting land-scapes, exotic birds and formal abstract designs. An unusual rack plate has an Ancient Egyptian scene and the inscription 'Tutankhamen's Treasures Luxor'.

Over fifty different shapes of vases and bowls are recorded. Production had been practically discontinued by 1925 but a few items were made to special order into the early 1930s. Wholesale prices recorded in 1915 are almost unbelievably low for wares of such outstanding quality. Here are some examples:

Vase, *Swan*, painted by H. Allen; 6 in. (15 cm.) high: 75p
Vase, *Young Flycatcher*, painted by H. Allen; 6¾ in. (17 cm.) high: £1.05
Vase, *Peacock*, painted by H. Allen; 13½ in. (34 cm.) high: £4.20
Cylinder vase, *Chill October*, painted by H. Tittensor; 8 in. (20 cm.) high: £1.50
Vase, *Seagulls*, painted by F. Henri; 8 in. (20 cm.) high: £1.05

Vases with Titanian colour effects but without formal decoration, 8¼ in. (21 cm.) high were priced at 12.5p plain and 15p if lustred! No price record has been found of Titanian Wares with raised gold and acid gold treatments but these would naturally have been more expensive.

(During the early twentieth century a tableware pattern known as Titanian, and depicting fairies, is said to have been made at Burslem. No other information is available but if such a pattern did exist it probably had no connection with the Titanian Wares introduced in 1916.)

IX

Figures and Other Ceramic Sculptures

This chapter includes a much condensed version of part of the introduction to *Royal Doulton Figures*, (Eyles and Dennis) published by Royal Doulton Tableware Limited in 1978. This book of 432 pages, containing some 850 colour plates and many black and white illustrations, gives details of well over 2,000 figures, including miniatures, made at Burslem between 1913 and 1978. It describes their size, colour, dates of introduction and withdrawal, designer and any other information relevant to their manufacture and naming. It contains also a reference list of some 700 animal and bird models included in the HN series.

Royal Doulton figures have made a major contribution to the history of modern ceramic sculpture, establishing in our day a reputation comparable with that of their Meissen, Sèvres, Chelsea, Derby and Staffordshire predecessors of the eighteenth century. More extensive in range of subjects than those of any earlier china-works in England or on the Continent, they reflect in their diverse styles the versatility of their designers and modellers, and in their fine finish the skills of the artists and craftsmen who produce them. While not overlooking the influence of earlier traditions, they have created an unmistakeable and refreshingly new *genre* all their own, combining in a remarkable way an impression of timelessness with a reflection of changes in popular tastes and trends since their inception right up to the present day. At the same time they generally avoid the 'fussiness' and over-ornamentation that marked, and sometimes marred, the work of many earlier figure-modellers in both the china and earthenware media. In creating a Royal Doulton figure the designer, sculptor, potter and painter fuse their talents. The result of their collaboration is an impeccably finished example of ceramic art.

Tradition

The English figure tradition began in Staffordshire, where figures were made from about 1720 onwards by several potters whose names are honoured in ceramic history – John Astbury, Thomas Whieldon, the Woods, Humphrey Palmer, Felix Pratt, John Walton, the Mintons and others.

Between about 1745 and 1793 famous English china-works – Chelsea, Bow, Lowestoft, Derby, Longton Hall, Bristol, Plymouth, Worcester, Spode and Minton among them – were also founded and at all of these, in addition to tablewares, china figures formed part of the production. During the nineteenth century, with a few exceptions, there was a sad falling-away from the high standards set by Ralph Wood and other earlier potters and the revival, early this century, of the once famous Staffordshire figure-making traditions, albeit in quite a new form, must rank high among Charles Noke's many contributions to the fame of Royal Doulton. The story of Doulton figures begins, however, in Lambeth.

George Tinworth

The first Doulton figures were made at Lambeth in terracotta and salt-glaze stoneware by George Tinworth. He was the first student from the Lambeth School of Art to come to work for Henry Doulton in 1866; with his advent the story of the Doulton art wares may be said to have begun.

Born in 1843, the son of an improvident and often intemperate wheelwright, Tinworth had little or no formal schooling but was taught to read and recite the Bible by his God-fearing mother. In face of abject poverty, a slum environment, his father's disapproval, and other disadvantages, he yet managed to work his way through the Lambeth Art School and the Antique School of the Royal Academy, winning several important awards. During his subsequent career at Doulton's Lambeth Pottery he became renowned for his ceramic sculpture, especially his large and small terracotta and stoneware panels, almost all of them illustrating, in his own unique fashion, subjects taken from the Old and New Testaments. Examples of his work are to be found in cathedrals, churches and chapels in many parts of the world.

From the late 1870s until his death in 1913 Tinworth found relaxation from the labour of his larger works in an intermittent flow of small ceramic figures, especially of children, and amusing little studies of mice, frogs, birds and other creatures, parodying all manner of human situations and activities. He would doubtless be amazed, were he to come back today, to find that his once famous religious sculpture arouses scant general interest while his little figures find an ever-increasing host of admirers.

The renaissance of Staffordshire figure-making

Ceramic sculpture had fascinated Charles Noke since childhood days in his father's antique shop. At the Chicago Exhibition of 1893 he exhibited a few well-modelled figures and during the next decade designed perhaps a dozen or so more, but they were rather large, and subtly-coloured, besides being expensive, and failed to arouse much interest. Noke later became deeply absorbed in various new projects, such as the highly successful *Dickens* and other Series Wares, and the Holbein, Rembrandt, *flambé* and Kingswares. These demanded all his time to bring them to successful fruition. Any thoughts he cherished of reviving the Staffordshire figure-making tradition had to be temporarily set aside. During his regular visits to Lambeth, however, he took a particular interest in the figures which not only Tinworth but other Lambeth artists – notably John Broad, Mark Marshall and Leslie Harradine – were creating, and he acquired examples of some of these for his own collection of examples of ceramic sculpture.

According to Joseph Mott, Art Director of the Lambeth Pottery, it was these figures which revived his dormant desire to bring about a renaissance of figure-making in Staffordshire itself, leading eventually to the launching of a new series of Doulton Burslem figures (now known as the HN-series) in 1913. He would have liked Tinworth to create some further child models for reproduction in bone china but unfortunately the sculptor died suddenly on the way to work in 1912, just at the time the first figures in the new series were being prepared. Some of Tinworth's mice models, however, were reproduced in small quantities at the Burslem factory.

Many of the figures produced in England in the nineteenth century had been somewhat garish and naïve representations of famous (or infamous) contemporaries – royalties, politicians, admirals, generals, preachers, actors, murderers and their victims, prize fighters and so forth – or outmoded and often poorly modelled imitations of the conventional nymphs and swains of Meissen, Chelsea and Bow. These have a considerable social-historical interest and a peculiar fascination which appeals to some collectors but few could be called 'things of beauty'. Between the 1840s and the end of the century many well-modelled but conventional figures in classical and pseudo-classical style were made in a parian body. A Doulton type of parian had been used for some of Noke's earlier figures, for example the *Jester*, which later appeared in the HN range and is still made today. By the early 1900s parian figures had largely gone out of favour, and in the absence of good English china figures, large numbers were being imported from Germany, France and other countries.

The history of china-figure production in England up to the time of Noke's revival had been an unfortunate one financially, several of the factories which were involved going bankrupt after a few years. It had been said of the Worcester factory that one reason it outlasted several other eighteenth-century potteries was because

69

figures never represented more than a small part of its output; the same would apply to Spode, Minton and Wedgwood.

Noke moved cautiously in the light of his earlier disappointments. He realized that the revival he had in mind was an ambitious undertaking and would require the collaboration of other experienced sculptors and artists. He therefore invited several contemporary modellers to contribute suggestions; they included Phoebe Stabler, Charles Vyse, William White, George Lambert and F. Stone, all of them established sculptors or art school teachers.

The new range of some twenty models had been completed by the end of 1912, some even earlier. They included *The Diligent Scholar, The Sleepy Scholar* and *Coquette* by White; *Elizabeth Fry* and *Return of Persephone* by Vyse; *Picardy Peasants* and *Madonna of the Square* by Phoebe Stabler. (The original of *Elizabeth Fry* had been exhibited earlier in 1912 at the Royal Academy.) Noke himself contributed *Dunce, Pedlar Wolf, An Arab, Moorish Minstrel* and one or two other models. They were all held back from public exhibition and sale until after the visit of King George V and Queen Mary to the Burslem factory in April 1913.

At that time the little figure now known as *Darling* had been named *Bedtime*. The Queen, picking it up, exclaimed, 'Isn't he a darling!' She ordered copies for herself and some of her friends, and the figure has ever since been known to many thousands of collectors all over the world as *Darling*. Although it was not in fact the first of the new series to be completed, it was, because of its Royal 'christening', given the number HN–1 when this system of numbering was introduced. Each new figure or colour version produced thereafter has been given an HN–number, a sequence that runs in more or less chronological order up to about 1940 when a different system was introduced. The initials HN, incidentally, are those of Harry Nixon, who was in charge of the first small group of artists concerned with painting the figures.

Between 1914 and 1920 several other sculptors contributed to the range, among them Albert Toft, L. Perugini and two resident artists, Harry Tittensor and E. W. Light (both of whom were also local art teachers). Tittensor's *The Gainsborough Hat, Pretty Lady* and *The Parson's Daughter*, Light's *Lady of the Fan, Lady with Rose, The Curtsey* and *The Flounced Skirt*, Perugini's *Shy Anne, A Child's Grace* and other child studies and Noke's *Carpet Vendor, Guy Fawkes, King Charles, Omar Khayyam* and *The Old King* opened up new directions which were to influence many subsequent creations. With some of the figures previously in production they established certain basic themes – children, 'fair ladies', quaint 'characters', and legendary, historical and literary personages – which still predominate today.

The Crystal Palace fair

For several years progress was slow and production remained on a restricted scale. Records show, for example, that between June 1913 and September 1917 the total number of figures completed was 680 – an average of about three a week. These early figures have naturally become very valuable collectors' pieces.

The slow development was partly because of the repercussions of the First World War, during which many artists and craftsmen were engaged in the Armed Forces or other branches of war work. It was due also to the fact that much experimenting – with different subjects and styles of modelling, different kinds of costume, dress and colour schemes – was found necessary before the factors influencing popular response to the new offerings could be gauged with any degree of accuracy. Market and design research as we know them today had not then been born.

The first marked impact upon the press, the critics and the buying public was undoubtedly at the British Industries Fair held in the Crystal Palace, Sydenham, London in 1920. Here was shown the whole range of figures by then available, including those already mentioned and others such as the *Welsh Girl*, *A Lilac Shawl*, *A Mandarin*, *Guy Fawkes*, *Tony Weller*, *Blighty*, *Digger*, *A Geisha*, *Dolly*, *Contentment*, *Puff and Powder*, *Betty* and *Marie*. The last four were the creations of the former Doulton Lambeth artist, Leslie Harradine.

It was after this display that a discerning writer in the *Staffordshire Sentinel* described it as heralding 'A renaissance of Staffordshire figure-making after long neglect. . . . Since the days of Ralph Wood there had been produced in Staffordshire nothing so craftsmanlike and so eminently right.' This verdict was echoed by many English, Australian, Canadian and American collectors. Queen Mary visited the exhibition and again bought copies of *Darling* as well as of *Contentment*. She became a great admirer of Harradine's work and subsequently bought many of his models at other exhibitions.

By 1927 the number of figure painters was still only ten. Taking into account the fact that the figures were all hand-painted and that many separate moulds and several firings and fusings of colour were needed to obtain the beautiful effects which differentiate them from those of other makes, it is clear that the total output could not have been great. The studios were extended in the mid 1930s but even by 1939 there were only twenty-seven painters. The Second World War brought many problems including the calling-up of many of the artists and craftsmen. Between 1941 and 1949 many of the earlier models were discontinued for ever. They are now among the most sought after by present-day collectors. It is unlikely that as many as 2,000 of any one of them had been made, probably far fewer of most of them. They would rank today as 'limited editions'.

Leslie Harradine

Asking Arthur L. Harradine (usually known by his second name, Leslie) to create some models for him was, as things transpired, the most important step in the successful development of the new range that Noke could possibly have taken. Harradine had joined Doulton's Lambeth studios in 1902 as an apprentice modeller, working at different times under the guidance of Tinworth, Broad and Marshall. He studied also under the well-known sculptor, Albert Toft, at the Camberwell School of Art. Between about 1907 and 1912 he produced some excellent pieces in salt-glaze stoneware. These included spirit flasks (inspired by John Doulton's 1812 'Reform Flasks') depicting Arthur Balfour, Lord Haldane, D. Lloyd George, H. H. Asquith, John Burns and Sir Austen Chamberlain; also one of Dr Johnson. Among several other creations revealing an original and vigorous talent, those which particularly attracted Noke, a great lover of Dickens, were models of *Pickwick*, *Micawber*, *Sam Weller*, *The Fat Boy* and other well-known characters from the novels.

In 1912 Harradine emigrated to Canada. Four years later, having enlisted in a Canadian Regiment, he was in action in France. When he left the army he decided to return to England and work as an independent artist. Noke tried to entice him to Burslem but this he refused to consider; he agreed, however, to send Noke some figures, which he would model at home, to see if these could be reproduced in bone china. Thus began one of the most successful and enduring collaborations between a sculptor and a china factory in the whole history of figure-making – one which was to continue unbroken for nearly forty years, first with Charles Noke, then with his son Jack who succeeded him as Art Director in 1936, and finally, after 1955, with the present Director of Design, Joseph W. Ledger, ARCA.

The porcelain figure offered Harradine scope for depicting a wonderful variety of expressions, forms and poses. He had a great gift for suggesting movement – wind-blown out-of-door girls, flouncing and gliding indoor ladies. Among his first models for Noke, apart from the four already mentioned, were *The Goose Girl*, *Fruit Gathering*, *The Balloon Seller*, *The Flower Seller's Children* and a famous series – *Polly Peachum* and other characters from *The Beggar's Opera*. These, like the first Dickens figures, had been modelled earlier in stoneware. Six large and sixteen small Dickens characters (later increased to twenty-four) were developed in close collaboration with Noke. And through the succeeding years new Harradine models came regularly one after another. 'I sent at least one model a month, sometimes two or three, for nearly forty years,' he said, shortly before his death in Gibraltar in 1965.

Noke and Harradine between them consolidated the revival of Staffordshire figure-making which the former had initiated in 1913. The *Chelsea Pair*, *The Perfect Pair*, *The Mask*, *Harlequinade*, *A Yeoman of the Guard*, *A Chelsea Pensioner*, *Mam'selle*, *A Victorian Lady*, *The Belle*, *Lady Jester*, *A Wandering Minstrel*, *Sweet Anne*, *Darby*, *Joan*, *Sweet and Twenty* – these are just a few of the many Harradine models which have given endless joy and pleasure to a host of collectors of ceramic sculpture. It is a great tribute to his flair for creating figures which do not date that so many of them are still in production today, just as popular as decades ago. His child studies still evoke a world of innocence. His *Top o'the Hill*, *Autumn Breezes*, *Old Balloon Seller* and the Dickens characters are among the most popular china figures ever made.

Freelance sculptors

Charles J. Noke's interest in the work of established sculptors continued into the 'twenties and 'thirties and he regularly visited London galleries and exhibitions to keep up to date with new developments and generally to talent spot. It was no doubt on such a visit that he came across the work of David Evans, a promising young *Prix de Rome* sculptor. In particular his bronze figure *Diana* had attracted favourable attention at the Royal Academy and elsewhere. With the help of the artist this design was adapted in 1928 for limited reproduction in white glazed earthenware. At about the same time, Richard Garbe, recently appointed Professor of Sculpture at the Royal College of Art, began to work for Doulton. Some of the models he produced were adapted from existing sculptures in stone or ivory, but others were designed specifically for Doulton. The liaison between Garbe and the Nokes, father and son, lasted from around 1934 until 1939 and during this time they produced a number of very distinctive figures and other ceramic sculptures entitled *Beethoven*, *Spring*, *The Spirit of the Pines*, *The Cloud*, *West Wind*, *Lady of the Rose*, *Lady of the Snow*, *The Spirit of the Wind*, *Macaw* and *Salome*.

Garbe also modelled a number of wall masks. All these pieces were first produced in limited editions ranging from twenty-five to one hundred, in an ivory-glazed special porcelain body. Coloured versions were later produced; these were not limited in numbers but sales of both the limited and unlimited editions were surprisingly disappointing. The ivory and coloured figures, masks and other sculptures are all rarities today.

Wall masks

The titles of the Garbe wall masks referred to above are given in the records as *Saint Agnes*, *Fate* and *Lion of the East*. There was a limited edition of one hundred of each in matt white and an unlimited edition of each in green. The masks did not appeal to many people at the time and not more than five hundred of each of the unlimited editions were sold.

Between 1934 and 1935 Charles Noke, Harry Fenton and Leslie Harradine also modelled some twenty-eight other wall masks. A *Jester* by Noke was produced in large, small and miniature sizes in two different colourings. *A Friar of Orders Grey*, ascribed to Fenton, was made in one size only. Some of the other wall masks – all of girls – were probably by Harradine; those to which names were given in the records were: *Baby* (large and small sizes), *Pompadour* (brown eyes) and *Pompadour* (blue eyes) (in large and small sizes), and *Marlene Dietrich* (two colourings, large size). The others, which included three miniature masks of girls in three different colours, are not named in the records and it is possible that only prototypes of these were made.

All the masks were withdrawn during the Second World War and are becoming quite rare items, likely to appreciate considerably in value.

Margaret May Davies

During the Second World War severe restrictions were imposed by the Government on the manufacture and sale of decorated English ceramics. This, and the fact that many artists were in the Forces, or otherwise involved in the war effort, prevented many new additions to the Royal Doulton figure range. Since 1945, however, under the direction of Jack Noke, Jo Ledger and, more recently, Eric Griffiths, there has issued forth from the Nile Street studios a procession of exquisitely modelled and delicately decorated figures – some of them new variations of well-established themes, others introducing entirely fresh concepts both in theme and techniques – and all of them adding fresh lustre to the Royal Doulton annals.

Margaret Davies (Peggy, as she is known to friends and admirers all over the world) has, during the past thirty years or so, made a magnificent contribution to the Royal Doulton Collection which for originality, creative talent, artistry and popular appeal matches that of Harradine, and she is, in fact, catching up on him as regards the number of different models she has by now designed.

Peggy was born in Burslem, the mother-town of the Staffordshire Potteries. When she was only twelve she won a scholarship to the Burslem College of Art, where the gift for modelling she had already displayed at school had scope to develop. After some years, first as a junior student, then as a senior under Gordon Forsyth – a distinguished designer, craftsman and teacher – she became an assistant to Clarice Cliff, a successful local designer and modeller. In 1939 she went to Doulton's Burslem studios as an assistant to Jack Noke, thus beginning a long and fruitful association which still endures.

A small studio which Peggy had set up at home was destroyed by incendiary bombs. As her contribution to the war effort she then became a nurse. After the war she established herself as an independent artist but has continued, under contract, to create for Royal Doulton a host of delightful figures as well as several large figures and groups, in a very individual style of modelling. She delights in producing complicated pieces such as *The Matador and Bull, Indian Brave* and *The Palio*, taking great pains to research her subjects thoroughly, whether they involve the attire of medieval English Queens, the techniques of a Spanish bull-fighter, or the costume of a sixteenth-century Italian knight. Her group, *The Marriage of Art and Industry*, was the centre-piece of the Doulton stand at the Brussels International Exhibition of 1958, at which Royal Doulton was the only British pottery firm to win a *Grand Prix*. Modelled by Peggy, to a suggestion by Jo Ledger, this group symbolized the theme of the exhibition; it depicted a young man and woman by the tree of knowledge with doves of peace and, at the base, symbols of the arts and sciences.

Peggy's bevy of 'fair ladies', each a distinct individual portrayal of archetypal femininity, carries on the Royal Doulton pre-eminence in this field, yet each is an original conception quite distinct from the work of Harradine who was also a brilliant exponent of the manifold variations possible in this *genre*. The *Enchantment* of the figure thus aptly named, the fantasy of *Sea Sprite*, the mature beauty of *Southern Belle*, the lively freshness of *Sweet Seventeen*, endearing studies such as *Sweet Dreams, Nanny* and *Golden Days* – these show but a few aspects of Peggy Davies's versatility as a sculptor. She is, not surprisingly, considered by many collectors to be one of the world's best figure artists in the ceramic medium. Besides these single subjects she has given the world of collectors several outstanding series featuring themes such as *Period Figures in English History, Ballet, Figures of Williamsburg* and *Lady Musicians*. Among her most recent contributions to the Royal Doulton Collection are the *Kate Greenaway* figures, capturing the infinite delicacy, tenderness and grace of the famous artist's sketches of children, and *Dancers of the World*, a new series of limited edition figures which bring to life dance forms – formal and informal, classical and popular – from many lands. The recent introduction of *Cleopatra* has launched yet another exciting range, *Les Femmes Fatales*.

Mary Nicoll

To the many admirers of her work the news of the death of Mary Nicoll in 1974, at the early age of fifty-two, came as a great shock. Her work will undoubtedly continue to give pleasure to future collectors as it has done to those of the recent past. It has the indefinable quality which is the result of close observation of many different types of human nature, combined with wholesome imagination, vitality and considerable artistic and technical ability; it reflects her own unique blend of human sympathy, tenderness, romance and humour, with now and then a touch of lovable eccentricity.

Mary's artistic gifts, especially in the field of sculpture and modelling, like those of Peggy Davies, manifested themselves at an early age. Her first 'professional' commission came when she was only twelve from the architect Mr Guy Church, who asked her to model seven figures for him. Her artistic education was guided by her father, Gordon Nicoll, RI, a well-known and gifted painter in oils and water colours. After a period of study at the Central School of Arts and Crafts in London, she began to exhibit at the Walker Galleries, the Royal Academy and other art centres. Several examples of her work were shown at the Festival of Britain in 1951. She began to model for Jack Noke in 1955. *The Fiddler, Jolly Sailor, The Tailor* and *The Organ Grinder* were among her earliest Doulton productions.

In a tribute to Mary and her work Eric Griffiths wrote:

To her family, in their Devon home, she was a loving wife and mother. In her studio she created another family from lumps of raw clay – dream children from a world full of cheer and gentle humour. A motherly old lady, pouring a saucer of milk for her tabby cat, grows into *The Favourite*; the companionship between a shepherd and his dog gives us *The Master*. . . . She drew inspiration, too, from the small Devon harbour she knew so well, portraying the characters she observed with a kindly but discerning eye – as in *Sea Harvest, The Boatman* and *Tall Story*. To thousands of homes *The Lobster Man* brings a salty tang of sea air. Whether an artist's worth is to be judged by the esteem of her fellows or by the appreciation of her public, the name of Mary Nicoll can justly claim to rank high indeed.

Past Glory, Thanksgiving, Make Believe, the *Clockmaker, Tuppence a Bag, The Wayfarer, a Good Catch, Twilight, Parisian, The Cup of Tea* – these are just a few of the many other figures which Mary Nicoll added to the Royal Doulton Collection, figures which reflect her versatility, and keen powers of observation.

Eric J. Griffiths

Under a reorganization of the design centre for the Royal Doulton Group in 1972, design activities were separated into three main divisions, each with its own Art Director, under the over-all direction of Jo Ledger as Design Director. Eric J. Griffiths then became the head of the Ceramic Sculpture Division.

It was during a long convalescence of two years after a serious accident which almost cost him his life that Eric Griffiths, who had spent his childhood in a North Wales mining village, discovered his true vocation – that of an artist. There followed some years of study at Shrewsbury Art School and Wolverhampton Art College but he was not the type to take readily to conventional academic teaching; he regards himself as a largely self-taught artist.

For a time he earned a living as a cartoonist while training as a portrait painter. There was no great demand for his portraits but an evident talent for modelling found him an opening with a manufacturer of toys and ornaments. This was the beginning of his successful career as a sculptor in industry. During the next twenty years he worked for several concerns as chief designer, head of development or design consultant, modelling all manner of subjects from tractors to toy dogs, from life-size figures to merry-go-round horses, from portrait busts to inch-high toy soldiers. He created sculptures in ceramics, plastics and metals, played a leading part in developing several new industrial processes and obtained patents on two inventions. He has also undertaken independent research into technological processes used in industry in the reproduction of shapes – such as mould-making materials and methods and the lost-wax casting of metals.

To his new appointment as head of sculpture at Royal Doulton Eric Griffiths thus brought not only his considerable and varied experience as a sculptor, but also an essentially practical outlook gained in leading teams of talented craftsmen to success in the competitive world of commercial achievement. To have at his disposal the skills developed over generations at Royal Doulton has been for him, he says, a marvellous experience.

During the few years he has been at Burslem Eric Griffiths has already made some notable contributions to the Royal Doulton range of figures. Among these are *Cavalier, The Detective, Buddies,* the *Haute Ensemble* series of elegant ladies, and the magnificent *Soldiers of the Revolution* series.

The detailed military sculptures that make up the latter were produced to celebrate the bicentenary of the United States, the thirteen soldiers representing the regiments of the original thirteen states. Made in limited editions of 350 of each figure, and available only in North America, the series was designed in close association with the Colonial Williamsburg Foundation. Long and careful research has ensured that each figure is historically correct down to the smallest details of uniform and equipment. This unique collection has given Griffiths a wonderful opportunity, which he has grasped with great enthusiasm, to make a significantly new statement in the somewhat neglected field of ceramic military figures.

On the shelves of the Griffiths studio are numerous new models, by himself and other sculptors whom he has commissioned, in various stages of preparation, including some intriguing experimental pieces. In his department one may see enthusiastic young modellers at work developing their own ideas and following up suggestions made by their Art Director. The collector may evidently look forward to some interesting new developments in the field of Royal Doulton figures.

'Heirlooms of tomorrow'

To no Royal Doulton product can this description be more appositely applied than to the figures. The total number of these made since 1913 well exceeds 2,000 (not including animal and bird models which will be described later). Few models were actually withdrawn altogether until about 1938 but by then only some 370 were on the active list. Since the mid 1940s the whole method of production has been changed, as a result of which only 200 to 300 models are now in production in any one year. Each year some new models, usually half a dozen or so, are introduced to replace others which are withdrawn – generally because they have not sold in sufficient numbers to justify continued production. Obsolete models rapidly become collectable. Rarity largely depends on the number of years during which they were being made, this naturally affecting the quantity likely to be still in existence. More and more collectors are building up quite extensive assemblages of figures in the certainty that in years to come these will have proved not only a source of much pleasure but also an excellent investment.

It may interest collectors to know a few wholesale export prices of figures in 1938: M–38 and 39 *Robin* – 30p; HN–1319 *Darling*, HN–1370 *Marie*, HN–1482 *Pearly Boy* and HN–1677 *Tinkle Bell* – 45p each; HN–1365 *Mendicant* – 95p; HN–728 and 1345 *Victorian Lady*, HN–1517 *Veronica*, HN–1606 *Falstaff*, and HN–1699 *Marietta* – all £1.00 each; HN–1712 *Daffy-down-Dilly* – £1.25; HN–1820 *Reflections* – £1.50; HN–1745 *Rustic Swain* – £2.00; HN–1747 *Afternoon Tea*, and HN–1493 *The Potter* – £2.25 each.

The following were the prices in the same year for Garbe *limited edition* figures: HN–1774 *Spring* – £3.00; HN–1775 *Salome* – £1.50; HN–1776 *West Wind* – £8.40; HN–1777 *Spirit of the Wind* – £4.20; and HN–1778 *Beethoven* – £15.

Animal and bird models

In addition to figures, there have been produced at Burslem since 1912 some 700 animal and bird models in bone china, fine earthenware and, occasionally, in *rouge flambé* and Titanian Ware. They were produced in naturalistic, stylized, whimsical and other styles and embrace a great many different species. It would, in fact, be possible to create a well-populated 'ceramic zoo' from the Royal Doulton models. This is a field which, until fairly recently, had not been as fully explored by collectors as some others, and it still offers opportunities for building up a fascinating collection.

In introducing animal models as well as figures, Charles Noke was again reviving an earlier Staffordshire tradition. From the mid eighteenth century onwards several potters in the Stoke area began to produce miniature representations of cats, dogs, cattle, sheep, horses, poultry and other domestic fauna. These, as Bernard Rackham, formerly Keeper of Ceramics in the Victoria and Albert Museum, remarked in his little book *Animals in Staffordshire Pottery* (Penguin 1953), represent 'a peculiarly English byway in the history of ceramic art'. It has to be borne in mind, he points out, 'that these little figures in earthenware were made not for the world of fashion but to find a place among clocks, jars and sundry other articles of use on the mantelpiece or dresser, chiefly in the farmhouses and cottages of country districts. . . . The approval betokened by purchase when the pedlar came on his round, or "on the stones" of the market-place, would thus be given in the first place to creatures endeared by their familiarity as companions of the daily round.' By the 1870s, Rackham points out, the standards of modelling and colouring had greatly declined and all aesthetic quality was lost.

It is thought that many of the earlier Doulton animal models were designed by

Noke himself; certainly this applies to the larger ones, such as elephants, tigers, lions and leopards, and probably also to the 'character' models such as monkeys, owls and foxes. The names of other modellers are not recorded but it is likely that Light and Tittensor were responsible for some. Harradine is believed to have modelled some of the birds.

A list of all known animal and bird models with their HN-numbers is given in the book referred to at the beginning of this chapter. The animals include one or more examples of the following species: apes, bears (polar and brown), cats and kittens (several), dogs and puppies (many – see below), dolphins, elephants, foxes, frogs, hares, horses (several – see below), ibex, lambs, leopards, lions, mice, monkeys, pigs and piglets, rabbits, squirrels, tigers and tortoises. Among the birds may be found Baltimore orioles, blue birds, blue tits, budgerigars, cardinal birds, chaffinches, cockatoos, cockerels, drakes, ducks and ducklings, eagles, falcons, gannets, great crested grebes, guinea fowl, hens and chicks, herons, Indian runner drakes, kingfishers, mallards, owls, parrots, peacocks, pelicans, penguins, pheasants, terns, thrushes, toucans, turtle doves, swallows, swans, wrens (ordinary and golden-crested) and yellow-throated warblers.

The variety of subjects outlined in the above lists (which do not claim to be complete) will probably surprise many readers, for, apart from the *Championship Dogs* mentioned below and some whimsical, miniature character models the name Royal Doulton is not nowadays associated with this particular field of ceramics. Most of the animal and bird models were in fact produced between 1912 and 1930.

Noke was a dog-lover and from the start dogs played an important part in the collection. The named *Championship Dogs* were introduced in the early 1930s but before and since then there have been many *unnamed* varieties including Airedales, American Foxhounds, American Great Danes, Bloodhounds, Cairns, Chows, Cocker Spaniels, Collies, Dachshunds, Doberman Pinschers, Fox Terriers, French Poodles, Gordon Setters, Great Danes, Greyhounds, Pekinese, Pointers, St Bernards, Scottish Terriers, Staffordshire Bull Terriers and West Highland White Terriers. About twelve models of dogs' heads only were produced both with and without plinths.

The *Championship Dogs* were introduced by Jack Noke in the early 1930s and proved to be the most successful line of animal models produced by Doulton. For the next twenty years they were all modelled by Frederick T. Daws, a former student of the Lambeth School of Art, who had gained a world-wide reputation as a sculptor of animals. He visited the kennels and worked from life with the dog posed for him. The first model produced was invariably submitted to the owner for approval. Daws also executed many works for private individuals in Britain and America; his animal sculptures were exhibited in the Royal Academy and the Paris Salon.

The first *Championship Dogs* produced in 1931 were *Crackley Startler*, Rough-haired Terrier; *Albourne Arthur*, Scottish Terrier; *Biddee of Ifield*, Pekinese; *Crackley*

Hunter, Fox Terrier; and *Lucky Pride of Ware*, Cocker Spaniel. Since then other breeds represented by outstanding champions have included the Airedale Terrier, the Alsation, the Black Labrador, the Boxer, the Bull Terrier, the Cairn, the Collie, the Dachshund, the Dalmation, the English Setter, the Foxhound, the Sealyham, the Smooth-haired Terrier and the Springer Spaniel. Almost all of these have been made in three different sizes.

Besides birds and dogs Royal Doulton produced in the 1940s a limited number of horse models sculpted by W. M. Chance, another well-known animal modeller whose works were commissioned by many important breeders on both sides of the Atlantic, and were exhibited in the Royal Academy and other Galleries. His first models for Jack Noke appear to have been *Pride of the Shires*, mare and foal; *The Gude Grey Mare*, hunter and foal; *The Farmer's Boy* on dappled shire (and the same shire without the boy); *The Dapple Grey*, girl on shire; *The Chestnut Mare* and *Merely a Minor*.

Chance's most important model for Doulton was that of *Monaveen*, the famous steeple-chaser owned jointly by H.M. the Queen Mother and Princess Elizabeth (as she then was). This was specially made to present to the Princess after her visit to the Burslem factory. During the design of the model Chance worked closely with Captain Peter Cazalet, the horse's trainer. Twenty-six separate moulds and five firings were necessary to complete the finished model. Shortly after the presentation a letter was received at Burslem from the Queen's Equerry, which said: 'As you already know, this model has given Her Royal Highness very great pleasure. She would be very happy if you would convey her thanks and gratitude to all who had anything to do with this very beautiful model.' The only other examples of *Monaveen* were made for display in the Royal Doulton Showrooms.

All horse models were withdrawn by 1966.

Reference to a current Royal Doulton catalogue will show that out of over 700 animal and bird models produced since 1912, fewer than 50 are now being made. The great majority of the others had already been withdrawn by 1946. This is therefore a branch of Doulton productions of very great significance to the discerning collector.

The following wholesale export prices are from a 1938 list: HN–999 *Cat* – 50p; HN–1001 large size *Cocker and Pheasant* – £1.25; HN–1010 large size *Biddee of Ifield* – £1.35; HN–1118 large size *Lion on Rock* – £4.00; HN–1192 *Duck*, and HN–1196 *Seagull* – 50p each; HN–1199 large size *Penguin* – £3.30; *Dogs of Character* were from 20p to 25p each.

The Raoh Schorr models

The beautiful, lively animal models by the well-known sculptor, Raoh Schorr, were commissioned by Jack Noke for Doulton in 1936 and 1937. Unfortunately, although highly regarded by the art critics, they did not meet with much public response and had to be withdrawn during the war years. The quantities made were therefore limited and these models are today rare and valuable collectors' items. The animals represented were a mouflon lamb standing and also lying; a sleeping calf and a standing calf; a buffalo; a donkey in two sizes; a Swiss goat; a horse; a jumping goat; a suspicious doe, and an antelope. These models were produced in different finishes: black matt and white matt, green–bronze, and natural colours.

The Chatcull Range

Another very distinctive range of animals, delightfully modelled and coloured, was introduced by Jo Ledger, the present Director of Design in 1959. These represented three Siamese cats; a pine marten; a Langur monkey; a white-tailed deer; a brown bear; a mountain sheep; a river hog; a Nyala antelope; a llama and a badger. Like the Schorr models, for some reason several of them met with poor public response and only the three cats are still in production. As always happens, the models which did not sell so well are now greatly in demand by collectors.

Butterflies, brooches, jewellery

Not often seen today is a set of six butterflies made before 1939: the Peacock, Camberwell Beauty, Swallowtail, Red Admiral, Copper, and Tortoiseshell. These were also made into brooches, as were little clusters of beautifully modelled and painted flowers. There also exist some now rare examples of bracelets, necklaces, lockets, pendants, ear-rings, parasol handles and the like, incorporating Doulton ceramics in the form of flowers, jewel-like insects, cameos and miniature paintings.

Book-ends, fountain-pen stands, lamps and other sundries

During the 1930s, alabaster book-ends were marketed, mounted with china dogs' heads depicting: English Setter, Irish Setter, Cocker Spaniel (liver and white), Cocker Spaniel (black), Foxhound, Alasatian, Smooth-haired Terrier, Sealyham, Airedale, Scottish Terrier, Cairn, and Pekinese. The same dogs' heads were also supplied mounted on oval wooden plaques.

The following *small-size* models of dogs, not just their heads, were supplied mounted on mahogany book-ends: Cocker Spaniel, Sealyham, Cairn, Scottish Terrier, Bulldog, English Setter, Irish Setter, Rough-haired Terrier (Champion *Crackley Startler*), Pekinese and *Cocker and Pheasant*. Some of the dog models were made in *rouge flambé* as well as natural colours, as was a small fox model.

Any of the miniature and small china figures in the current range could be supplied mounted on wooden or alabaster book-ends. Book-ends mounted with heads of *Pickwick*, *Micawber*, *Tony Weller* and *Sairey Gamp* were also available.

Miniature figures and small animal models were mounted on white, blue, deep amber and green alabaster fountain-pen stands, calendars, and on variously shaped ashtrays. Many large-size figures and animal models were mounted to order on alabaster lamp bases; prices, including shades, ranged between about £1.80 and £3.15.

All the above were withdrawn in the mid 1940s.

Floral pools and other 'fancies'

Other items made in the 1930s and withdrawn in the mid 1940s were the so-called floral pools – clusters of delicately hand-made ceramic flowers arrangèd in bowls. These were described in a 1932 advertisement as 'fashioned in various irregular and formal shapes, in multi-colour, some almost iridescent in effect, embellished with favourite wild flowers'. There are records too, during the same period, of 'floral rocks', 'floral napkin-rings', 'floral brooches', and powder-boxes with covers encrusted with groups of kingcups, primroses, roses, wild roses, violets and forget-me-nots. Pot-pourris were made in eight designs on five different shapes. There was also a variety of menu-holders and napkin-rings with and without modelled floral decoration.

Art sculptures by Robert Jefferson

To conclude this chapter a brief reference must be made to the superb contemporary animal and bird sculptures recently modelled by Robert Jefferson. This is another project begun under Eric Griffiths' aegis as head of sculpture. Jefferson's studies of wild life subjects such as the *Fledgling Bluebird*, the *Colorado Chipmunk*, *Harbor Seals*, and the *Blue-Throated Loon* – to mention but four of his beautiful limited edition sculptures produced for the North American market – are the product of meticulous observation by a greatly gifted sculptor who has been an active naturalist since boyhood. They are modelled with extraordinary delicacy and exquisite detail. Their translation into porcelain, demanding the preparation of special ceramic colours to capture the right tones and, in one case, 114 individual castings, has been a real challenge. That the Royal Doulton artists and craftsmen have been able to meet this challenge is a great tribute to their skill, as well as being yet another indication that the high standards of design and quality, with which Royal Doulton has been so long traditionally associated in the field of ceramic sculpture, are being sustained and, indeed, enhanced under the present leadership.

X

Character and Toby Jugs and Associated Wares

A complete list of all known Character and Toby Jugs and associated wares produced by Doulton of Burslem between 1934 and 1979, together with dates of introduction, dates of withdrawal where relevant, details of designers, and background information about the characters depicted, will be found in the book *Royal Doulton Character and Toby Jugs* (Eyles) published in 1979 by Royal Doulton Tableware Limited, Stoke-on-Trent. Some sections of this chapter are a condensation of part of that book.

Charles Noke in 1934 followed up his earlier success with the by then widely acclaimed Royal Doulton figures and animal models by reviving in a distinctly new and vigorous vein the eighteenth and early-nineteenth-century vogue for figure-jugs of which the Toby Jug was the most famous example.

Toby's origins

The Toby Jug, as we know it today, was almost certainly the creation of some unknown mid-eighteenth-century Staffordshire potter. Droll and endearing, and a worthy container for generous potations, it reflected the spirit of a boisterous and convivial age. Within a few years of its first appearance it had become the most popular jug ever produced in human likeness. Despite its essentially English aura, its fame soon spread abroad and today Toby Jugs, and – still more – the Character Jugs derived from them by Noke and his colleagues and successors, are avidly collected in many parts of the world.

Collectors frequently ask questions such as: 'What was its origin?' 'Why are they called Toby?' and 'Who made the first Toby Jug?'

The honour of designing the first Toby Jug has been ascribed to various Staffordshire potters – John Astbury, Thomas Whieldon, Ralph Wood the First and Aaron Wood, among others. Another theory is that a somewhat intemperate Frenchman, John Voyéz, who modelled for several potters of the period, was the original designer. The facts are that the earliest Toby Jugs were not marked with the makers' names; there are no written records concerning them; and one potter often copied the successful designs of another. It has proved impossible so far to unravel the truth as to Toby's creator. One thing that can be said with certainty is that the famous Wood family of Burslem played a leading part in establishing the fame of the Toby Jug.

Toby was the descendant of a long line of jugs in human likeness fashioned by potters in earlier times, stretching back to Ancient Greece and beyond. In Staffordshire, in the early eighteenth century, some quaint and now very rare small earthenware figures and figure-jugs were made depicting midshipmen, soldiers, musicians and other characters. Generically known as 'Astbury-type' they were in fact made by several different potters. They appear to have been the immediate forerunners of the Toby Jug.

The name 'Toby' was used originally to describe those jugs which were in the form of a seated male figure in a tricorne hat, holding a beer jug on his knee and a pipe or glass in his hand. The hat was so fashioned that each corner formed a convenient spout. Many of the early jugs had a hollow cap which fitted into the top to complete the hat, and which could be used as a cup. The early Toby was dressed in typical mid-eighteenth-century attire – full-length coat with low-set pockets, broad waistcoat, cravat, knee breeches, stockings and buckled shoes.

The name Toby

Before long several variations were introduced, including standing figures and female figures but *Toby* has persisted as a generic description. It is not known with any certainty why this name – a familiar form of the biblical name Tobias – was given to these jugs. The word 'toper', describing one who imbibes strong drink too freely, was in common use long before the Toby Jug was created. Bearing in mind the native genius for coining apt nicknames it is not difficult to imagine how the designations *Toper Fillpot*, *Toby Fillpot* or *Toby Philpot* could come into existence. Certainly the name Toby was unquestionably associated with conviviality by Shakespeare in the person of the rascally Sir Toby Belch (in the comedy *Twelfth Night*) for whom 'not to be a-bed after midnight' was 'to be up betimes'.

The name Toby Fillpot is thought to have appeared in print for the first time in a song called *The Brown Jug* (also known as *The Metamorphosis or Toby Reduc'd*) published in 1761, but it is likely to have been in conversational use before then. Some years later the song was also printed under a mezzotint depicting an enormously fat toper dressed in much the same style as that adopted for the first Toby Jugs, with a foaming jug in one hand and a clay pipe in the other. Perhaps this was the inspiration for the figure-jug.

Noke's revival

During the second half of the nineteenth and the early part of the twentieth century there was, with a few exceptions, a similar falling-off in the standards of designing, modelling and painting Toby Jugs as occurred with china figures and animal models.

Charles Noke, according to his son Jack, had for many years nursed the idea of reviving, in a rather different form, the Staffordshire figure-jug tradition but he did not find time actively to pursue the project until the early 1930s. By then Charles Noke was in his mid seventies and it says much for his ever-fertile imagination and creative energy that he should at such a late stage in his life have launched what was to prove another great Royal Doulton success.

Just before the first Character Jugs appeared the *Pottery Gazette* for December 1933 published an account of the celebration by Charles Noke and his wife of their Golden Wedding. It contained the following well-deserved tribute: '[He] is not only everywhere regarded at the present time as the doyen of pottery modellers and designers but we believe that, by virtue of his exceptional talents, and the consistently enthusiastic manner in which he has utilized them to the full *to give himself joy whilst at the same time disseminating it to the world at large*, he has enshrined his name in future ceramic history. [He] enjoys a fertility of ideas to encourage him ever onwards as well as a disciplined master-hand to do his instant bidding.'

To give himself and the world at large *joy*. This was indeed eminently true of Noke's figure-jug revival. He and his staff spent many months in modelling, casting, painting, glazing and firing experiments before he felt satisfied that he had produced a set of what he called 'Character Jugs' which fulfilled his ideas. What he envisaged was a much more colourful style of jug *in a far more varied range* than the somewhat stereotyped Toby, depicting a series of original character studies in English song, literature, legend and history. These he hoped would appeal to his and future generations just as the original Toby Jugs did to our ancestors and, indeed, still do to many today. Unlike the seated and standing Tobies, the Character Jugs depicted the head and shoulders only of the various subjects.

The first two jugs to appear were *John Barleycorn* and a still immensely popular study of *Old Charley*, the night-watchman of earlier times, whose job it was, before a regular police force was created, to patrol the streets during the night, calling out the hours and the weather – thus: 'Eleven o'clock of the night; fine night; all's well.' The jug shows him winking, one may imagine, at some of the odd goings-on he sees as he makes his nightly round. John and Charley were quickly followed by

Sairey Gamp, Dickens's immortal bibulous midwife and sick nurse; *Parson Brown*, a personification of the sporting cleric of earlier days, and the notorious *Dick Turpin*, most famous perhaps of all highwaymen. These were the prelude to a long and still continuing procession of fascinating finely finished character studies by Charles Noke and several of his colleagues and successors.

While remaining true to the spirit of the earlier Staffordshire traditions, the Doulton modellers, from Noke's time down to the present day, have succeeded in creating styles distinctly their own, usually more detailed than the earlier types but conceived in the same fanciful, humorous and convivial vein. Reginald G. Haggar, one of the greatest authorities on English ceramic sculpture, has written of them: 'They are of outstanding quality. Their vigorous modelling exhibits a liveliness of observation, shrewd characterisation and humour which worthily continue the tradition of John Voyéz and Ralph Wood.'

Two other names which are associated with the figure-jug revival are those of Leslie Harradine and Harry Fenton. Harradine had already designed, while still at Lambeth, some salt-glaze stoneware figure-jugs, depicting Dickens characters, also a series of figure-flasks with necks in the likenesses of Dr Samuel Johnson and several well-known early-twentieth-century politicians. He and Harry Fenton collaborated in designing and modelling for Noke a number of Dickens characters in jug form. Fenton too contributed *John Peel*, *Granny*, *Old King Cole*, *Auld Mac*, *The Cavalier*, *'Arry*, *'Arriet*, *The Beefeater*, *The Clown* and several others. Fenton died in 1953 and his last model *Johnny Appleseed* was produced in that year.

Later developments

Four years before Harry Fenton's death, another talented modeller, Max Henk, had joined the Burslem Pottery, working under the direction of Jack Noke. Henk came of a distinguished line of ceramic modellers and the continued and ever-growing success of the Character Jugs since the 1950s owes a great deal to his abilities as a creative ceramic sculptor. His first model to be produced was *Long John Silver*; others among the many which have been equally great successes are: *The Apothecary*; *Aramis*, *Athos*, *Bacchus*, *The Falconer*, *The Guardsman*, *The Mad Hatter*, *The Pied Piper*, *Porthos*, *Tam O'Shanter*, *The Viking* and *The Walrus and the Carpenter*.

In more recent years, under the direction of Jo Ledger and Eric Griffiths, a new generation of modellers have been ably continuing the tradition, among them Gary Sharp (now no longer at Burslem), David Tootle (a free-lance modeller), Alan Moore and Peter Gee. The most prolific so far has been David Brian Biggs, who studied at the Shrewsbury School of Art and joined Royal Doulton in 1958 as an assistant to Max Henk. The first of his Character Jugs to be produced was *The Town Crier* in 1960, and since then he has created some twenty others including *Regency Beau*, *The Golfer*, *The Jockey*, *The Gardener*, *The Veteran Motorist*, *Gulliver*,

The Lobster Man and several of the *Jugs of Williamsburg*.

Thanks to the craftsmanship and versatility of the Royal Doulton modellers, a host of fascinating characters created during the past forty-five years have become available for the collector. Such is their appeal that anyone acquiring one or two – whether by way of gift, purchase or inheritance – is generally fired with the urge to obtain others, both current and obsolete. In addition to the Character Jugs (many of which were made in up to four different sizes – large, small, miniature and tiny) – sixteen Toby Jugs (in the traditional sense of seated or standing figures) were produced, of which six only are still in production today. The ten which were withdrawn ten to twenty years ago are now of course collectors' prizes as are certain other rare character items – musical jugs, air-tight tobacco jars, teapots, wall vases, match-stands and ashtrays, ash bowls, busts, sugar bowls, miniature sugars (described by some American collectors as 'toothpick holders'), table cigarette lighters and liqueur containers.

Since 1934 some 125 different characters have been created in various sizes, making nearly 300 jugs in all. (Full details will be found in the book referred to at the beginning of this chapter.) It is the practice, as with the Royal Doulton figures, to withdraw certain models from time to time and to add others. The jugs which have been withdrawn quickly become collectors' items and naturally increase greatly in value compared with their original cost. Broadly speaking, the shorter the period during which any particular jug was made, the rarer it is likely to become.

Another factor has to be taken into account concerning jugs introduced before the First World War and withdrawn in 1960 or earlier, as many were. This is that during the war years, and for several years afterwards, production was on a very limited scale indeed – and then only for export. This accounts for the relative scarcity of such jugs as the twelve tinies, *Churchill*, *Jan Smuts*, *Mephistopheles*, and *The Clown*.

In 1937 the wholesale prices of large jugs varied between about 19 and 25p; those of the small size between about 9p and 12p. The retail prices would have been higher by 50 per cent or more. In 1947 miniature models were 7½p and tinies 6¼p.

On the basis of past experience many of the jugs now in current production are destined in time to increase greatly in value. Already jugs withdrawn as recently as the mid 1970s have greatly appreciated.

XI

Rack Plates, Series Wares, Nursery Wares and Tablewares

One of the most popular, abundant and still relatively inexpensive fields for forming an interesting collection of Doulton Burslem Wares is that which embraces rack or wall plates and what used to be described as fancy lines but are now termed Series Wares. Among the best-known series are those depicting characters and scenes from the works of Shakespeare and Dickens.

A series might embrace anything from a few items to over a hundred, including in some cases dinner, tea and coffee ware, bowls, vases in several shapes and sizes, tobacco jars, trays, trinket sets, fern and flower pots, plaques, loving cups and miniatures. Most of the series included one or more plates which had either been specifically designed as rack plates or could be used as such. An idea of the variety of items covered by some of these series may be gained from the illustrations.

Rack plates and Series Wares

Rack plates or wall plates (also known as rail plates), have long been popular as a colourful adjunct to interior decoration. The use of pottery plates, plaques and chargers (large circular dishes) for display on walls, chests, dressers and buffets dates back many centuries. On the London Thames-side site of Doulton's Lambeth pottery, examples of delftware chargers, including some depicting William III and Mary, have been found.

In the early 1840s, the then Duchess of Sutherland is said to have introduced the notion of displaying decorated pottery plates on the mouldings along the walls of her rooms, two or three feet below the ceilings. By the 1850s the vogue had spread from palace and mansion to farmhouse, cottage and suburban villa.

In this chapter we are concerned with plates which are designed for display in

Charles Noke in the studio surrounded by animal and figure models, c.1932

Cleopatra, from a new series of figures, *Les Femmes Fatales*, designed by Peggy Davies, introduced in 1979. 7¼ in. (18.5 cm.) high

A Good Catch, Lobster Man, Sailor's Holiday, The Captain and *Shore Leave* designed by Mary Nicoll and introduced in the 1960s. *The Captain,* 9½ in. (24 cm.) high

The Clown, The Doctor, The Chief and *The Wizard* designed by Eric Griffiths, introduced in 1979
The Wizard,
9½ in.(24 cm.) high

Figure painter at work on the series *Soldiers of the Revolution* designed by Eric Griffiths and introduced in 1975

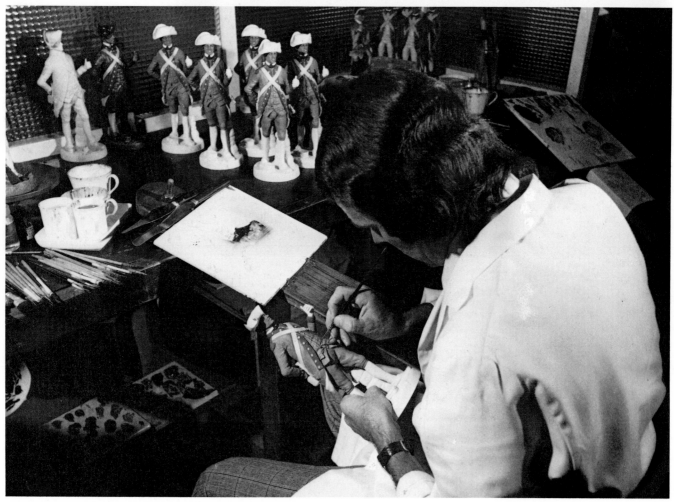

H.N. 197.	H.N. 163.	H.N. 133.	H.N. 205.	H.N. 158.
H.N. 116.	12. H.N. 147.	H.N. 125.	H.N. 176.	H.N. 151.
H.N. 117.		231. H.N. 168.		61. H.N. 802.
H.N. 181.	H.N. 27.	H.N. 128.	H.N. 134.	H.N. 132.
H.N. 276.	H.N. 161.	H.N. 118.	H.N. 280.	H.N. 137.	H.N. 145.

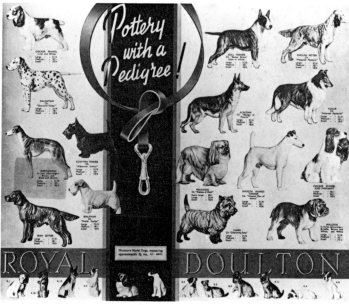

Top: A group of dogs introduced c.1940
Largest model, 8¼ in. (21 cm.) high

Above right: Publicity leaflet showing a range of dog models, c.1935

Catalogue page showing a range of bird and animal models, 1927

Gude Grey Mare designed by William Chance, c.1940 7 in.(13 cm.) high

Right: Advertising photograph showing *Pride of the Shires* and *Chestnut Mare* designed by William Chance, c.1940

Below: Catalogue page showing a range of animal studies designed by Raoh Schorr, 1936

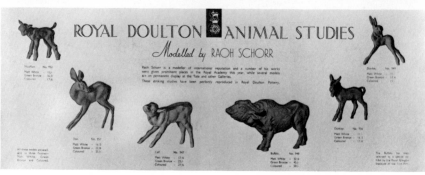

Left: Earthenware pastile burner in the form of a watermill, 1928
8½ in.(21.5 cm.) high

THE CHATCULL RANGE

SIAMESE CAT (STANDING) 2650 5 in.

SIAMESE CAT (SITTING) 2655 5½ in.

LANGUR MONKEY 2657 4¾ in.

PINE MARTEN 2656 4¼ in.

BROWN BEAR 2659 4⅛ in.

SIAMESE CAT (LYING) 2662 3¾ in.

Above: Brooches; the orchid design painted by David Dewsberry c.1910, the Kingfisher design c.1930
Largest brooch, 2⅛ in.(5 cm.) high

Catalogue page showing animal models in the Chatcull range designed by Jo Ledger, 1959

Right: Harbor Seals, designed by Robert Jefferson and introduced in 1975
8½ in.(21 cm.) high

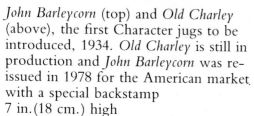

John Barleycorn (top) and *Old Charley* (above), the first Character jugs to be introduced, 1934. *Old Charley* is still in production and *John Barleycorn* was re-issued in 1978 for the American market with a special backstamp
7 in.(18 cm.) high

Right: Paintress at work on Lem Ward decoy ducks introduced in 1979 for sale in North America only

Top: Some Doulton Character Jugs. From left to right: *Smuts, Scaramouche, Mephistopheles, Clown* (white hair) and *'Ard of 'Earing* Tallest jug, 7 in. (18 cm.) high

Above: A group of Character Jug derivatives. From left to right: *Cap'n Cuttle* Toby, introduced in 1948; *Paddy* tobacco jar, introduced in 1938; *Parson Brown* ash bowl, introduced in 1939; *Old Charley* teapot, introduced in 1939; *Buz Fuz* bust, introduced in 1939; and *Poacher* liqueur jug, produced during the 1960s. All except the latter were withdrawn in 1960 Teapot, 6½ in. (17 cm.) high

Left: Whisky decanters made for Asprey & Co. in the form of a Scotsman and an Irishman, c.1935 9¼ in. (23.5 cm.) high

Catalogue page showing examples from the *Dickensware* series D2973 introduced in 1908

Catalogue page illustrating a range of rack plate designs available in 1914

Top: Catalogue page showing examples from the *Shakespeare* series D3746 introduced in 1914

Publicity
photograph
showing the set of
Head rack plates
introduced in 1938

Earthenware rack
plates from the
series *Coaching
Days, Izaac
Walton,
Dickensware* and
Shakespeare,
c.1910

English translucent china rack plate from a series decorated with photographic views, introduced in 1957
10½ in.(26.5 cm.) in diam

Below right: English translucent china rack plates decorated with photographic views of historical Britain, introduced in 1967
10½ in.(26.5 cm.) in diam

Catalogue page showing a range from the *Coaching Days* series, introduced in 1906

Above left: Earthenware jugs from the *Canterbury Pilgrims* series, introduced in 1909, *Dickensware* series, introduced in 1917 and *Rip van Winkle*, introduced in 1906
Largest jug, 7½ in.(19 cm.) high

Earthenware jugs with relief moulding, one from the *Jackdaw of Rheims* series and the others showing subjects from *Dickens*, introduced in 1937
6¾ in.(17 cm.) high

Catalogue page illustrating the *Gaffers* and the *Egyptian* series, introduced in 1921 and 1923 (adapted version)

Publicity photograph showing a selection from the series *Under the Greenwood Tree*, introduced in 1914

Publicity photograph showing a group from
the series *Famous Ships*, introduced in 1938

Top: Bone china rack plate and cat model
based on John Souter's cartoon cat *Kateroo*,
c.1906
Cat, 13 in.(32 cm.) high

Publicity photograph showing cigarette boxes and ash
trays in the *Dickensware* and *Hunting* series, c.1938

Right: Cartoon by John Souter published in the *Bulletin*,
an Australian magazine of current affairs, c.1925

DESIGN FOR WALL PAPER.
SUITABLE FOR A BACHELOR APARTMENT.

Top: Rack plates and vases decorated with
Gibson Girl subjects, the plates introduced
c.1901, the vases c.1905
Plate, 10½ in.(25 cm.) in diam

Above right: Wallpaper design by Charles Dana
Gibson featuring the famous *Gibson Girl* heads

Earthenware rack plate and teapot from the *Old English Scenes* series based on sketches by Cecil Aldin, introduced in 1925
Plate, 9½ in.(24 cm.) in diam

Below right: Bone china rack plate, the first in a series of Valentine scenes, 1976
8¼ in.(21 cm.) in diam

Earthenware rack plate, *Ye Knave of Hearts*, designed by Augustus Jansen, c.1915
10½ in.(26.5 cm.) in diam

Right: Newspaper advertisement for miniature Christmas novelties which were marketed as a ceramic alternative to Christmas cards and were sold complete with postal box. 1902

TRAY. 7924   8051.A   8051.B   7119.A

7922 TRAY

BOX 8148 & TRAYS

7922 TRAY

"Aldin's Dogs."

CECIL ALDIN is the acknowledged Master in the drawing of the comic dog, and in this series a number of his clever studies are adapted to a full line of interesting and useful articles. The general effect is bold and decorative and each piece bears the artist's signature.

WITH SANTA CLAUS SUBJECTS IN ENAMEL COLOURS ON PORCELAIN.

Each little Vase is decorated with one of the above mentioned subjects and mottoes; also with a border of Christmas Bells or Holly and the handle and edge is finished in solid Sevres Green.

Above: Catalogue page advertising Cecil Aldin's *Dog* series, introduced in 1926

Top: Publicity photograph showing the range of wares decorated with cartoons by Henry Mayo Bateman, introduced in 1937

Above left: Earthenware rack plate printed with a scene entitled *The Young Folks*, based on a cartoon by Randolph Caldecott published in *The Graphic* of 1876. 1908 10½ in.(26.5 cm.) in diam

Collector's International plates; *A Brighter Day*, from the series *All God's Children* by Lisette De Winne, and *Rounding the Horn*, from the series *Log of the Dashing Wave* by John Stobart, 1978 10 in.(25 cm.) in diam

Group of blue and white ware. From left to right: jug from the *Eglington Tournament* series introduced in 1902; clock in the *Watteau* pattern c.1905; teapot in the Blue Children design introduced c.1890; and a facsimile English delft plate, 1910

this way. In this collecting field there is a vast range of subjects from which to choose if one wishes to specialize: there are hunting, coaching, golfing, motoring and similar themes, portrait heads, and many characters from song, legend, history and literature, animals, birds and flowers, national monuments and landscapes.

Collectors interested in decorating techniques used in the ceramic industry will find that the rack plates and series offer interesting examples of underglaze, in-glaze and overglaze decoration; printing from engraved plates; slip-painting with coloured semi-liquid clays; painting with ceramic pigments; combinations of printing and hand-painting (known in the industry as 'print and tint'); lithograph and silk-screen printing. Most unusual and extremely attractive are the block-printed designs, especially of intricate geometrical and stylized floral and foliate patterns. This process, used in the late 1840s for colour printing on pot-lids, was a development from colour letterpress printing, whereby three or four colours in succession are printed on paper and exactly registered to obtain a colour print. The Doulton factory at Burslem kept a block-printing department going until the mid 1950s, long after practically every other pottery in Britain had given it up for economic reasons.

Some collectors confine their interest in these wares exclusively to rack plates; others try to find as many different items as possible in one or more particular series. The *Shakespeare, Dickens,* coaching, hunting and golfing series offer great scope in this respect; there are, for instance, at least forty different characters from the novels depicted on the various items in the *Dickens* series. At least one collector of Doulton rack plates has amassed in the past few years some four hundred different examples. There is, at the time of writing this, still a good supply of both rack plates and Series Wares if one browses around, and prices are still modest, except for some exceptionally rare types which were in production for only a short period.

To attempt to comment at any length on all the known subjects of both Series Wares and rack plates would be pointless; most of them require no elucidation. What collectors especially need is, firstly, some guidance in establishing when patterns were introduced and withdrawn; secondly, information about the significance and origins of some of the *more unusual* subjects, as, for example, the *Gibson Girls* or the *Aeronautical* and *Egyptian* series.

One of the earliest known and now rarest of all series is that known as the *Isthmian Games* featuring Ancient Greek chariot races, processions and mythological themes. This was already being produced by Pinder, Bourne in the late 1870s before Doulton took over the factory in Nile Street. Production went on probably intermittently until the early years of the present century. Examples are found with the Pinder, Bourne trademark and both the pre–1901 and post–1901 Doulton marks. Comparatively few seem to have survived.

THE GIBSON SERIES

Two early Doulton series of rack plates, first produced in 1900/1901, feature illustrations by the well-known American artist, Charles Dana Gibson (1867–1944). Both because of their priority and the numerous questions asked about them, their story merits being told in some detail. Gibson first became famous for his pen and ink drawings contributed to the magazine *Life*. His strikingly attractive 'Gibson Girls', as they were popularly called, with their *bouffant* hair styles and provocative features, had a tremendous vogue – being reproduced as signed proofs, and on china, pillow covers and wall paper. They depicted typical sophisticated beauties of the 'Gay Nineties' and inspired fashions and trends throughout America. Three of the models for these and other Gibson drawings were his sister, his future wife Irene Langhorne (sister of Nancy Astor who, as Lady Astor, was the first woman to sit in the British House of Commons), and Mary Leiter (destined to become Lady Curzon, Vicereine of India). Many of the drawings and cartoons satirized the manners, wealth, social pretensions, dilemmas and prejudices of American 'upper-class' society.

Doulton had been approached by the American firm George Bassett and Co. with the idea to reproduce Gibson cartoons on plates. Initially they produced two ranges, one of twelve rack plates depicting Gibson Girl heads in different attitudes and one of twenty-four plates decorated with illustrations from Gibson's book *A Widow and her Friends*. The success of these rack plates prompted a further series around 1904 which included vases, bowls and other fancy items mainly featuring Gibson's humorous golfing situations. Some legal problem seems to have arisen over the copyright which belonged to the Life Publishing Co., for on 2 November 1904 Doulton wrote direct to china dealers saying: 'We are pleased to tell you that the legal difficulty which caused us to withdraw the plates from the market has now been most amicably settled, and we have not only acquired the right to reproduce the twenty-four subjects of the "Widow" series and the twelve Girls' Heads but all other subjects that this celebrated artist sends to this country.' The letter goes on to say that the price of either 'Widow' or 'Heads' is 7s 6d (37.5p) per dozen, packing and carriage extra, cash discount 5 per cent. Although many thousands of both series were made, the Gibson plates are now among the most difficult to find of all Doulton rack plates. The collector who possesses all twelve 'Girls' and all twenty-four of the 'Widow' series is singularly fortunate.

OTHER FAMOUS ILLUSTRATORS

C. J. Noke was quick to realize the potential offered by popular illustrators, and so acquired the rights to reproduce a number of other series. David H. Souter (1862–1935) was well known in Australia for his decorative *Art Nouveau* drawings of cats which featured regularly in the *Sydney Bulletin*. A range of Souter drawings, as well as actual models of his comic cats, were reproduced at Burslem. Another rack plate series was based on the cartoons of Randolph Caldecott (1846–86), probably the best-known graphic artist of the period. Cecil Aldin (1870–1935) is remembered particularly for his book illustrations and travel posters; his humorous hunting scenes and ubiquitous comic dog series were effectively used by Doulton on a range of Burslem products. H. M. Bateman (1887–1970), the popular social satirist, contributed a range of humorous drawings of his familiar types which included the frustrated golfer and other well-known characters.

Although none of these artists achieved the cult following associated with Gibson, their popularity ensured a good sale for Doulton items decorated with their designs. It is therefore surprising that Doulton was one of the few potteries to exploit extensively this area of the market.

C. J. Noke's ever fertile imagination conjured up new ideas for rack plates and Series Ware every year from 1901 onwards. In 1902 came the *Eglington Tournament*; in 1903 a nursery ware series; in 1904 a *Shakespeare* series; and in 1905 *The Jackdaw of Rheims, Motoring* and *Isaac Walton* series. And so it continued for many years, sometimes as many as twenty new lines appearing the same year. Apart from Noke himself, the principal artists involved were Leonard Langley, Arthur Eaton, Walter Nunn, George Holdcroft, William Grace, Stanley Woodman and Noke's son, Jack.

After the Second World War, owing to changing fashions in home furnishing and interior design and decoration, the market for 'fancies' declined. This, coupled with other factors – the reconstruction of the Burslem factory; new marketing policies; the introduction of a new translucent fine china to take the place of earthenware for practically all products – led to almost all rack plates and series items being withdrawn by 1967, and the few that then remained in 1975. This has naturally made all of them, even those introduced in the last thirty years, desirable collectors' pieces. They have already appreciated considerably in value and this process will continue. It is interesting to note that with the recent reorganization of the Royal Doulton Group there have been signs in the past two or three years of a revival (now always in china) of the production of plates suitable, among other purposes, for use as rack or wall plates. The *Christmas Plates* and the *Valentine's Day Plates* are already established favourites, and the continuing series of *Collector's International Plates*, which reproduce designs by some of America's most acclaimed artists, are some of the finest examples of their kind that Doulton has ever made, a great tribute to Design Director Jo Ledger and all concerned in their production. These are now being made in editions of 15,000 and are only available in the USA.

A NOTE ON DATING

The great majority of rack plates and series made between 1901 and 1975 were in fine earthenware and bear D-numbers, e.g. D. 3930: *The Parson*. The relatively few made in china have E-, H-, V- or TC- numbers.

In the list which follows on the next page, the dates of introduction and withdrawal, together with comments where appropriate, are given for many of the best known rack plates and Series Wares. The exact dates of withdrawal are often not recorded; evidently those concerned with keeping records did not have collectors' interests in mind! Where approximate dates are given (in italics), withdrawal is likely to have taken place somewhat *before* rather than *after* the date indicated. Subjects based on Shakespeare and Dickens characters will be found under S and D respectively; other patterns are given in alphabetical order for easy reference.

As regards plates and series not included in the list, the following remarks should be useful:

(1)   Many items will be found to have either impressed or coded printed dates, giving the year of manufacture. Examples of both methods of dating will be found on pages 184–7.

(2)   There have been several changes of trade-mark between the 1890s and 1975. These can be helpful. Reference to the marks, with accompanying dates and notes, on pages 177–83 will establish the particular period during which a certain piece was made.

(3)   The D-and other numbers on pages 184–7 will indicate the period during which items so marked were *introduced*.

(4)   All items bearing numbers below D.4000 had been discontinued by 1936 except D.2716, *Coaching Days*; D.3647, *Countryside*; and D.3668, *Landscapes*. These were discontinued by the mid 1950s, production having been decreasing for several years.

(5)   All remaining items with D- numbers were withdrawn *in or before* 1967 except those few shown in the following list as having been withdrawn in 1968, 1969 and 1975.

(6)   All china items are believed to have been withdrawn by 1958 except V.2352, *Coaching Days*, withdrawn 1967, and those in the TC- series. The latter were in production only from 1967 to 1975 and are already becoming very rare.

Nursery wares

From the late nineteenth century until the present day, generations of British, American and Australian children have learnt to feed themselves from Doulton products. The earliest Doulton nursery ware so far known dates from about 1884 and reproduces two Pinder, Bourne subjects *Le Mouchoir Retrouvé* and *Bonjour, M'sieur le Marquis*. These isolated examples remained in production until 1913. However, their popularity was quickly superseded by the new Series Ware ranges designed specifically with children in mind. In 1903, C. J. Noke, well aware of the new consumer potential of the child, launched a *Nursery Rhyme* series decorated with designs by William Savage Cooper (1863–1943), a painter in oils and water-colours who exhibited regularly at the Royal Academy. Favourite rhymes in this series, such as *Little Bo-Peep* and *Mary, Mary, Quite Contrary*, were featured on children's beakers, bowls, mugs and baby plates for over thirty years. Equally popular were the various series depicting scenes from *Alice in Wonderland* and *Alice through the Looking Glass*, introduced in 1906 and 1908 respectively. The designer of this series has not been recorded, which is the case, unfortunately, with most of the nursery ware. Occasionally some of the leading Burslem artists, such as Harry Allen, painted baby plates with suitable nursery subjects, but most of the children's designs were in printed Series Ware. Subjects have included the cartoon characters *Pip, Squeak and Wilfred*, toy personalities such as *Dr Jumbo* and *Gollywog*, fairy stories, popular proverbs, and farmyard and comic animals. The range most commonly associated with Doulton is the *Bunnykins* series, first introduced in 1934. Within a few years of the introduction of this phenomenally popular ware, all the other nursery ware series still in production at that time were withdrawn. This whimsical rabbit family was originally the creation of Barbara Vernon, who has spent her life in a convent. She was one of the children of Cuthbert Bailey, then manager of Doulton's Burslem Pottery and pioneer of the Doulton *flambé* wares. For many years, from 1934 onwards, Mr Bailey paid regular visits to the convent to collect Sister Barbara's new batches of drawings which were then adapted by Burslem artists and transferred to beakers, mugs, jugs, plates and many other shapes destined to find their way, literally, to all parts of the globe. Queen Elizabeth, now the Queen Mother, was delighted with the *Bunnykins* ware exhibited at the British Industries Fair in 1937 and since then many orders have been received for royal nurseries in this country, as well as for others in Belgium, Holland and Scandinavia. *Bunnykins* indeed has such a universal appeal that it is found in every type of home.

In the late 1940s, designer Walter Hayward, now a Royal Doulton Art Director, took on the task of continuing the series, although until the 1950s the ware continued to bear Barbara Vernon's facsimile signature. To date there have been hundreds of different scenes portraying the adventures and exploits of the *Bunnykins* family and their friends.

Walter Hayward's designs can often be distinguished by the inclusion of a little mouse in a scene otherwise devoted to bunnies. Since 1970 *Bunnykins* has been made in a strong translucent china body, so it is easy to distinguish pre-1970 wares.

Rack plates and Series Ware

A Hundred Years Ago, D.5499: 1934–*1946*. A series including rack plates.

Aborigine with Hunting Weapons, D.6410: 1954–1967 and D.6421: 1954–1969. Rack plates with photographic image.

Aborigines in Corroboree, D.6409, 6420: 1954–1960. Rack plates with photographic image.

Admiral, The, D.5902: 1938–*1948*, D.6278: 1948–1967 and TC. 1045: 1968–1975. Rack plates.

Aeronautical, D.3205: 1901–1914. There are at least three versions of a rack plate featuring these. Issued to commemorate the First International Air-race, 1909, held at Bethany race-course near Rheims.

African Girl and Kraal, D.6153: 1940–1967. Rack plate and plaque with photographic image.

Aldin's Dogs, D.4629: 1926–1946. A series including rack plates. (Cecil Aldin, 1870–1935, illustrated several books including *A Dog Day, Dogs of Character* and his witty autobiography *Time I Was Dead.*) Each piece in the series – featuring comical drawings of the dogs – bears his facsimile signature. Some of these designs were also available in Titanian glaze effect.

Alice in Wonderland and *Alice through the Looking-Glass,* E.4021: 1906–1932 and E.4090: 1908–1932. Two series decorated with incidents from these well-known books by Lewis Carroll. D.5180, 5187: 1932–1942. A new 'Alice' series of some fifteen pieces. D.2883, 2863: 1907–1935. A similar series to D.5180 including sixteen pieces.

All Black Cricketers, D.2864: 1907–*1930* (earthenware) and E.4336: 1907–1928 (china). A humorous series depicting piccaninnies playing cricket, with comments such as 'Ready for Chances', 'The Boss', 'There's Style', 'I wasn't ready', 'Next Man In', 'Out for a Duck', and 'Good for Fifty'.

American Statesmen (and other personalities), D.2054: 1904–1928. A series including at least seven rack plates depicting David R. Francis, Benjamin Franklin, Ulysses S. Grant, William McKinlay, Theodore Roosevelt, George Washington and Martha Washington. Very rare.

American Views, D. ? : Between about 1913 and 1928 several rack plates and other items in underglaze blue were issued depicting The White House; The Capitol in Washington, D.C.; Washington Mansion, Mount Vernon; The Kip-Beekman-Livingston-Heermance House, Rhinebeck (souvenir of Banquet, Duchess County Society 1913) and possibly other views.

An Open Door may tempt a Saint, D.3427: 1911–*1929*. Rack plate depicting a Cavalier and a Puritan.

Anemone, D.4251 and D.4252: 1923–*1945*. A colourful series, including rack plates.

Ann Hathaway's Cottage, D.4149: 1921–1950 and TC.1027: 1967–1975. TC.1027 is in translucent china and decorated with a photographic image. Rack plates.

Arabian Nights, D.3198: 1909–1928, and D.3420, 3534: 1911–1928. Rack plates, plaques and various other items depicting scenes from the famous Persian collection of tales known as *The Thousand and One Nights*. This series had its own special mark.

Athens, D.3302: 1910–1928. A series designed by Walter Nunn, depicting Ancient Greek festivals and processions. Including at least three rack plates. (D.3475: 1911–1928 also features Greek scenes.)

Australian Aborigine, D.6411: 1954–1967 and D.6422: 1954–1975. Rack plates with photographic image.

Australian Bush, D.5633: 1936–1950. Rack plates with photographic image.

Autumn Glory, D.4713, 4714: 1927–*1942*. A series including at least two rack plates.

Balmoral Castle: see *Castles*.

Bateman, D.5813: 1937–*1950*. A series of several plates and other items featuring humorous sketches of golfers and other subjects by H. M. Bateman (1887–1970), one of the best-known caricaturists of the first part of this century.

Bayeux Tapestry, D.2873: 1907–*1930*. A series including at least three rack plates. Inspired by scenes from the famous so-called 'tapestry' which depicts the story of the Norman Conquest of England in 1066. It was commissioned by William the Conqueror's half-brother, Odo, Bishop of Bayeux, for the cathedral there. The fabric, which has 79 scenes, is 231 feet long but only 19 inches wide and is worked in eight colours. It is an important historical document, an Anglo-Norman secular work of art.

Bears, D.2879: 1907–1928. Rack plate. (See also *Koala*.)

Bermuda Scenes, D.6342: 1951–1967. Rack plate with photographic image.

Birds, D.3080: 1909–*1930*. An extensive series including at least five rack plates.

Birds, D.4586: 1926–*1950*. Another large series, including at least six rack plates. The sketches of game birds were drawn by Fred Hancock and engraved by C. Vyse. Printed and hand-tinted in underglaze colours.

In addition to rack plates in the above two series, others featuring birds of many kinds have been noted under the following numbers: D.1501–1505, 1517, 1518, 1754, 1755: 1903–1928; D.1929:1904–1928; D.2408, 2415–2417: 1905–1928; D.4206: 1921–*1935*; D.4639: 1926–*1940; D.4758: 1928–1940*; D5038: 1930–*1940*. (Some of these incorporate proverbs.)

Birds of Paradise, D.4222: 1922–*1935*. A series including at least one rack plate.

Bison, D.2880: 1907–1928. Rack plate.

Blue Children: Between the late 1880s and about 1928 some very attractive plates and other items were issued, printed in overall blue and depicting children playing various games, skating, sledging, cycling, dancing, sheltering under an umbrella in a snowstorm, walking in the woods and by the sea, and so forth. The engravings recall the style of some of the illustrations in women's and children's journals of the 1890s and early 1900s. Besides young children, older girls and women with muffs are depicted in similar underglaze blue on plates, jugs and other pieces. Quite a number of collectors are attracted by the *Blue Children*, as these items have now been christened, although none of those noted have either titles or numbers except D.2955 and D.2956: 1908–1928. Some of the subjects are attributed to James Boulton, Louis Bilton and A. Pearce.

Blue Iris, A.1147: 1886–1914. A series including two rack plates.

Blue Persian, D.4031: 1917–1942. Registered No. 597783. A large and colourful series including two or more rack plates. (See also *Persian*.)

Blue Ships, D.2273: 1905–1932. A series depicting coastal ships, barges, etc. There are five or more rack plates showing variations in the disposition of the ships due to the use of different sections of the print edition.

Bluebell Gatherers, D.3812: 1914–1928. A series illustrating woodland and country scenes; two or more rack plates.

Bookworm, The, D.3089: 1909–*1930* and D.5905: 1938–1949. Rack plates.

Bow Falls, D.6471: 1957–1969. Rack plate with photographic view of these falls in Banff National Park, Canada.

Bow Valley, D.6475: 1957–1975. Rack plate giving another photographic Canadian view.

Broom-Man, D.4835: 1929–*1942*. A companion rack plate to D.4834: *Roger Solemel, Cobbler*.

Brown Ships, D.2274: 1905–1932 and D.2872: 1907–1932. A similar series to *Blue Ships* (above), the only difference being in the predominant colour. The *Brown Ships* are apparently much more often seen than the blue.

Burns, Robert, D.3368: 1910–*1924* and D.4419: 1924–1951. Both these series, with scenes and quotations from the works of Scotland's most famous and beloved poet, included at least one rack plate.
  There are also the following rack plates with a portrait of Burns in the centre and characters from his poems round the rim:
D.2964: 1908–?; D.3392: 1911–*1940*; D. 6344: 1950–1967; and TC.1040: 1968–1975.

Canada, Centennial Map, TC.1037: 1967–1975. Rack Plate.

Canterbury Pilgrims, D.3188: 1909–*1933*. A large series including at least two rack plates. It depicts scenes and characters inspired by Geoffrey Chaucer's *Canterbury Tales*, published c.1386, presenting what has been called 'the first great picture gallery in English literature'. The tales are told by a group of pilgrims on their way to the tomb of Thomas à Becket, saint and martyr, in Canterbury Cathedral.

Castles and Palaces: These have long been a favourite subject with Doulton artists and have been depicted again and again in several large and small series. The following all include rack plates: D.3471: 1911–*1929*; D.4643: 1926–*1950*; D.4728 (coupe shape): 1927–*1950*; E.7239 (china): 1911–1926; H.2948 (china): 1926–*1950*; and V.2352 (china): 1947–1957. In addition other rack plates have been noted under the following numbers: D.3425, 3426 and 3491: 1911–*1932*; D.3599: 1912–*1932*; D.3610: 1912–*1930*; D.4391: 1924–*1952*; D.4504: 1925–*1952*; D.4941: 1929–*1952*; D.5413: 1933–*1952*; D.6112: 1940–1967; D.6308: 1950–1967; TC.1092, 1095: 1972–1975. (The last two, depicting Edinburgh and Balmoral, are becoming as hard to find as some earlier ones.)

Cathedrals and Churches: The *Pottery Gazette* for March 1908 refers to a set of china rack plates 'decorated with exquisite views of English cathedrals by W. Nunn'. Other plates depicting cathedrals, abbeys and churches occur, including D.2654 (1906–?) and D.2846 (1907–?).

Cats: There are several series depicting cats, including D.3730: 1914–? which shows a cat in a cottage doorway with a fireside. D.4538: 1926–*1942* shows just a cat at a cottage door. (See also *Souter's Cats*.)

Cattle, D.2091, 2092 and 2108: 1904–*1919*; D.3943: 1916–*1942*. Rack plates.

Cavaliers, D.3103: 1908–*1929*. A series depicting Cavaliers and proverbs, including at least two rack plates. D.2875: 1907–*1929*, D.3045: 1908–1930 and D.3084: 1909–1928 also depict Cavaliers but without accompanying proverbs.

Children Scenes: In addition to the *Blue Children* already referred to, there are at least another dozen rack plates (besides a variety of other items) depicting children (in full colour) at play, etc., in Kate Greenaway and similar styles. D.2391: 1905–1930. A series of different sized jugs with coloured sketches of children at play. Proverbial sayings on the backs. D.2955, D.2956: 1908–1928. A series depicting children sledging and playing found in an underglaze blue and an over-all yellow glaze. Some of the designs incorporate mottoes and sayings such as: 'East West, home is best', 'He has enough who is content', 'He who takes a child by the hand takes a mother by the heart', 'One false move may lose the game', 'When the wind is high, the kite will fly', 'A word once out flies anywhere', 'A little neglect may breed great mischief', 'Love grows with obstacles', 'It's an ill wind that blows nobody good', 'Good words without deeds are but rushes and reeds', 'A little leak will sink a great ship'. These are found without numbers and also under various numbers such as D.1506–1508, 1515, 1516, 2232, 2233, 2391, 2394, 2884, and 3119. They were introduced between the 1890s and 1909. All had been withdrawn by 1932, as had D.3884, introduced in 1915.

Christ with Crown of Thorns (no number): *1937–1945*. One of the few Doulton rack plates depicting a religious subject. (A companion to one of the *Virgin Mary*.)

Christmas Plates: 1977 and still issued annually. Rack plates with embossed decoration and Christmas scenes.

Chrysanthemums, D.6299: 1949–1967. A series including at least one rack plate.

Clovelly, TC.1028: 1967–1975. Rack plate.

Coaching Days, D.2716: 1906–*1955*. A large series in the style of Cecil Aldin including rack plates inspired by Charles Dickens' description of Mr Pickwick's journey to Dingley Dell by the Muggleton Telegraph Coach. There was a similar series in china under E.3804: 1906–*1945* and another V.2352: 1948–1967. D.2682: 1906–*1930* also depicts a coachman.

Coats of Arms: A series of three rack plates has been noted, dated 1905, illustrating invented humorous Coats of Arms.

Cobbler, D.4234: 1922–1950; D.4834: 1929–1950; and D.6302: 1950–1967. Rack plates.

Cock-a-Doodle-Doo, D.3659, D.3660: 1913–1930; D.4686: 1927–1939. A series based on the nursery rhyme.

Collectors' International Plates: 1973 and still in production. A series of bone china plates with transfer-printed decorations designed by well-known American artists including: Edna Hibel, who has interpreted the Mother and Child theme; Le Roy Newman, who has chosen subjects from *Commedia dell'arte*; Doug Kingman, who has taken *Ports of Call* as the title of his series, and Hahn Vidal, who has painted mixed blossoms as part of his *Flower Garden* series.

These plates are all produced in an edition of 15,000. Each plate is sequentially numbered and all bear the signature of the artist.

Cornfield and Churches, D.2654: 1906–?. Series including rack plates.

Cotswold Shepherd, D.5561: 1935–1950. A series including rack plates.

Cottage Door, D.3617: 1912–1935. A series including rack plates.

Country Garden, D.4932: 1929–?. Rack plate depicting a milkmaid in a flower garden.

Country Side, D.3634, 3647: 1912–*1945*. A large picturesque series including rack plates.

Days of Chivalry, D.5030: 1930–*1945*. A large series, designed by Walter Nunn, including rack plates. It has its own mark in addition to the usual one.

Deadwood Crackle, D.3399: 1911–?. Stylized landscape series with simulated crackle effect printed on the surface. Special backstamp.

Deer, D.4644: 1926–*1950*. A large and very attractive series including rack plates. D.5193 and D.5194 rack plates also depict deer.

Desert Scenes, D.3192: 1909–1929. A large series with its own special mark. Probably designed by Harry Allen, it includes rack plates.

Dickens: The Dickensware was undoubtedly the most popular of all the series and, as it is the subject of so many enquiries, it will be considered in some detail.

There have been several different Dickens series and this has caused some confusion. The earliest recorded in the Doulton archives is numbered both D.2973 and D.3020. Introduced in 1908 and referred to in the *Pottery Gazette* for March 1909, this is really one series though given two distinct numbers. In preparation for the centenary of Dickens's birth in February 1912, the number of shapes and the number of characters depicted on these shapes were both gradually augmented. By 1911, the following characters had made their appearance, set usually against a London street background:

Alfred Jingle	*Fagin*	*Sairey Gamp*
The Artful Dodger	*The Fat Boy*	*Sam Weller*
Mrs Bardell	*Little Nell*	*Serjeant Buzfuz*
Barkis	*Mark Tapley* (two	*Sidney Carton*
Barnaby Rudge	versions)	*Mr Squeers*
Bill Sykes	*Mr Micawber*	*Tom Pinch*
Cap'n Cuttle	*Old Peggotty*	*Tony Weller*
Mr Chadband	*Mr Pecksniff*	*Trotty Veck*
Dick Swiveller	*Mr Pickwick*	*Uriah Heep*
Mr Dodson	*Poor Jo*	

All the above were depicted on rack plates and on other items in the series.

By 1915 (perhaps even earlier), the series was expanded to include the following characters:

Betsy Trotwood	*Dora*	*Poll Sweedlepipe*
Bumble	*Jonas Chuzzlewit*	*Snubbin*
Daniel Quilp	*Mr Mantalini*	*Mr Winkle*
David Copperfield	*The Marchioness*	
Dombey	*Mrs Nickleby*	

Apart from pieces depicting single characters there are others with groups of two or more figures. Some of these embrace other Dickens characters not yet mentioned, e.g. the Pickwickians – *Tupman*, *Snodgrass* and *Winkle*; *The Artful Dodger* with *Oliver Twist*; *Pecksniff* with his daughters, *Charity* and *Mercy*. The sketches were described by an unknown writer in 1915 as 'no mere mamby-pamby representations of wooden inanities vacantly simpering in rainbow colours, such as are to be constantly met with in miscalled "artistic" pottery. They are virile portrayals of the outer aspects of Dickens' personalities, reproduced mainly from original designs by an artist who has devoted the whole of his life to a sympathetic and reverent study of the great master's creations.'

The *Dickens* series were originated by Charles Noke and he played the major part in their development. Many of the original sketches bear his signature as Art Director, but some were possibly the work of William Grace, Walter Nunn, Leonard Langley or Harry Tittensor. Although Noke doubtless 'master-minded' the whole series to ensure a continuity of style, collectors have noticed certain differences of backgrounds and techniques.

The earliest components of the series appear to have been teapots, coffee pots, cups, saucers, round and square plates in several sizes, milk jugs, sugar bowls and cream jugs, candlesticks, bowls, trays and at least a dozen differently shaped vases with and without handles. By 1917, if not earlier, the range of articles in the D.2973, D.3020 series, and in D.4030 introduced in that year, included toilet jugs, basins, soap dishes, toothbrush holders, chamber-pots, hatpin stands, pintrays, trinket boxes, several more vases, ashtrays, wall plaques, tobacco jars, biscuit barrels, fruit bowls, oatmeal bowls, porridge plates, tea-caddies, punch bowls, salad bowls, sweet trays, comports, covered jars, soup tureens, bowls and plates, bulb bowls and jardinières. Probably other items were added before the above-mentioned series were withdrawn c.1930. Compared with later series, the colours in the three earlier ones were more restrained – browns, tans, dark blues and greys and blacks usually predominating. These early series are especially sought after by collectors; in addition to the usual Royal Doulton trademark they carry a special backstamp featuring a portrait of Dickens in a circle, with 'Royal Doulton' at the top and 'Dickensware' at the bottom.

In 1931 a new series in brighter colours but a more limited range of articles was introduced. This was numbered D.5175. It is thought (but no record has been found) that the D.2793, D.3030 and D.4030 series were withdrawn at the end of the previous year. The D.5175 went on until about 1951 but, for several years before this, demand, and hence production, had been on a steadily decreasing scale.

Meanwhile in 1937 a small additional series, D.5833, had been introduced. The designs of scenes and characters in this were moulded in low relief and hand-tinted. This series, probably because of production problems, was withdrawn during the Second World War. Examples are not seen so often as those of the other series. In 1937 also, a series of jugs and vases numbered D.5864 was introduced, having rather higher relief moulding and with buildings as backgrounds to the characters.

In the early 1950s all previous series were superseded by a new range numbered D.6327. This included eight plates, suitable for use as rack plates, depicting *Cap'n Cuttle*, *The Fat Boy*, *Sairey Gamp*, *Micawber*, *Mr Pickwick*, *Bill Sykes*, *Sam Weller* and *Tony Weller*. The number of articles was much more limited than in the early series, comprising – apart from the rack plates and plaque – teacup and saucer, two square plates, fruit saucer, coupé soup, comport, salad bowl, two fruit dishes, four trays, ashtray, covered cigarette box and beer mug. The D.6327 series was withdrawn completely in 1960.

China plates featuring Dickensian scenes, and with Art Deco borders, have been noted dated 1927 and 1930. No other details available.

Charles Dickens rack plate: In addition to the several series already mentioned there have been, over the years, at least five different versions of a rack plate featuring a portrait of Dickens himself in the centre with, around the rim, several characters from the novels. The first one recorded was D.2964, a blue print, produced in 1908. In 1916, this was superseded by a full colour version numbered D.3948. This in turn gave way in 1937 to a new colour version, D.5900. Then, in 1949 came D.6306 which went on until 1967. From 1968–75 there was a translucent china version TC.1042.

Doctor, D.3189: 1909–1915; D.3931: 1915–1938; D.5906: 1938–1948; D.6281: 1948–1967; TC.1048: 1968–1975. Rack plates.

Dr Johnson at the Cheshire Cheese, D.3123: 1909–1938 and D.5911: 1938–1952. Plaque, rack plates, ashtrays and other items.

Dogs: There are several rack plates depicting dogs: D.5386: 1933–1950; D.5759, 5769: 1937–1952; D.5770, 5781: 1937–1950; D.6304, 6313: 1949–1967. (See also *Game Dogs* and *Aldin's Dogs*.)

Don Quixote, D.4965: 1929–1946. A series including rack plates. Don Quixote is also featured on the following rack plates: D.2692, 2709: 1906–1928; D.2768: 1907–1928; D.3120: 1909–1928; and D.3683: 1913–1930.

Drake, D.2788: 1907–1915; D.3053: 1908–1915; D.3940: 1916–1929; and D.4849: 1929–1956. Rack plates.

Sir Francis Drake took part in several expeditions against the Spaniards in the West Indies and Central America. Between 1577 and 1580 he completed a voyage round the world in the *Golden Hind*. He was largely responsible for the defeat of the Spanish Armada in 1588.

Dutch Scenes: See *Harlem*.

Eglington Tournament, D.1425, 1461, 1462, 1496: 1902–1928; D.3054, 3055: 1908–1928. This series, including rack plates, was introduced in 1902 and added to in

1908. It depicts jousting knights and other scenes from the tournament held at Eglington Castle which Disraeli described in his novel *Endymion*.

Egyptian, D.3419: 1911–*1929*. This series, including rack plates, was introduced originally in 1911. In 1923, a year after the discovery of Tutankhamen's tomb in the Valley of the Kings by the Earl of Caernarvon and Mr Howard Carter, it was adapted to commemorate this event and the sub-title 'Tutankhamen's Treasures, Luxor, Egypt' was added.

Some rack plates and other items in Titanian Ware were also made in 1923 under D.4263.

Elephants, D.6155: 1944–1960; D.6477: 1957–1967; and D.6481 (photographic image): 1957–1975. Rack plates and plaques.

Explorers, D.2787: 1907–1915; D.3941: 1915–1928; D.4852: 1929–*1942*. Amongst the famous explorers depicted on these rack plates are Samuel de Champlain (1567–1635), who discovered Lake Champlain in Canada and became French Governor of the surrounding area, and also Sir Martin Frobisher (1535–1594), the first British navigator to seek the North-West Passage from the Atlantic to the Pacific. On some plates his name is mis-spelt 'Forbisher'. These are particularly prized by collectors. There may be other explorers in this range.

Fairy Tales, D.3606: 1912–1930. Rack plates with nursery subjects including *Little Red Riding Hood*.

Falconer, D.3576: 1912–1936; D.5907: 1938–1947; and D.6279: 1948–1967; TC.1046: 1968–1975. Rack plates.

Falconry, D.3696: 1913–*1930*. A large series with several rack plates. Special mark in addition to usual one.

Famous Ships, D.5957: 1938–*1958*. Series depicting in relief the following famous ships of earlier days: *Victory, Sirius, Cutty Sark, Active, Acorn, Matthew, Revenge, Henri Grace à Dieu, Bounty, Golden Hind, Hydra, Sussex, Fernande, Heemskerck, Endeavour, Ark Royal* and an *East Indiaman*.
The series comprises over 40 items including rack plates. Special backstamp.

Fisherfolk, D.4405: 1924–*1942*. Series including rack plates depicting Breton fisherfolk. D.2420: 1905–1918 also depicts a fisherman.

Flowers and Foliage: There is a great variety of rack plates featuring floral and foliate designs – naturalistic, stylized and combined with geometrical designs. They include: D.2204–6, 2208: 1905–*1918*; D.2544, 2546, 2701, 2702 and 2710: 1906–*1918*; D.3056–8, 3060, 3062: 1908–*1918*; D.3143, 3225–7: 1909–*1924*; D.3430, 3439: 1911–*1920*; D.3579: 1912–*1924*; D.3700: 1913–*1929*; D.3808, 3814: 1914–*1924*; D.4049: 1917–*1930*; D.4176–4180: 1921–*1940*; D.4361: 1923–*1940*; D.4546–4551:

1925–*1940*; D.4602: 1926–*1942*; D.4792–5, 4814 and 4819: 1928–*1942*; D.4860–4, 4881, 4882, 4900–4902: 1929–1942: D.5308, 5309: 1930–*1942*; D.5107, 5112–4: 1931–*1942*; D.5208, 5209: 1932–*1942*; D.5359–61, 5408–10: 1933–*1950*; D.5436, 5437, 5460: 1934–*1950*; D.5990–6: 1938–*1959*; D.6118, 6119: 1939–*1959*; D.6298, 6299, 6312, 6325, 6402: 1952–1967.

The last five are named flowers: nasturtium, pansy, chrysanthemum, poppy and magnella. *Magnella* was the name of a series containing other items besides the rack plate.

Flower-sellers in Flemish Setting, D.4785: 1928–*1945*. A series including rack plates.

Footballers: See *Old English Scenes*.

Fox-hunting: See *Hunting*.

French Courtiers, D.5497: 1933–?. A large series.

Gaffers, D. 4210: 1921–*1949*. A large series with rack plates. A 'gaffer', probably contracted from 'grandfather', is the name used by Charles Noke, who designed this series, to denote an aged, talkative rustic. The series is sub-titled: 'I be all the way from Zummerzet.' Special backstamp.

Gallant Fishers, D. 3680: 1913–*1936*. Another large series with rack plates. Special backstamp.

Game at Drinking Pool, D. 5712: 1936–1952; D. 6349: 1952–1960; D. 6361 1952–1967. Rack plates with photographic image.

Game Birds, D. 4586: 1926–1950. A large and much admired series including rack plates. Drawn by Fred Hancock and engraved by C. Vyse; hand-painted in underglaze colours.

In addition to those in this series, collectors who are interested in this particular genre will find many other plates, often unnumbered, depicting game birds. A list published in 1934 gave the names of the subjects then available: Pheasant, Partridge, Grouse, Teal, Pintail, Hybrid Black Game, Moor Hen, Capercaille, Quail, Ruff, Prairie Hen, Bob White, Wood Duck, Widgeon, Snipe, Landrail, Coot, Black Game, Red Legged Partridge, Ruffed Grouse, Mallard, Shoveller, Sheldrake, Pink Footed Goose, Garganey, Teal, Plover, Oyster Catcher, Turkey, Canada Goose, Hybrid Grouse, Woodcock, Water Hen and Ptarmigan (two subjects – winter and summer plumage). Another series, D. 2071: 1904–? depicts game birds.

Geometrical and Stylized Designs: Between about 1905 and 1955 probably more than 100 unusual and extremely attractive rack plates were produced, decorated by various processes: hand-painting, litho prints, prints from engraved copper plates, a combination of print and tint, and, particularly pleasing, block printing. These plates featured geometrical designs, crystal forms, abstract designs, stylized floral and foliate designs and other non-naturalistic themes; they give scope for forming an 'out of the ordinary' collection and are still available at quite reasonable prices. Among those either recorded or noted are plates bearing the following numbers: D.2204–6, 2208, 2218 and 2268: 1905–*1930*; D.2701, 2702, 2710 and 2780: 1907–*1930*; D.3018, 3019, 3056–8, 3060: 1908–*1930*; D.3087, 3088, 3143: 1909–*1930*; D.3430: 1911–*1930*; D.3546, 3572, 3579: 1912–*1930*; D.3699, 3700: 1913–*1930*; D.3969, 4031: 1916–*1930*: D.4174–80: 1921–*1942*; D.4361, 4365, 1924–*1942*; D.4546–51: 1925–*1942*; D.4602: 1926–*1942*; D.4792–5, 4814, 4819, 4820: 1928–*1950*; D.4859–64, 4881, 4882, 4900–2: 1929–*1950*; D.5038, 5039, 5106, 5107, 5112–4: 1931–*1950*; D.5207–10: 1932–*1950*; D.5293, 5294, 5297, 5408–11: 1933–1950; D.5436, 5437, 5460, 5473: 1934–*1950*; D.5659, 5661: 1936–*1950*; D.5990–6: 1938–*1950*; D.6118, 6119: 1940–*1955*; D.6297: 1949–*1960*.

Gibson Girls: In 1900, an American firm, George Bassett and Company of New York, asked Doulton to reproduce twelve of the Gibson Girls and twenty-four illustrations from Gibson's book *A Widow and her Friends*. This was done and the first plates were supplied in 1901. Each of the 'Girl' series had a head printed underglaze in the centre in black, with a border of blue lover's knots alternating with ribbon-encircled hearts. The 'Widow' series had captioned reproductions of Gibson's drawings framed within a stylized foliate border. (On some plates in both sets the illustrations appear to be dark sepia rather than black.)

The plates were at first sold exclusively to Bassett who in turn sold them to china dealers in various parts of the United States, the retail price being 50 cents. Some of the early plates, taken from undecorated stock, have impressed dates in the clay for 1888, 1889 and 1900, although not actually supplied until 1901.

THE WIDOW SUBJECTS

Collectors often ask for a list of the twenty-four subjects of the *Widow and her Friends* series. Here they are:

1 She contemplates the cloister.
2 She finds that exercise does not improve her spirits.
3 She decides to die in spite of Dr Bottles.
4 Miss Babbles, the Authoress, calls and reads aloud.
5 She finds some consolation in her mirror.
6 A message from the outside world.
7 A quiet dinner with Dr Bottles, after which he reads aloud Miss Babbles' latest work.
8 Some think that she has remained in retirement too long. (Others are surprised that she is about so soon.)

9   She is the subject of more hostile criticism.
10   She looks for relief among some of the old ones.
       (A pile of books on the floor.)
11   Mrs Diggs is alarmed at discovering what she imagines to be a snare that threatens the safety of her only child. Mr Diggs does not share his wife's anxiety.
12   She longs for seclusion and decides to leave town for a milder climate. While preparing for the journey she comes across some old things that recall other days.
13   The day after arriving at her journey's end.
14   They go fishing.
15   She goes into colours.
16   Failing to find rest and quiet in the country she decides to return home.
17   Mr Waddles arrives late and finds her card filled.
18   They take a morning run.
19   She becomes a trained nurse.
20   Miss Babbles brings a copy of a morning paper, and expresses her indignation and sympathy over a scurrilous article. Meanwhile other friends are calling upon the editor.
21   They all go skating.
22   She is disturbed by a vision which appears to be herself.
23   She goes to the fancy dress ball as 'Juliet'.
24   And here, winning new friends and not losing the old ones, we leave her.

Other Gibson subjects: About 1905 a further series of Gibson subjects was reproduced on rack plates, vases, bowls, jugs, cups and saucers and probably other pieces, covering amusing golfing and other situations mostly involving a courting couple. A complete record has not been found but the following titles to the illustrations have been noted: 'Golf – a good game for two', 'Is a Caddie always necessary?', 'Don't watch the player, keep your eye on the ball!', 'Fore', 'Who cares?', 'The girl he left behind him', 'A little incident', 'Wasting time', 'From 10.00 a.m. to 6.45 p.m. this dog has been kept out. Where is the S.P.C.A.?', 'One difficulty of the game – keeping your eye on the ball', 'The last day of summer', 'Here it's Christmas and they began saying good-bye in August'.

Giraffes, D.6154: 1945–1967; D.6478: 1957–1967; D.6482: 1957–1975.

Gleaners and Gipsies, D.3191: 1909–1929; D.4983, 4984: 1930–*1945*; D.6123: 1940–*1955*. There are also two rack plates showing gipsies in a modern setting, D.5003 and D.5027: 1930–1945.

Gnomes, D.4697: 1927–*1950*. A delightful series, including two or more rack plates, designed by Charles Noke. Other rack plates depicting gnomes are D.2876: 1907–*1919* with fairy, and D.3919: 1915–1930 with girl.

Golfers, D.3391, 3394, 3395, 3481: 1911–*1932*. A series introduced and added to during 1911 containing several rack plates, some with and some without proverbs and views on the rims. Rack plates depicting golfers have also been noted under D.1396 and D.1398: 1902–*1916*. (See also *Bateman, The Nineteenth Hole* and *Gibson*.)

Gondoliers, D.3039: 1908–1930; D.4981: 1930–*1945*. Series containing rack plates.

Good-Morning Zulu Girl, D.6355: 1952–1967; D.6387: 1952–1975; D.6479: 1957–1960; D.6483: 1957–1967. Rack plates and plaque with photographic image.

Governor Phillip's Statue, D.5852: 1937–*1950*. rack plate with photographic image. (See also *Phillip*.)

Green Grow the Rushes, O, D.3368: 1910–*1934*. Rack plate.

Gugnunc, D.4741: 1928–1939. Series of 17 pieces.

Gulliver, D.2707: 1906–*1928*. A large series with rack plates.

Gum Trees, D.6309: 1949–1967. Rack plate.

Harlem, D.1886: 1904–*1928*. D.3388–90: 1911–1928 and D.4828: 1929–1943. Series including several rack plates depicting Dutch scenes and figures. Some items were specially marked for sale at Liberty. Also biscuit barrels in this design were produced for McVitie and Price.

Head plates: A series of rack plates depicting heads of the following characters: *Jester, Admiral, Falconer, Parson, Doctor, Hunting Man, Mayor* and *Squire*. These designs were made in various colourways and printing techniques on earthenware, bone china and English translucent china. See also under individual names.

Hiawatha, D.3044: 1908–1930; D.5965: 1938–1949. Series including rack plates depicting North American Indians from the poem *Hiawatha* by H. W. Longfellow.

Highwayman, D.4729: 1927–1942; D.4833: 1929–1942. Rack plates.

Historic England, D.5940: 1938–*1952*. A large series containing several rack plates depicting views with appropriate characters including *Nottingham Castle, Chelsea Hospital, Hampton Court, Canterbury Cathedral, Kenilworth Castle, Bootham Bar* (one of the Gateways to the City of York), *HMS Victory at Portsmouth, Stratford Church, Haddon Hall, Plymouth Hoe, The Tower of London* and *Temple Bar, London*.

Historical Britain: A series of photographic views printed on English translucent china. See *Ann Hathaway's Cottage, Clovelly, The Houses of Parliament, Little Moreton Hall, The Tower of London*.

HMS Lion, D.?: *1916*–1920. Rack plate produced during the First World War.

Home Waters, D.6434: 1954–1967. A popular series designed by W. E. Grace, including rack plates and a plaque.

Horses, D.2777 and D.2778: 1907–1929. Two rack plates and possibly other items.

Houses of Parliament, TC.1029: 1967–1975. Rack plate.

Hudson-Fulton Celebrations 1909: Two unusual rack plates have been noted, apparently unnumbered – one with aeroplane, airships and river scene, entitled the *Aero* (sic) *Plate*; the other called the *Half-Moon Plate*, depicting Henry Hudson landing from his ship, the *Half-Moon*. (Hudson, the English navigator, is credited with the discovery of the Hudson River and Hudson Bay. Robert Fulton was an American engineer who experimented in the application of steam to navigation and in 1807 launched the *Clermont* on the Hudson.)

Hunting: There have been several hunting series. D.1321: 1902–*1928* depicted hunting and coaching scenes based on works by George Morland (1763–1804), well-known for his paintings of animals, landscapes, 'galanteries' and rustic scenes. This series includes rack plates. D.4988: 1930–*1945*. A series with rack plates. D.5104: 1931–*1950* entitled *Fox Hunting*, another series with rack plates. A similar series is believed to have been done in china. D.6185, 6186, 6231, 6326: 1947–*1960*. A series, including rack plates, designed by Charles Simpson, a well-known painter of hunting scenes. The subjects include *Across the Moor, Post and Rails, In the Vale, Gone to Ground, Over the Grass, Changing Horses, Hot Scent, The Master, Going to Covert,* and *The Brook*. There are several other rack plates with fox-hunting and deer-hunting scenes by Morland, Aldin, Simpson and other artists. These include: D.1375, 1376: 1902–*1928*; D.2215, 2397–9; 1905–*1928*; D.2778; 1907–*1928*; D. 3636, 3695: 1913–*1928*; D.4475: 1925–*1940*; D.4507: 1925–*1942*; D.4990, 4994, 1930–*1946*.

Hunting Man, D.3349: 1910–*1938*; D.5904; 1938–*1950*; D.6282: 1948–1967; TC.1049: 1968–1975. Rack plates.

I Say a Stoop of Wine, D.1978: 1904–*1918*. Rack plate.

Isaac [sic] *Walton*, D.2312, D.2704: 1905–*1928*. A large series with six or more rack plates and a plaque, designed by Charles Noke. Quotations from Isaak Walton's famous book *The Compleat Angler*. Special backstamp in addition to usual mark.

Isthmian Games, D.1440. A series based on Pinder, Bourne engravings produced during the early part of this century. Probably withdrawn by 1918.

Italian Landscape, D.5021:1930–?. Rack plate.

It's a Long Way to Tipperary, D.5945: 1916–*1920*. A series including a rack plate, produced during the First World War.

Jackdaw of Rheims, D.2532: 1906–*1930*. A large series including rack plates and a plaque. Based on the legend recounted in Thomas Ingoldsby's poem of the same name. The Jackdaw stole the Cardinal of Rheims's ring and hid it. For this he was cursed. When he returned the ring the curse was removed. When he died he was canonized. Some of the scenes were reproduced also on china (E.3505; 1906–*1940*). Some earthenware items are misnumbered D.2352 and some china ones E.3305.

Jessopeak Pressgang, D.2541, 2542, 2761: 1906–*1930*. An unusual series with three rack plates. The three scenes featured show men being press-ganged, sailors in action, and reunion in a tavern after the battle.

Jester, D.3684: 1913–1939; D.5903; 1938–1948; D.6277: 1948–1967; TC. 1044: 1968–1975. Rack plates.

Jock of the Bushveld, D.5463, 5464, 1934–*1942*. Rack plates.

Justice's Late Meeting, D.4832: 1929–*1942*. Rack plate.

Kang-He, D.4162: 1921–*1942*. A series with rack plates.

Kensington Gardens, D.4467: 1924–*1942*. An attractive series with rack plates. The series depicts riders, coaches and sedan chairs in the park in silhouette against a rich yellow background.

King Arthur's Knights, D.2961: 1908–*1930*; D.3120: 1909–? Series with rack plates, an adaptation of the *Eglington Tournament* design.

King of Hearts, D.3969: 1916–*1932*. Rack plate.

Koala Bears, D.6413: 1953–1967; D.6424: 1953–1975. Rack plates with photographic image and wattle flowers.

Kookaburra, D.4205, 4206: 1920–*1949*. A series including rack plates. (See also *Young Kookaburra*.)

Lake Louise and Victoria Glacier, Canada, D.6474: 1957–1975. Rack plate with photographic image.

Lambeth Horseferry, D.6160: 1941–1950. A rare rack plate of which only between 1,000 and 1,500 copies were made.

Landscapes, D.2538: 1906–*1928*; D.2846: 1907–*1928*; D.3668: 1913–*1940*. Series containing several rack plates. Landscapes are found also on numerous other rack plates. The following have been noted: D.2452, 2652, 2654, 2683: 1906–*1928*; D.2882: 1907–*1928*; D.2938, 3040: 1908–*1928*; D.4385, 4390: 1924–*1942*; D.4914: 1929–*1942*; D.5007, 5008, 5021: 1930–*1942*; D.4883: 1929–1950; D.4368: 1933–1950; D.5506: 1934–1950.

The two early series are apparently based on sketches after George Morland and

Teniers by Walter Nunn. (See also *Moonlight Landscape*.)

Leda and the Swan, D.2545: 1906–?. Rack plate in *Art Nouveau* style.

Lion, D.5723: 1936–*1951*; D.5750: 1937–*1951*; D.6347, 6356: 1952–1967; D.6359: 1952–1975 (photographic image). (Also a plaque D.6191: 1945–1967.) Rack plates.

Lion, HMS: see *HMS Lion*;

Lioness, D.5724: 1936–*1951*; D.5751: 1937–*1951*; D.6348: 1952–1960; D.6360: 1952–1967 (photographic image). Rack plates.

Little Moreton Hall, TC.1031: 1972–1975. Rack plate. (See also *Old Moreton 1589*.)

Loch Lomond, TC.1093: 1972–1975. Rack plate.

Log-hauling, D.4533: 1925–*1941*; D.5364: 1933–*1945*; D.5928: 1938–*1945*. Rack plates.

Lorne, Scene at, D.5816: 1937–1948; D.5895: 1938–1948; D.6310: 1950–1967. Rack plates.

Magnella, D.6298: 1949–1967. A series with rack plates.

Man with Scythe, D.3356: 1910–*1928*. Rack plate.

Maori Girls, D.6058: 1939–1960; D.6305: 1948–1975. Rack plates with photographic image.

Maori Woman with Child, D.4930, 4931: 1929–*1955*. Rack plate.

Maple Tree, D.5652, 5653, 5657–61: 1936–*1945*. Seven rack plates in different block-printed colours with maple tree in centre; rose, thistle, shamrock and fleur-de-lys underneath; inscription and short history of Doulton on back.

It is thought that these plates were in production for only a few years and then mainly for Canada. They are much admired and sought after by collectors.

Maritime Provinces, Canada, D.6493: 1957–1975. Rack plate with photographic image.

Mayor, D.3348: 1910–1938; D.3933: 1915–1938; D.5899: 1938–1948; D.6283: 1948–1967. TC. 1050: 1968–1975. Rack plates.

Medallion, D.3193: 1909–1928. A series with rack plates.

Minstrels, D.4243: 1923–*1940*. A series with rack plates.

Monks, D.2567: 1906–1919. A series with rack plates. D.2385: 1905–1919. Same design but different colourway. Monks are also depicted, sometimes with mottoes and proverbs on several other rack plates. Those noted are: D.2567: 1906–1919; D.2877: 1907–1928; D.2976: 1908–1928; D.3084; 1909–1928; D.3429; 1911–1928;

D.3571: 1912–1928; D.4617; 1926–1940; D.6099: 1939–1950 (two rack plates and a plaque).

Monks are also depicted on two or more china rack plates.

Montmorency Falls, Canada, D.6472: 1957–1967. Rack plate with photographic image.

Moonlight Landscape, D.3697: 1913–1930. A series including rack plates.

Moorish Gateway, D.4601: 1926–1945. An unusual series with relief decoration designed probably by Harry Allen. It included several rack plates. Another rack plate D.4742: 1928–? has been reported with a Moorish scene.

Mother Kangaroo with Joey, D.6412: 1954–1967; D.6423: 1954–1975. Rack plates with photographic image.

Motoring, D.2406: 1905–1928. A series with nine or more rack plates. The amusing scenes noted on rack plates (designed by George Holdcroft) are entitled: *Deaf, The New and the Old, After the Run, A Horse, A Horse!, Blood Money, A Nerve Tonic, Room for One, Itch Yer on Guvnor?, Outside the Chequers Inn.*

A china rack plate E.3247 (specimens dated 1905 and 1907) has been reported entitled *The Wise Motorist,* illustrating the limerick:

> There was a young man of Dacota
> Who went to get wed in a motor;
> Said he to his bride:
> My horse is inside –
> We prepare for events in Dacota.

(He has fitted up the back of the car as a horse-box.)
(See also *Willow Pattern.*)

Mount Egmont, New Zealand, D.6417: 1953–1960; D.6434; 1953–1975. Rack plates with photographic image.

Murray River Gums, Australia, D.6414: 1953–1967; D.6425: 1953–1975. Rack plates with photographic image.

Nelson, Admiral Lord, D.3514: 1911–*1928*: D.3616: 1912–*1928*. Rack plates.

New Cavaliers, D.3051: 1908–1928. A series including rack plates. (See also *Cavaliers.*)

New Guinea Native, D.6416, 6437: 1953–1960. Two rack plates with photographic image.

New South Wales: see *Phillip.*

Niagara Falls, D.6476: 1957–1975. Rack plate with photographic image.

Night Watchman, D.3190: 1901–1928. A series with rack plates. D.4746: 1928–1945 also features a watchman.

Nineteenth Hole, D.3755, 3770: 1914–1930. Rack plates.

Nursery Rhymes, E.1441: 1903–1936. A series designed by William Savage Cooper, a regular exhibitor at the Royal Academy, including the following titles: *Old Mother Hubbard, Little Tommy Tucker, Little Bo Peep, Where are You going. . .?, Hey Diddle Diddle, Simple Simon, Ride a Cock Horse, Tom, Tom the Piper's Son, Old Mother Goose, To Market, to Market, There was an Old Woman. . ., Peter Piper, There was a Little Man, Mary, Mary Quite Contrary, Jack and the Beanstalk* and *Queen of Hearts.*

Supplies of this series were ordered by Queen Alexandra for use by her grand-children. A 40-piece tea-set cost just under £1.50 in 1905.

D.1513: 1903–1930. Jug depicting *Old King Cole*.

D.1712–14: 1903–1930. Three *Jack and Jill* jugs noted of different colourings. Proverbs on back in a shield, e.g. 'Nothing is troublesome that we do willingly'.

D.1811: 1903–?. Similar designs but with gold edges.

D.1909, 1914: 1904–1932. A teapot with illustration of *Polly put the Kettle on* and a baby plate with blue print *Willow Pattern* have been recorded.

D.2404: 1905–1930. A series with different single lines from the nursery rhyme *Where are You going to My Pretty Maid?*

D.2515: 1906–1930. Cups and saucers and plates with illustrations of *Here we go gathering Nuts. . ., Hark, hark the Dogs do bark*, and *Tom, Tom the Piper's Son*.

D.2539, 2540: 1906–1930. A series illustrating nursery rhymes including *Little Bo Peep, Tom, Tom. . ., Little Miss Muffet, The Pied Piper, To buy a fat Pig* and *Old King Cole*.

D.2921, 2922: 1908–1930. Rack plates, including *Baa, Baa, Black Sheep, Where are You going. . .?*

D.3082, 3083: 1909–1930. A plate, porridge dish and baby plate have been recorded featuring *Baa, Baa, Black Sheep, Little Bo Peep* and *Little Miss Muffet* respectively.

D.3300, 3312, 3357: 1910–1930. Mugs and plates illustrating *Baa, Baa, Black Sheep*.

D.3606: 1912–1930. Rack plates, including *Old Mother Hubbard* and *Little Red Riding Hood*.

D.3659, 3660: 1913–1930; D.4686: 1927–1939. A series based on the nursery rhyme *Cock-a-doodle-do*.

D.3918: 1915–1934; D.4064, 4083: 1919–1934. A series of black-printed nursery rhymes, the cups and jugs having black handles. Subjects include *Jack and Jill, Little Boy Blue, Little Tommy Tucker, Where are You going. . .?, Simple Simon, See saw, Margery Daw* and *Queen of Hearts*.

D.4016: 1917–1934. A nursery rhyme series including *Three Blind Mice, Little Miss Muffet,* and *There was a little Man*.

D.5444: 1934–1942. A series of mugs depicting nursery rhyme illustrations and printed with a variety of forty or more popular children's names.

E.5773: 1909–1932. A small series of jugs featuring nursery rhymes.

Nursery Subjects, A.2115, 2116: c.1885–c.1910. Plates, cups and saucers bearing these two numbers depicted cats, bears, ducks and dogs and subjects entitled *Dr Jumbo's School* and *The Gollywog's Joyride*.

D.2433, 2434: 1905–1934. A series depicting toy figures motoring.

D.5604–7: 1935–1942. A series of mugs embossed with chicken, chanticlere, duck and squirrel respectively.

Old Balloon Man: 1980. Rack plate with embossed decoration.

Old Balloon Seller: 1979. Rack plate with embossed decoration.

Old Bob ye Guard, D.2724: 1906–1928. Rack plate and plaque.

Old Bristol Series, C.1904. At least ten different views of Bristol on jugs and other items, designed by Walter Nunn.

Old English Coaching Scenes, D.6393: 1953–1967. A series designed by W. Grace.

Old English Country Fairs, D.3611: 1912–1928. A series designed by Walter Nunn.

Old English Inns, D.6072: 1939–*1955*; V.2353 (china): 1947–*1958*. Series including rack plates depicting The Bell, Hurley; The Leather Bottle, Cobham; The Fighting Cocks, St Albans; The Peacock, Rowsley; The Cat and Fiddle, Hinton Admiral; The Royal Oak, Winsford; The King's Head, Chigwell.

Old English Proverbs Illustrated, Old English Sayings, D.3354, 3427, 3428, 3435, 3544, 3545. A series of rack plates was produced under these titles and numbers between 1910 and 1928. Special backstamp on *Old English Proverbs Illustrated*.

Old English Scenes, D.3191, 3611 and 3470: 1909–*1940*; D.4507: 1925–*1950*; D.4960, 4983, 4984: 1930–*1950*. A series based on sketches by Cecil Aldin, including rack plates. Special backstamp.

Old Jarvey, An, D.3118: 1909–1928. A series designed by Walter Nunn including rack plates depicting a coachman whose popular name was Old Jarvey.

Old London, D.2105, 2351: 1904–1928. A series by Nunn with at least 18 different views of Old London.

Old Moreton 1589, D.3822, 3842, 3858: 1915–1933; D.5490: 1934–1949. Series depicting aspects of the visit of Queen Elizabeth I to the Hall in 1589, during which a pageant was held. The present Hall, originally known as Little Moreton Hall, was built in 1540 by Sir William Moreton. The Hall is situated about eight miles from The Potteries. The series includes four or more rack plates and at least one plaque; one is also reported on china. Special backstamp.

Old Quebec, TC.1035: 1967–1975. Rack plate.

Old Salt, D.3059, 3085: 1908–1928. Two rack plates.

Old Sea Dogs: D.2160: 1904–?. A series with rack plates.

Old Wife, D.5966: 1938–*1955*. A series depicting tropical fish.

Oliver Goldsmith, D.?: 1905–*1914*. A rack plate with Goldsmith's head and scenes based on *The Deserted Village*.

Omar Khayyam, D.3287–89: 1910–1928. Three rack plates and a plaque; possibly other items.

Open Door, D.3754: 1914–*1936*. A series including rack plates.

Ottawa Peace Tower and Houses of Parliament, TC.1036: 1967–1975. Rack plate.

Owls, D.3607: 1912–1930. A series with rack plates.

Pan, D.4784: 1928–*1940*. A series with rack plates.

Parson, D.3303: 1910–1928; D.3930: 1915–1928; D.5901: 1938–1948; D.6280: 1948–1967. TC. 1047: 1968–1975. Rack plates.

Paxton, D.3204: 1909–1930. Rack plate with classical female head.

Persian, D.3550: 1912–1917. A similar design to *Blue Persian*.

Persian Tree, H.1790: (china) 1923–*1946*. A series with rack plates.

Phillip, Captain Arthur, D.5852: 1937–*1942*; D.6201: 1938–*1942*. Rack plates issued for sesquicentenary of the Founding of New South Wales by Captain Phillip in 1788.

Pip, Squeak and Wilfred, H.3485: 1927–1935. A series based on the exploits of the then popular cartoon characters. D.4762, 4763: 1928–1935. A similar series.

Piping down the Valleys Wild, D.4977: 1919–*1940*. A series with rack plates.

Ploughing, D.5650: 1936–1948. A pair of rack plates. Ploughing is also represented on D.4934: 1929–?.

Polar Bears, D.3127: 1909–?. A series.

Poplar Trees (Sunset), D.3301, 3305, 3416: 1910–*1940*. A series with rack plates, also in Titanian glaze effect, D.4274: 1923–1929. Poplars are also depicted on D.5369: 1933–*1940*.

Proverbs: Several series include rack plates incorporating proverbs. In addition to some already mentioned – *Birds, Cavaliers, Dogs, Golfers, Monks, Old English Proverbs*, there is the D.3391 series (1911–1928) with rack plates depicting figures in

113

Eastern and other styles of costumes, and also an early series D.2982: 1908–?. Between all of these different series, 24 different proverbs and sayings have been noted.

Prunus, D.3832, 3833: 1915–*1935*. A series with rack plates with different coloured backgrounds.

Queen's View, Loch Tummel, TC.1094: 1972–1975. Rack plate.

Quorn Hunt, D.4468: 1924–*1945*. A popular series with rack plates.

Raleigh, Sir Walter, D.2787: 1907–1915; D.3053: 1908–1915; D.3939: 1915–1928; D.4843: 1929–1955. Rack plates.

Refectory Bell, D.3608: 1912–?; D.3717: 1914–1930. Series including rack plates.

Rhodes Centenary, D.6379–82: 1952–1955. Four rack plates in different colours, with portrait centre of Cecil John Rhodes (1853–1902).

Rip Van Winkle, D.2553, 2788: 1906–1928. A large series with rack plates. Some items bear facsimile signature of Walter Nunn.

Robert Burns: See *Burns*.

Robin Hood: See *Under the Greenwood Tree*.

Roger Solemel, Cobbler, D.4834: 1929–1942. Rack plate. (See also *Broom-man*.)

Royal Mail Coach, D.4490 or 4498: 1925–*1940*. Rack plate.

Rustic England, D.5694: 1936–1960; D.6297: 1949–1960. Series designed by Walter E. Grace, including rack plates.

Sailing Barges, D.2551: 1906–1930. Two rack plates.

St George and the Dragon, D.5108–5111: 1931–*1945*. Four rack plates in various colours. There is also a china version.

St Mary's Aisle, Dryburgh, D.5412: 1933–*1940*. Rack plate.

St Vincent, Admiral Earl of, D.3514, 3617: 1911–1928. Rack plate.

Sampler, D.3749: 1914–*1936*. A series including rack plates. Special backstamp.

Sayings, D.2799: 1907–*1930*. A series including rack plates illustrated with sketches of women drinking tea with captions such as 'The Cup that cheers' and 'Heart's Content'.

Sedan Chair, D.3597: 1912–*1940*. A series with rack plates.

Shakespeare: In the *Pottery Gazette* for June 1901 there is a reference to a Shakespeare dessert set, each plate having in the centre a painting of a scene from one of

Shakespeare's plays. Further details of this service have not so far been traced but the plates were presumably the forerunners of a long series of Shakespearean items.

D.2129: flow blue rack plates depicting *King Lear, The Merchant of Venice, Othello,* and *A Midsummer Night's Dream.*

D.2137: scene from *The Tempest.*

D.2493: rack plate, *Sir Toby Belch.*

D.2494: rack plate, *Sir Andrew Aguecheek.*

D.2495: rack plate, *Sir John Falstaff.* (*Belch, Falstaff* and *Aguecheek* also appear on jugs and tankards.)

D.2543: rack plate featuring scenes from *Romeo and Juliet, Merchant of Venice, As You Like It* and *The Winter's Tale.*

D.2881: rack plates – *Falstaff and Prince Henry, Falstaff and Dame Quickly,* and *Falstaff and Bardolph.*

D.2644 and

D.2721: *Dogberry's Watch,* rack plates.

D.2779: *Falstaff* scene, rack plate.

D.2874: pair of rack plates featuring *Snout* and *Bottom.*

D.3199: rack plate, *Lear and his daughters.*

All the above were introduced between 1904 and 1912 and had been withdrawn by 1928.

D.3596: 1912–1928. Rack plates with coloured backgrounds depicting *Shylock, Portia, Hamlet, Ophelia, Romeo and Juliet, Anne Page and Falstaff, Katharine and Wolsey, Orlando and Rosalind.* (Possibly others.)

D.3746: 1914–*1930.* A large series of over 50 items including rack plates featuring characters as above with *sepia* background.

D.3835: 1914–*1930.* Coupé plates depicting characters as above. (Possibly also *Titania* and others.)

D.3882: 1915–*1930.* Rack plate, *Anne Page.*

D.3934: 1914–*1930.* Rack plate, scene from *A Midsummer Night's Dream.*

D.4149: 1921–1939. A series entitled *Shakespeare's Country.* The following subjects have been noted on rack plates: Papist Wixford, Beggarly Broom and Ann Hathaway's Cottage.

A number of Shakespeare subjects appear also on china series E.7267: 1911–*1930.*

Shakespeare Portrait: The following rack plates were produced with a portrait of Shakespeare in the centre and sketches of characters around the rim: D.3194, 3195: 1909–1937; D.5910: 1938–1948; D.6303: 1948–1967; TC.1041: 1968–1975.

Shepherd, D.3356: 1910–*1930;* D.3601: 1912–*1930.* Rack plates.

Ships: See *Blue* and *Brown Ships.*

Silhouettes, D.3577, 3598: 1912–*1930.* Series with rack plates.

Sir Roger de Coverley, D.3418: 1911–1936; D.5814: 1937–*1949*. Series with rack plates. Special backstamp.

Skating, D.2789, 2865: 1907–1928. Series with rack plates.

Sketches from Teniers: Sketches by the Flemish painter David Teniers the Younger (1610–1690) were adapted by Walter Nunn for a series of rack plates and other items. The following have been noted on rack plates: *Tavern Scene*, D.2440: 1905–?; D.2648: 1906–*1930*; D.2785, 2786, 2790: 1907–*1930*; D.3477: 1911–*1930*; D.3716: 1914–*1930*; D.5001: 1930–*1942*. *Village Fete*, D.2780: 1907–1930. Other reproductions of sketches from Teniers are believed to have included *The Five Senses, Meeting of the Civic Guards* and *The Prodigal Son*.

Souter's Cats: A popular series including rack plates, revived at intervals between 1906 and 1939, featuring humorous studies of cats, by the famous Australian cartoonist David H. Souter (1862–1935). 'The Tiff', 'Trust not him that seems a Saint', 'The Lovers', 'The Honeymoon', 'The Gay Bachelor', 'O Perfect Love', 'Better alone than in bad company', 'Here we go round the Mulberry Bush'.

Spanish Armada, D.3086: 1909–1928. Two rack plates, different colourings. Another rack plate with same number features the *Battle of Trafalgar*.

Squire, D.3117: 1909–1938; D.3932: 1915–1938; D.5898: 1938–1948; D.6284: 1948–1967. TC.1051: 1968–1975. Rack plates.

Stag, D.2214: 1905–1928; D.2410: 1905–1928; D.3694: 1913–*1940*. Rack plates.

Stirrup Cup, D.3045, 3046: 1908–1929. Rack plates.

Surfing, D.4645, 4789: 1926–*1942*. A series introduced in 1926 and added to in 1928. It includes rack plates.

Swans, D.3570: 1912–1932; D.5206: 1932–1945. Rack plates.

Sydney: see *Phillip*.

Tea in the Garden, D.5439: 1934–1949. Rack plate.

Teniers: See *Sketches from Teniers*.

Three Musqueteers, D.4006: 1917–1939. Rack plate.

Tiger, D.6190: 1946–1967. Rack plate and plaque.

Timber Logging, D.5157: 1931–1958; D.5367: 1933–1958. Rack plates.

Timber Waggon, D.6307: 1950–1967. Rack plate.

Tomorrow will be Friday, D.3429: 1911–1930. Rack plate.

Tower of London, TC.1030: 1965–1967; TC.1039: 1967–1975. Rack plates.

Town Crier, D.2716: 1906–*1928*; D.3682, 3688, 3716: 1913–1941. Rack plates.

Trafalgar, Battle of, D.3086: 1909–1928. Rack plate.

Treasure Island, D.6376: 1951–?. Series.

Tudor Lady (head), D.3946, 3990, 3991: 1916–1932. Rack plates.

Tudor Sailing Ships, D.2677: 1906–1920. Rack plates.

Tunis, D.3538, 3578: 1912–*1940*. A series with rack plates.

Uncle Toby, Old English Games, D.3111, 3121: 1909–1930; D.3470 and D.3547: 1911–1928. A series designed by Walter Nunn containing rack plates, based on Laurence Sterne's well-known character in *Tristram Shandy*. Special backstamp.

Uncle Tom's Cabin: A series under this name was mentioned in an American trade journal for 1904.

Under the Greenwood Tree, D.3751: 1914–*1936*; D.5808: 1937–*1948*; D.6094: 1939–*1948*; D.6341: 1951–1967. Series with special backstamp.

Urn and Flame, D.3018, 3019: 1908–1930; D.4820: 1928–1958. Rack plates.

Valentine's Day, 1976 and still issued annually. Rack plates with embossed decoration and Valentine scenes.

Van Riebeeck Statue, D.5714, 5759: 1936–1958; D.6350: 1952–1960; D.6362: 1951–1967. Rack plates with photographic image.

Venice, H.2945 (china): 1926–1958. A series including rack plates.

Vermillion Lake and Mount Rundle, Canada, D.6473: 1957–1975. Rack plate with photographic view.

Victory and Peace, D. ? : 1919–1920. Rack plate issued at the end of the First World War.

Viking Ship, D.3569: 1912–1928. Rack plate.

Virgin Mary, (no number) c. 1937; a companion rack plate to one of *Christ with Crown of Thorns*.

Voortrekker, D.5979, 5980: 1938–1950. Rack plates.

Waratah, D.5207, 5295, 5296: 1932–1948. Rack plates.

Washington, George, D.2707, 2708: 1906–*1916*. Rack plates entitled *Marching on Trenton* and *Crossing the Delaware*. D.3375, D.3376 (portrait): 1911–*1918*. Rack plates. (See also *American Statesmen*.)

Watchman and Minstrel, D.4273: 1923–1939. Rack plate.

Water Buck, D.6156: 1940–1956; D.6480, 6484: 1957–1967. Rack plates with photographic image.

Wattle Frieze, D.3811: 1914–1930. A series with rack plates.

Wedlock, D.2395: 1905–1928. A series including rack plates illustrating titles such as *Wedlock's joys are soft and sweet*, *Wedlock's joys do sometimes change*, and *Wedlock is a ticklish thing*.

Weeping Rock Waterfall, D.5851: 1937–1950; D.6311: 1950–1967. Rack plates.

Welsh Women, D.2717, 1906–1928; D.3208: 1909–1928; D.3363: 1910–1928. Series containing rack plates.

William and Mary, D.3207: 1909–1919. Rack plate inspired by an old Lambeth delftware plate.

William ye Driver: Rack plate c.1907.

Willow Pattern: Between the 1880s and the 1930s this famous pattern has been reproduced several times in different versions, including a set of six plates telling the Willow Pattern story in underglaze blue earthenware and polychrome bone china. Plates numbered D.653, 3382, 3393, 3866, 3867, 4478, 4841, 4851, 4872 have been noted. All withdrawn by 1945. There is also a comical 'Motoring Medley' adaptation of the Willow Pattern, D.3625: 1912–1928.

Wiltshire Moonrakers, D.4635: 1926–*1946*. A series with rack plates.

Witches, D.2673, 2735, 2903: 1906–1928. A series with rack plates.

Women's Voluntary Service: A plate was produced in 1962 with the crest of the WVS and the motto 'Not why we can't but how we can'. Edition of c.3,000.

Woodland, D.5815: 1937–1956. Series with rack plates.

Woodley Dale, D.5195: 1932– ? . A view in Staffordshire.

Ye Knave of Hearts, D.3655: 1913–?. Rack plate designed by Augustus L. Jansen.

Ye Squire ye Passenger: Unnumbered rack plate c.1907.

Young Kookaburras, D.6415: 1953–1967; D.6426: 1953–1975. Rack plates with photographic image.

Zodiac, D.3112: rack plate noted dated 1909.

Zulu Girl at Waterhole, D.5711, 5747: 1936–1951; D.6351, 6363: 1951–1967. Rack plates with photographic image.

Zulu Warrior, D.5713, 5748: 1936–1951; D.6352, 6364: 1951–1960. Rack plates with photographic image.

Zunday Zmocks, D.5680: 1936–*1950*. A series with rack plates.

Tablewares

Tablewares have already been discussed in several earlier chapters. It remains to be said that throughout the whole history of the Doulton Burslem Pottery they have played a major part in building up its world-wide reputation. While the *flambé,* Sung, Titanian and other special wares naturally won a great deal of publicity and soon became 'collectables', it was on the steady production of readily saleable domestic tablewares in bone china, stone china and fine earthenware that the factory mainly depended to pay its way. Without the sustained underlying support afforded by the success of the tablewares in their several different price ranges, many of the other developments described in previous chapters would not have been viable; this applies also to the early years of figure production.

The range of tableware patterns and shapes during the existence of the Burslem Pottery has been immense. It includes costly services with rich raised gold and acid-gold decorations, combined often with the finest hand-painting and coloured grounds, for English and foreign royalties, Indian potentates, American million-aires, British and other embassies; more moderately-priced services decorated by a combination of outline prints from engraved copper plates and hand-painting ('print and tint'); and a great variety of inexpensive but attractive services decorated mainly with multi-colour lithographic and silk-screen transfers. From about 1901 to 1956, some delightful designs were produced also by 'block-printing'.

The Burslem designers, led in turn over the past century by John Slater, Charles Noke, Jack Noke and Jo Ledger, have been remarkably catholic in their outlook, never adhering too narrowly to a particular school of design or abstract aesthetic theory; and although some such as Raby, Hancock, Curnock and Dewsberry have become closely associated in collectors' minds with a certain style and choice of subject, one not infrequently comes across examples of their work which, without the evidence of their signatures, one would not have ascribed to them. The majority of the Doulton designers and artists have always been extremely versatile.

While Chinese, Japanese, Greek, Renaissance, Meissen, Sèvres, Chelsea, Leeds, Bristol, early Worcester, Derby and other periods and styles, including the impact of the *Art Nouveau* movement at the turn of the century, are reflected in certain designs, there is seldom any direct copying except in a few cases where an inscrip-tion on the ware indicates that the design is a reproduction of some earlier work. And, in addition to designs that can be described as traditionally-based, for which there seems ever to be a great demand, many others have been produced, and are still being produced today, which strike new and original notes in ceramic decoration.

Until fairly recently a china manufacturer had always to cater for a greater diversity of tastes, not only in different overseas markets (where, for instance, what would sell well in Australia would hardly sell at all in the United States, and vice-versa), but also even in different parts of the British Isles. There are still naturally some differences but, broadly speaking, and although some would say regrettably, a greater consensus of opinion has developed in many important markets as to the types of patterns and shapes with the greatest appeal.

It is interesting to read in Charles Noke's notes some of the varied requests which he had to try to meet from overseas' agents and representatives: 'china plates in Adams style'; 'more designs with rococo borders'; 'teas in modern French style'; 'plates and teas in Empire style'; 'tea-sets with more profuse floral patterns'; 'patterns with Australian flora'; 'sets in early Worcester style'; 'Chinese Chippendale'; 'more Old Leeds patterns', etc., etc. Noke sometimes found it difficult to reconcile some requests with his own predilections. The same problem of trying to meet many demands – often conflicting ones – faced all ceramic designers in those not so very distant days before such modern concepts as 'rationalization', 'market surveys' and 'design surveys', 'variety reduction' and the like began to make their impact.

Considering the literally thousands of different patterns of dinner, breakfast and tea services, mocha and other coffee sets, dessert, game and fish sets produced at Burslem over the past hundred years, it is remarkable how seldom one comes across a design which prompts the thought, 'How on earth could Doulton have *made* or anyone have *bought* a thing like that!' From the present-day collector's point of view their profuse variety adds greatly to the attraction of the Doulton tablewares; variety not only of shapes and designs but also of methods of decoration and types of ceramic body, the latter including both feldspathic and bone china, fine earthenware and – less well-known – 'stone china'. (Several stone china patterns are illustrated in late-nineteenth- and early-twentieth-century catalogues.) This material, like 'granite china', Mason's 'ironstone china' and Spode and other types of 'stone china' is really an extra strong and heavy form of earthenware.

BRANGWYN WARE

One of the most interesting and original tableware experiments at the Burslem factory involved the versatile designer Frank Brangwyn, RA (1867–1956). This well-known and popular painter had already produced furniture, textile and ceramic designs for many firms before he began to work with Doulton. It is said to have been Charles Noke's old friend from his Worcester days, the composer Sir Edward Elgar, who introduced Brangwyn to him in 1928. He soon began submitting designs and the first fruits of his work appeared in the showrooms and china shops in 1930. Further designs were produced during the next four or five years but, though praised by the critics, they failed to meet with the hoped-for popular approval and production seems to have ceased during the Second World War and was not resumed.

Noke was in his seventies at the time the Brangwyn Ware was introduced and it says much for his sustained freshness of outlook and open-mindedness that he was ready to sponsor something so utterly unusual. The new products were a complete breakaway from any of the traditional styles then in vogue. The *Pottery Gazette* described the ware as 'something in pottery the like of which has never been seen before – something immediately arresting because of its uniqueness'. Speaking to a reporter, Noke said he considered 'new and original themes and fresh branches of technique as important to maintain a pottery concern's valued reputation as the production of established lines'. This was in keeping with his general philosophy that too narrow an adherence to accepted tradition could have a deleterious effect on twentieth-century ceramics.

Brangwyn wanted the ware he designed to be 'within the reach of people of quite moderate means'. A strong robust earthenware body rather than the more expensive fine bone china was therefore chosen as the medium. This was buff-coloured, splashed and painted underglaze with coloured slips – especially matt blue, pink, lemon yellow, ivory, jade green, blue-green, olive green, and golden brown. The outlines of the main features of many patterns were formed in the moulds; others were incised in the clay by hand. Block prints were used for some of the designs. No two pieces, not even the ten-inch plates of a dinner service, though broadly conforming to an over-all colour scheme, are exactly alike.

Besides the dinner, tea and coffee services, vases, ashtrays, biscuit barrels, beakers, plaques, candlesticks, sandwich trays, covered boxes and lamp bases were produced in Brangwyn Ware. No fewer than sixteen different shapes and decorations of vases are recorded. In addition to the Royal Doulton trade mark these items all bear the words 'Designed by Frank Brangwyn, R.A.' and/or 'Brangwyn Ware'.

The prices for such an unusual ware were incredibly low even for the 1930s. A dinner service for twelve people could be bought, for instance, in London stores for just over £8, a tea-set for twelve for £3.15. Vases ranged from 25p to 75p according to size and a lamp cost £1.60 complete.

In overcoming the problems which inevitably arose in expressing Brangwyn's unusual designs in the ceramic medium, Jack Noke, Harry Nixon and Harry Fenton successfully collaborated with Charles Noke.

ENGLISH TRANSLUCENT CHINA

The universal reputation of English tablewares since the late eighteenth century had depended on two traditional materials developed by Staffordshire master-potters, namely fine earthenware and bone china – the latter so-called because up to about half the composition of the body is calcined bone ash which gives the ware its unique combination of whiteness, translucency and strength. Since the early 1800s, although increased control over uniformity of raw materials and new production and firing techniques had brought about refinements in appearance and finish, there had been no great changes in formulae.

Broadly speaking, fine earthenware met the demand for everyday services at moderate prices, while the much more expensive bone china was, for most people, something to be reserved – if they possessed any at all – for special occasions. Careful research indicated clearly, however, that in countries where living standards had risen since the war, there was a growing preference for translucent china for *everyday use* if it could be obtained at prices comparable with those for good earthenware. (Fine English earthenware was regarded as the best in the world but even it lacked both the strength and the translucency of china and, a serious disadvantage from the point of view of hygiene, it was porous under the glaze so that if this were damaged it would gradually absorb liquids.)

The demand for a less expensive china than English bone china was being met on a growing scale in such important markets as Australia, Canada and the United States by German, Japanese and other feldspathic china. It was in order to meet this competition at the right time, foreseeing that it would increase, that the long and costly research programme was initiated which resulted in what was first named 'English Translucent China' but is now known simply as Royal Doulton Fine China (as distinct from Royal Doulton Fine Bone China). This programme was begun and developed under the direction of J. Kenneth Warrington who had succeeded Cuthbert Bailey as General Manager of the Burslem Pottery in 1953 and three years later was appointed Managing Director of Doulton Fine China Limited (a subsidiary of the parent company of Doulton & Co. Limited, created in 1956). The research team which made the idea of the new china a reality was led by Richard J. Bailey, then Technical Director of Doulton Fine China Limited and now Managing Director of Royal Doulton Tableware Limited.

The idea of an intermediate English tableware was not new, but previous attempts to create such a material had concentrated merely on developing variations of earthenware which, like the old delftwares, simulated china to some degree in appearance but lacked its most essential qualities. The new translucent Doulton china evolved by Richard Bailey and his team after several years' research, brought for the very first time a true English fine china within the reach of millions. Delicate in appearance and yet astonishingly tough, whiter than most foreign feldspathic chinas, and truly translucent, it lends itself to a wide range of colours and decorative treatments, including the use of gold and platinum. It is a natural evolution from traditional English pottery methods and no attempt was made to imitate oriental or continental methods of production which differ radically in many fundamental respects. While English bone china still remains 'the aristocrat of all chinas', the demand for English Fine China has increased each year since its introduction was announced to the world's press in December 1959, by Mr Warrington. For this technological innovation Doulton Fine China Limited received the Queen's Award to Industry in 1966.

LAMBETHWARES

In 1974 Royal Doulton launched their new Lambethware, an oven-to-table range designed to meet the needs and suit the mood of the contemporary home. This robust ware is machine washable, oven proof, freezer-proof and detergent-proof yet still perfectly in keeping with the modern table-setting. As the name implies, Lambethware was inspired by the Doulton Lambeth stoneware tradition. New designs to suit a variety of tastes are added to the range each year, the most recent *Prairie* pattern being particularly effective.

Tablewares and the collector

The successful development of the new china led to the decision to discontinue the manufacture of fine earthenware tableware by 1965. From the collector's point of view this means that every earthenware tableware item produced before then – including the many new designs introduced since the 1950s – have virtually become collectable.

It would be quite impossible, even if records were available (and in all but a very few instances they are not), to try and give dates of both introduction and withdrawal of all the many thousands of china and fine earthenware tableware patterns produced at Burslem since 1878. Fortunately, however, for the great majority of pieces this information can be arrived at if the collector will follow the indications given on page 92 for the rack plates and Series Wares. Two other points may be added: no pattern has apparently ever lasted without some modification (*involving the use of a new pattern number*) for more than about forty years, and this applies even to such well-known old favourites as *Norfolk, Old Leeds Spray, Countess, Watteau* and *Paget*; and, as already mentioned, all earthenware patterns become obsolete in 1965.

XII

Commemorative Wares, Presentation Jugs, Loving Cups and Other Special Editions

Recent years have seen a phenomenal increase in the number of collectors of commemorative wares – so much so that there are now special societies and journals devoted solely to their interests. This is a fascinating field in which the Doulton Wares offer an astonishingly varied range of items, probably unequalled by any other pottery firm in the world.

The earliest known dated English pottery commemorative is a tin-glazed delftware dish made by some unknown Thames-side predecessor of John Doulton. Painted with a view of the Tower of London, it bears the date 1600 and the legend: 'The Rose is Red: The Leaves are Greene: God Save Elizabeth: Our Queene.' This was the forerunner of many other Lambeth delftware pieces commemorating Kings and Queens, and notable events such as the Union of England and Scotland, and the American War of Independence.

The first Doulton Commemoratives were also made at Lambeth in the early nineteenth century. They include salt-glaze stoneware figure jugs, mugs, and flasks depicting Queen Caroline (wife of George III), William IV, Queen Victoria and her Consort, Prince Albert, and other royalties; also Nelson, Wellington, and Napoleon. These are all rare and valuable today, as are the figure flasks and bottles made by John Doulton and his men to celebrate the passing of the First Reform Act in 1832. These portray King William IV and the Lords Grey, Brougham and Russell who were associated with the Bill. In later years Doulton of Lambeth produced many other interesting items. Over 200 of these are described in the companion volume to this, *The Doulton Lambeth Wares*.

Doulton Burslem Commemoratives

The following list of Doulton Burslem Commemoratives has been compiled in response to many requests. While it is certainly the longest list of its kind yet published it cannot claim to be complete, for new items are constantly coming to light. None the less, as it stands, it should be helpful to collectors, many of whom may still be unaware of the vast range of the Doulton productions in this field.

1887   As far as is at present known, it was for Queen Victoria's Golden Jubilee that the first commemorative was issued by Doulton of Burslem. This was an earthenware beaker about 3¾ in. (95 mm.) high, of simple but well-proportioned shape, decorated with a brown print showing medallion heads of the Queen at the time of her accession and at the time of the Jubilee, surmounted by a conjoined scroll bearing the Royal Cypher V.R.I, the dates 1837 and 1887, and the Imperial Crown.

A variant of this decoration has the word *Jubilee* instead of Cypher under a much larger and differently drawn Crown, both scroll and Crown being separated from the heads. Variants with the decoration in green, blue and puce are also known but brown appears to have been the favourite colour.

This type of beaker, which was subsequently used (with sometimes very slight alterations in the height) to celebrate other Royal occasions – coronations, silver jubilees, births and weddings – had an interesting origin. The then Prince of Wales (later King Edward VII) had undertaken to arrange a party in Hyde Park for thousands of children, to celebrate the great occasion. Henry Doulton, who was 'By Appointment Potter to H.R.H. The Prince of Wales', was asked to submit some ideas for a souvenir which could be given to the children. None of those put forward was found suitable for the occasion – although several were approved for sale to the general public and were made in salt-glaze stoneware.

It happened that during a visit to Russia the Prince had seen a beaker (whether in pottery, glass or metal is not recorded) which had been made to celebrate some Royal event in that country. Taking a piece of paper and making a quick sketch, the Prince handed this to Doulton, saying: 'Something simple like this is what I want.' John Slater designed the decoration to go on the beaker, some 100,000 of which were subsequently produced. Of these about 45,000 were distributed as gifts to children at the giant party and others in hospitals and elsewhere. The rest were sold through the trade and to special bodies, such as local councils.

At the Royal Jubilee Exhibition held in Manchester there was a demonstration of the beakers being made and printed. Queen Victoria herself, after touring the exhibition, returned to the Doulton pavilion to rest and watch the demonstration.

A number of municipal bodies, schools and other institutions ordered supplies of the beaker for presentations in their own districts. These were supplied with prints of coats of arms, seals, crests and even local views on the opposite side to the portraits of the Queen. Among those noted (there are no doubt several others) are beakers for Birmingham, Glasgow, Liverpool, Manchester, Scarborough, Chester, Chertsey, Kirkby Lonsdale, Cucklington, Stoke Trister, Walton-le-Dale, Preston, Skelton-in-Cleveland, Needham and New Brentford. Some have a roundel on the reverse containing a drawing of a stag and tree, surrounded by the letters L.S.B. and the date 1887; others have a view of Muncaster Castle. These 'locals' are naturally much rarer than the beakers with just the standard print. The quantities made with special prints probably ranged from 500 to a few thousand.

Very rare indeed is a similar beaker in fine bone china with the print and trademark in gold and also gold edging. These were made for presentation by Henry Doulton to the Queen and other members of the Royal Family, to the Archbishop of Canterbury and other important people and to friends and important customers. The quantity made is not known but would not have been very large.

1892   An earthenware jug to commemorate the death of Alfred Lord Tennyson, with plain black printed portrait, illustrations of open book, quill pen and coronet; inscribed 'Poet Laureate. In Memorium. Born 1809. Died 1892.'

Another jug, vellum ground dusted with gold, with moulded semi-relief bust of Tennyson.

1893   Standard earthenware beaker to commemorate the marriage of Princess May (Mary) of Teck to Prince George, Duke of York (afterwards King George V and Queen Mary). Printed in brown with portraits of the Royal Couple, encircled by rose sprays, and inscribed 'Royal Marriage 6th July 1893'. On the back, usually, the words 'Made for William Whiteley by Doultons'.

Variants are found in green, blue or polychrome prints, with 'manufactured' instead of 'made' on the base, or without any reference to Whiteley (a popular store in Bayswater, London).

Similar beakers were made with a portrait of H.R.H. Princess Henry of Battenberg; others with portraits of H.S.H. The Duke of Teck and H.R.H. The Duchess of Teck. Those noted are printed in brown and have the reference to Whiteley. They are much rarer than those with portraits of George and Mary which were apparently made in larger quantities.

Barrel-shaped gold-edged china mugs, with the same portraits of the Royal Couple as on the beaker, and the inscription 'Royal Marriage 6th July 1893', were also made. They are found usually with brown prints but blue, green and puce are also known. Some have one handle, others two. Most have the reference to Whiteley.

A similar mug with a brown print portrait of H.S.H. The Duke of Teck is a rare item, as is a jug with the same portrait.

1894   Standard earthenware beakers with the same portraits of the Royal Couple as in 1893, inscribed: 'In Commemoration of the Birth of a Son and Heir to Their Royal Highnesses the Duke and Duchess of York at White Lodge, June 23rd 1894.' Examples noted have brown prints and the reference to Whiteley.

An identical beaker is also known with the additional inscription: 'Borough of Richmond, Surrey.' (White Lodge is in Richmond Park, one of the Royal Parks.)

1897   *Queen Victoria's Diamond Jubilee*

This was the occasion of great rejoicing. No previous monarch had ever reigned for sixty years anywhere in the world. Doulton of Burslem produced several items to celebrate the event. The following are those so far noted:

Standard earthenware beaker, printed usually in sepia but also in green, blue and puce. On one side, Queen Victoria on the throne, holding sceptre and orb, with Royal Arms on shields each side; underneath national emblems and the words 'Dieu et Mon Droit'. On the reverse in old English lettering, a lengthy inscription which is so much of the period that it deserves to be quoted in full: 'Victoria, our Beloved Sovereign and Most Excellent Majesty, By the Grace of God Queen of Great Britain and Ireland, Empress of India, was born on the twenty-fourth day of May in the year of Our Lord eighteen hundred and nineteen. Ascending the Throne of England in the year eighteen hundred and thirty-seven, by the continued Blessing of the Most High she after sixty years yet sitteth on the throne of her ancestors and reigneth in the hearts of her beloved people. 1897. God Save the Queen.'

Another standard earthenware beaker, decorated in four colours. Cameo head of the young Queen with her hair in a bun (as on early Victorian coins) surrounded by a design of flowers and decorative scroll work. On the reverse, the Royal Arms, national floral emblems and inscription: 'Victoria the Beloved Queen of England ascended the Throne June 20th 1837 and By the Grace of God, yet reigneth, this present year of our Lord 1897.' This beaker, known familiarly to collectors as the 'By the Grace of God beaker' is found with several variations in the colour schemes.

Another standard earthenware beaker with, on one side, portrait of the young Queen surrounded by a laurel wreath, on the other, portrait of the old Queen with flags on either side and surmounted by a Crown. Inscribed: 'Diamond Jubilee. God Save the Queen. Victoria Queen of Great Britain, Ireland and the Colonies, Empress of India. She wrought her People lasting Good: 1837. 1897.'

This beaker is found printed from one-colour transfers in light and dark brown, green, blue and crimson. It was widely used for presentation purposes by private individuals, municipal and other local bodies, civic dignitaries and the like. Among names noted are Sir Henry Doulton, H. Lewis Doulton, Mr & Mrs Leeds Smith of Sandy, F. Davison of Blunham, Mrs Bartlett, Corporation of Edinburgh, Mussleburgh, Lower Bebington, Savile Town, Caledonian Free Schools, Leith Town Council, Castlemilk, and the Mayor of Grimsby. There are doubtless many more. The minimum order is thought to have been 500 to 1,000.

A variation of this design has the flags printed in full colour and Victoria is described as Queen of Great Britain, India and the Colonies. Some beakers with this variation have also printed on the base: 'Manufactured for the T. Eaton Co., Ltd., Toronto.'

Another standard earthenware beaker, decorated in brown with portraits of the young and old Queen in decorative frames, between which are the following inscriptions in frames surmounted by Crowns: '1897. This cup is a memento of the completion of the sixtieth year of the glorious reign of our beloved Queen Victoria. God save the Queen'; 'Victoria by the Grace of God Queen of Great Britain and Ireland, Empress of India, was born the 24th day of May in the year of our Lord 1819 and ascended the Throne June 20th 1837.'

A bone china beaker of slightly different shape, with gilded rim, on one side a fine colour portrait of Queen Victoria wearing Crown and, on the other, the Royal Cypher surmounted by the Imperial Crown and a scroll inscribed 'Diamond 1897 Jubilee'. Some beakers of this design also have a scroll *beneath* the Cypher containing the name of the individual or body presenting them. Examples have been noted bearing the names of Sir Henry Doulton and other members of the Doulton family, The Duke of Norfolk, Lady Iveagh and other donors.

The same portrait is found also on plates, wall plaques, cups, saucers and mugs. An engraved inscription within a laurel frame on some of the plates has been noted reading: 'From Sir Henry Doulton to . . . in Commemoration of Her Most Gracious Majesty's Diamond Jubilee 1897. She wrought her people lasting good.'

Bone china loving cup with moulded scroll and mask decoration, portrait of Queen Victoria and Royal Arms in gilt, presented only to members and friends of the Doulton family.

An earthenware mug with loop handle, with portrait of Queen Victoria in a leafy oval frame. To the left Sir Edward's Crown, the initials V.R.I. and the dates 1837:1897; to the right a Ducal Coronet, the letter N for Norfolk, and the words 'Arundel Park June 1897'.

Bone china candlestick, in the form of a drawstring purse with printed portrait of the Queen inscribed 'Her Majesty Queen Victoria 1897'.

1898 Jug in a parian body, vellum ground, pink and green sheen, to commemorate the death of the Rt. Hon. William Ewart Gladstone, the famous Liberal statesman. Portrait of Gladstone and replica of his coat-of-arms with motto 'Fide et Virtute'.

1899 Earthenware jug; on one side, black printed photograph of William Rathbone, inscribed around with his name and 'Greenbank Feb 11th 1899'; on the other side, poem commemorating his 80th birthday. Rathbone is believed to have been a Nonconformist local preacher.

1900 Bone china plate; in centre portrait bust of Lord Roberts in Military uniform, Victoria Cross, names of South African cities and names of Generals. On reverse side inscription: 'South African War: Field-Marshal Lord Roberts, V.C. Oct. 10th 1899.'

1900 Jug commemorating Canterbury (N.Z.) Jubilee Exhibition; on one side print of the Exhibition buildings, on the other portrait of William Reece with date 1900. Printed in sepia.

A flower bowl, wall plate and teapot were also issued in connection with this event.

1901   Bone china beaker, designed by John Slater and Doulton's Australian agent, John Shorter, to commemorate Australian Federation. Gold print; portrait bust of Queen Victoria (who died before Federation was consummated) within wreath surmounted by Crown and flanked on left by an Australian Light Horseman and on right by a British Infantryman. Underneath, on scroll resting on group of waratahs, is printed 'Australian Federation 1901'. On reverse side, scroll with lovers' knots and inscription: 'Tasmania, New South Wales, Victoria, Queensland, South Australia, Western Australia.' In centre, portraits of Lord Hopetoun and Sir Henry Parkes in rose medallion wreaths. Above them portraits of George, Duke of York and Mary, Duchess of York (later King George V and Queen Mary). On scroll at foot is inscription: 'May the union between the Colonies and the Motherland now cemented by their blood be forever maintained – Joseph Chamberlain.'

Although several thousand beakers were made, mainly for sale in Australia, they are now quite rare even there. Enquiries are often made concerning the quotation from Joseph Chamberlain. He was probably referring to the help given by contingents of Australian and New Zealand forces during the South African War when things were not going well for the British.

Other items issued to commemorate Australian Federation included a plate, jug, mug and jardinière. A beaker has also been reported commemorating the visit to Australia of the Prince and Princess of Wales.

1901   Bone china beaker with colour portrait of the Queen (as for the 1897 Jubilee), gold-edged, with inscription surmounted by Imperial Crown: 'In loving and loyal remembrance of Her Most Gracious Majesty Queen Victoria. Born at Kensington Palace, May 24th 1819, Acceded to the Throne June 20th 1837, Crowned at Westminster Abbey June 28th 1838, Died at Osborne, Jan. 22nd 1901.'

Similar beakers with one and two handles, and possibly other memorial items, were issued.

1902   Bone china plate inscribed: 'In commemoration of laying the Foundation Stone of the New Municipal Buildings and unveiling the Victoria Memorial Window in the Cathedral of Hereford, May 13th 1902.'

1902   *Coronation of King Edward VII and Queen Alexandra*

This, the first coronation to take place in Great Britain since 1838, naturally aroused tremendous interest and enthusiasm. Among other celebrations the King himself arranged for a special free 'Coronation Dinner' to be given at various centres to the poor people of London. At his wish and expense some 520,000 people, at the numerous dinners arranged by the Lord Mayor and the Mayors of the different London Boroughs, received each a Doulton beaker to use during the meal and to retain afterwards. A further half million beakers were provided at Doulton's expense for presentation to folk in hospitals, orphanages and other institutions; they cost less than one new penny each but the total amount involved ran into many thousands of pounds.

This beaker was of the standard earthenware type. When Mr Ronald Doulton was received by the King to discuss the design, he was told: 'I want something similar to those you did for my mother's jubilees.' On the front are conjoined portraits of the King and Queen in profile (designed by the well-known medallist, Monsieur Emil Fuchs) surmounted by a Crown and having a scroll underneath containing the date (see page 131). On the reverse the Royal Cypher and inscription: 'The King's Coronation Dinner. Presented by His Majesty.' The transfers were printed in at least five different single colours – light brown, olive green, blue, violet and maroon. Quantities of this type of beaker with appropriate arms and/or inscriptions (in place of the Royal Cypher etc.) were supplied for presentation purposes to many municipal and other bodies – minimum order 1,000.

At least one copy of this – perhaps the simplest but most famous of all Doulton commemorative items – was reproduced in gold by Gerrards, the famous jewellers and goldsmiths, and presented at a King's Dinner in Paddington, on behalf of the children of Paddington, to the King's young grandson (later King Edward VIII).

A more elaborately decorated gold-edged standard earthenware beaker was produced for sale to the general public through stores and china dealers. Some are inscribed as having been manufactured for William Whiteley. This beaker has front-face portraits of the King and Queen surmounted by Crown, lion and four standards. At the sides, the lion and unicorn, and underneath the portraits, the Royal Cypher and 'Coronation 1902'. On the reverse, in wreath of laurel and oak leaves, the inscription: 'Long life and happiness to King Edward VII and his beloved Consort Queen Alexandra – Crowned June 26th 1902.' (But see page 131.) The majority of these beakers were transfer-printed in brown, but some have been noted in olive green and crimson; also some with the portraits and flags printed in full colour. Quantities of this type of beaker (minimum one thousand) were supplied also to many public bodies and private individuals with appropriate inscriptions for presentation purposes.

Several gold-edged bone china beakers were also produced. Having been made in much smaller quantities than the earthenware beakers, they are naturally rarer. The following have been noted but there may be others:

(1) With half-length colour portraits of the King and Queen; in between them a small Crown. On reverse, wreath of oak and laurel leaves containing inscription 'Long life . . . 'etc. (As above.)

(2) Similar beaker but with half-length portrait of the King only. On the reverse the Royal Cypher surmounted by Crown, and the words 'Coronation 1901'.

(3) Similar beaker but with portrait and Cypher of the Queen only.

(4) Similar beaker with cobalt-blue ground with delicate raised gold foliate decoration, with Royal Cypher in raised gold surmounted by Crown in coral red; inscribed on reverse side 'Coronation King Edward VII' with date.

(5)   Similar beaker with yellow ground.

(6)   Similar beaker with *Rose du Barry* ground.

(7), (8) and (9)   Similar beakers to (4), (5) and (6) but with lion holding shield inscribed 'Coronation King Edward VII June 26th 1902'.

Earthenware plate with waist-length colour portrait of the King wearing red tunic. Above a small Crown and 'Coronation 1902', below Royal Cypher.

Similar earthenware plate but with portrait and Cypher of the Queen.

Bone china dessert plate with portrait of the King in colour with gold Crown.

Similar bone china plate with portrait of the Queen.

Bone china cup and saucer, lobed quatrefoil form, the cups decorated with full colour portraits of the King and Queen above gilt laurel sprays; gilded decorative border and handle. Saucer with gilded border and motifs of interlaced A's.

Earthenware mugs, cups and saucers were also issued.

Flat oval plaque. In centre colour litho portrait of the King, above it the Royal Cypher and below 'Coronation 1902'. Inscribed at top around the edge 'With Messrs. Moët and Chandon's Compliments' and at bottom 'Epernay (Champagne) France'.

Bone china medallions with colour litho portraits of the King and another of the Queen.

The King himself had been unable to attend any of the Coronation Dinners because of a sudden illness (leading to an operation for appendicitis). The Coronation had to be postponed from 26 June to 9 August, so that on all the pottery that had *already* been made bearing the former date *but not yet sent off* from the factory, the following additional wording had to be printed: 'Coronation postponed until the 9th August.' On the wares made after the new date had been fixed the correct date was of course substituted.

1902   Earthenware beaker inscribed: 'In commemoration of the End of the War and the inclusion of the two South African Republics within the British Empire.'

Also a jug with a similar inscription.

1903   China plate with scalloped edge with printed portrait in centre of Leo XIII who celebrated in 1903 twenty-five years as Pope. An unknown number was made; the plate is apparently now very rare.

1903   Bone china mug with sepia portrait of Sir George Livesey, reformer and promoter of Labour Co-partnership, knighted June 1902.

1904   Earthenware plate printed in blue with portrait of Ezra Cornell, founder of Cornell University. Inscribed: '1865 I would found an institution where any person can find instruction in any study.'

1906   Earthenware masonic jug, blue print, gold edge, inscribed: 'Ancient Landmark Lodge No 17, Portland, Maine, 1806–1906. Presented at Centennial Celebration June 10th 1906.'

1906   Bone china cup and saucer inscribed 'New Zealand International Exhibition 1906–7', with brown print of the Exhibition building.

1906   Earthenware beaker with portrait print of Richard J. Seddon (1845–1906) the well-known New Zealand statesman and reformer. Inscribed over the portrait 'He stood for Empire' and underneath 'Humanitarian'. On the other side, a verse from *Punch* by Owen Seaman.

   Also a small two-handled urn-shaped vase with similar portrait and inscriptions.

   Also cup and saucer with brown print portrait and inscription: 'Richard J. Seddon, Humanitarian. He stood for Empire.'

1907   Beaker inscribed: 'To commemorate the Marriage of Miss Dorothy Boughey to the Hon. Gerald S. Clegg Hill, April 3rd 1907.' Monogram of the couple's initials. (Mr Clegg Hill was a son of the third Viscount Hill of Coton Hall, Whitechurch, Shropshire.)

   This is one example of the *many* beakers, jugs and other items made for christenings, weddings, anniversaries, etc.

1907   Barrel-shaped earthenware mug with green printed portraits of King Edward VII and Queen Alexandra, inscribed: 'Empire Day May 24th 1907. Presented by WWN.'

1907   Earthenware jug presumably made to commemorate the centenary of the birth of the American poet, Henry Wadsworth Longfellow (1807–1882). Print of the Longfellow Mansion, Portland, Maine and inscription: 'Erected 1785 by General Wadsworth. Henry Wadsworth Longfellow made his home here in youth and early manhood.'

   It is possible that other items were issued to commemorate this centenary.

1908   Blue and white plate with portrait of Rev. Dr Carmichael, Bishop of Montreal. Scroll with dates 1835 and 1908; ecclesiastical symbols and arms.

1909   Standard earthenware beakers and mugs with portraits of Princess May and Prince George, as used in 1893 for the Royal Wedding, to mark their tour of the West Country; for example, a mug inscribed: 'To commemorate the visit of their Royal Highnesses the Prince and Princess of Wales to Newquay, June 8th 1909.'

   Another tour recorded on a Doulton beaker was 'Launceston'.

   These beakers and mugs, printed in green and sepia, were probably made in rather small quantities and are quite rare. Apparently, though sixteen years had elapsed since the Royal Wedding, it was not considered necessary to use fresh portraits!

1909   Aeronautical subjects featured on a variety of items to commemorate the First International Air Race held at Betheny race course near Rheims.

1910   Earthenware plate issued to commemorate the centenary in June 1910 of the

Primitive Methodist Connexion. Prints of the first Primitive Methodist Chapel at Mow Cop and of the 1910 Chapel. Portraits of James Bourne, Hugh Bourne, William Clowes and James Steel.

Jug with similar decoration. Both plate and jug were made with some variations in the number and disposition of portraits.

1911 *Coronation of King George V and Queen Mary.* Many more Doulton commemorative items were produced for this Coronation than for any other before or since. They included the following:

Standard earthenware beaker printed in brown, olive green or, less often, in blue or puce, with portraits and facsimile signatures of the King and Queen on opposite sides and, in between, the Crown, Royal Cypher and inscription: 'Coronation of Their Majesties King George V and Queen Mary June 22nd 1911.'

This is the best known of several differently decorated beakers and was the type presented to some 100,000 school children at the Royal tea-party held in the Crystal Palace. These have the additional inscription: 'Presented by Their Majesties King George V and Queen Mary Crystal Palace June 30th 1911.' Large quantities of this type (minimum order 1,000) with appropriately different arms, crests, inscriptions, etc., were supplied to municipal and other bodies. These beakers – which were also sold (without special inscriptions) to the general public through stores and china dealers – cost from four to five old pence each wholesale, according to the quantity ordered, plus a small charge for any special engraving involved.

This style of beaker is also found occasionally with only the one portrait of either the King or Queen with Cypher and facsimile signature.

Standard earthenware beaker decorated in the same general style as the gold-edged Edward and Alexandra beaker described on page 130. On one side portraits of the King and Queen surmounted by Crown, lion and four standards, etc., and, on the other, a similar inscription, in wreath of laurel and oak leaves, with the necessary change of names and date. This type was supplied with special inscriptions, etc., to local councils, schools, rifle clubs and other bodies and societies.

Standard earthenware beaker, simply decorated with, on one side, conjoined portraits of the King and Queen in a heart-shaped frame surmounted by Crown and, on the other, the Royal Cypher surmounted by Crown and 'Coronation 1911'. (Also found with special crests, inscriptions, etc.)

Standard earthenware beaker, gold-edged, decorated *all on one side* with two separate colour portraits of the King and Queen, surmounted by Crown and 'Coronation 1911', and with the Royal Cypher below the portraits.

This type is also found in two different sizes in bone china, and with special inscriptions on the reverse side.

Bone china barrel-shaped beaker, in two different sizes, with on one side colour portrait of the King in red tunic and, on the other, colour portrait of the Queen. Between the portraits Crowns, Royal Cyphers and 'Coronation 1911'.

Similar beaker but with the King in naval uniform.

Bone china plate, gilded rim, printed in full colour with portraits of the King and Queen against ermine drapes, with Rod and Sceptre, surmounted by Crown and Royal Cypher. Below a representation of St George and the Dragon with inscription 'Honi Soit Qui Mal y Pense'. The border decorated with the Orders of Chivalry, names of Commonwealth countries, oak leaves, etc.

Similar plate, printed in 'Royal Blue'.

Bone china dessert plate simply decorated with colour portrait of the King, with Crown in gold and 'Coronation 1911'.

Similar plate but with colour portrait of the Queen.

Bone china cup, saucer and plate. The cup decorated with colour portraits of the King and Queen against ermine drapes, surmounted by Crown and oak leaves. Swags of oak leaves linking laurel leaves, each containing a rose; printed beneath the swags 'South Africa, India, Canada, Australia'. On reverse 'Coronation George V 1911' in ornate cartouche; oak leaves and acorns to inner rim. Saucer decorated with swags, wreaths and roses; plate similarly decorated with, in addition, the Royal portraits.

In addition to the foregoing a great variety of inexpensive items made in large quantities was available. The following are recorded:

Earthenware, gold edge, brown Crown and Cypher, coloured portraits of King and Queen in four sizes of jugs, two of teapots, two of ashtrays, four of plates and one size of mug. Prices ranging from 6 old pence for a small plate to 15 for a large one.

Earthenware, no gold, plain prints of Crown, Cypher and portraits in two sizes of mugs at 2½ and 2¾ old pence each.

Bone china, gold edge, brown Crown and Cypher, coloured portraits of King and Queen in two sizes of plates, cream jugs, sugar bowls and dessert plates; four sizes of mugs and teapots; nine sizes of jugs; assorted miniatures, vases and sweet trays; cups and saucers; hair tidy; hat-pin stand. Some vases had portraits of both King and Queen, others King or Queen only. Prices ranged from 9 old pence for cup and saucer to 45 old pence for a large teapot.

Bone china, gold edge, brown Crown and Cypher, coloured portraits of King and Queen in panels in teacup and saucer; two sizes of mugs, teapots, cream jugs and sugar bowls; three sizes of plates; five sizes of jugs; assortment of sweet trays. Prices ranged from 12 old pence for a cup and saucer to 44 for a large teapot.

A commemorative jug with green/blue transfer decoration was produced for R. and H. Jenner and Sons, South London Brewery.

1913: Beaker to commemorate the Silver Wedding of Philip and Rita Berney-Ficklin, 18 July 1888–1913 with photos in brown and crest in colours. On reverse, portrait of their son who came of age also in 1913.

This is another example of the many beakers and other items produced for private individuals, this time for some Americans. Pieces have also been reported which were made for people in Belgium, France, Germany, Australia, Canada and New Zealand.

1919   Bone china beaker with brown print of standing Britannia holding shield inscribed 'Victory and Peace 1919'. Also, on reverse, soldier, tank and warship; 'Pro Patria' in scroll and names of Allies around the top.

Bone china mug with coloured portrait of King George V and similar inscriptions (but without Britannia, soldier, etc.).

Rack plate inscribed 'Victory and Peace 1919', with figure of Britannia with battleship, plane and soldier. Around the rim the names of the Allies.

There are several variations of the preceding items, e.g., mugs with seated Britannia instead of the King; beakers with field gun instead of tank; mugs and beakers without the names of the Allies; plates, mugs and beakers decorated in full colour and in other single colours besides brown. It appears that sets of several transfers both in full colour and in single colours were sometimes cut up and fitted to the beakers and mugs in different ways – the variation perhaps being due to supplies of one particular motif running out temporarily.

1920   Standard earthenware beaker inscribed in pale green: 'Metrogas Children's Party 1920: Metrogas A. C. established 1888.' With portrait of Mr J. J. Cooley, Founder and Chairman. On the reverse a shield with three feathers tied with bow.

One of several similar beakers and other items inscribed for special occasions.

1922   Standard earthenware beaker inscribed around the top: 'To commemorate the Wedding of Princess May with Viscount Lascelles at Westminster Abbey.' Printed with a very attractive design of wedding bells and flowers on one side, and on the other the Cyphers M and L above the date 28 February 1922.

A similar gold-edged beaker was produced in bone china. Both types are found decorated in full colour as well as in the single colours brown, blue and green. Some have the name of a store or china dealer on the base in addition to the Royal Doulton trade-mark.

1924   Standard earthenware beaker decorated with portrait of Edward, Prince of Wales and the inscriptions 'Our Prince' and 'H.R.H. The Prince of Wales South Africa 1924'.

Also jug similarly decorated.

1926   The Prince of Wales, HN 1217, a figurine designed by Leslie Harradine showing the prince in hunting dress.

1929   Standard earthenware beaker to commemorate the twenty-first birthday of the then Duke of Norfolk. On one side portrait of the Duke in a wreath of oak leaves and acorns, and the date 30 May 1929; on the other side, a view of Arundel

Castle, the Duke's ancestral home.

Some 3,000 of these beakers were ordered for distribution to workers, tenants and others on the Duke's estates.

1931   Cream earthenware plate, produced to commemorate the centenary of Christ Church, Harrogate. In the centre a view of the church seen across the Stray from the north-west. On the back, in addition to the Royal Doulton trade-mark, the words: 'Christ Church Harrogate Centenary 1831–1931.'

It is thought that fewer than 500 of these plates were made and although not among the more impressive of Doulton commemoratives they create considerable interest, especially locally, when they come on the market.

1932   Earthenware jug in limited edition of 1,000 to commemorate the bicentenary of the death of George Washington.

1934   Plate to commemorate the Diamond Jubilee of the firm Beatty Brothers. Portrait and inscription: 'George Beatty of Beatty Bros. founded 1874.' No further details recorded.

1935   *The Silver Jubilee of Their Majesties King George V and Queen Mary*

This appears to be the first Royal occasion for which one of the now famous two-handled Royal Doulton loving cups was produced. It was made in a limited edition of 1,000. On one side embossed relief-portraits of the King and Queen; on the reverse side, St George and Dragon against background of Windsor Castle.

On this occasion the long-established standard shape of earthenware beaker was produced for the last time. It was simply decorated with a joint portrait of the King and Queen in a rectangular frame, surmounted by a Crown, on one side and, on the other, the initials G and M separated by a Crown and, underneath, the dates 1910–1935. It was made in two sizes.

A similar earthenware beaker was also produced in two sizes with a handle. A small-size beaker without a handle and a large-size with handle were made in bone china.

In addition to the beakers, the following items, similarly decorated, were produced: In earthenware – cup and saucer and two sizes of mugs. In bone china – cup and saucer, three sizes of boxes and lids, two sizes of mugs and trays.

Old Charley, Sairey Gamp, Tony Weller and *Parson Brown* Character Jugs were made with a special backstamp commemorating the Silver Jubilee (small size only) and sold by Bentalls Ltd.

Beakers and mugs were made for presentation purposes with special inscriptions under the date.

1936   To mark the death of King George V a small (unlimited edition) earthenware two handled vase was produced. This has a sepia portrait of the King in a wreath of laurel leaves, and the inscriptions: 'Royal Exemplar King George V, The Friend

Left: Bone china cup and saucer with *Art Nouveau* pattern. Designed by Vincent Webster for the National Competition of Schools of Art, 1902
2 in.(5 cm.) high

Below: Bone china tea service with floral decoration in an *Art Nouveau* style, c.1905
Teapot, 5 in.(12.5 cm.) high

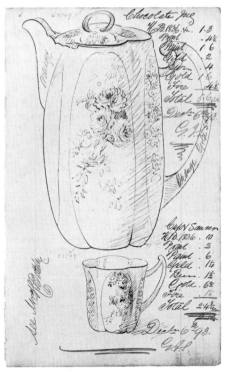

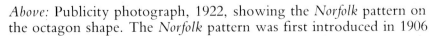

Above: Publicity photograph, 1922, showing the *Norfolk* pattern on the octagon shape. The *Norfolk* pattern was first introduced in 1906

Right: Drawing from a pattern book showing chocolate jug, as illustrated in the colour section, and cup with details of pricing

Publicity
photographs, c.1930,
showing a range of
Brangwyn Ware

Part of an earthenware
tea-set with incised and
printed decoration in the
Harvest pattern designed
by Frank Brangwyn,
1930
Plate, 10¾ in. (26 cm.)
in diam

Publicity photograph,
c.1930, showing the
Tango tableware pattern
and the figure *Clothilde*

Striking a Modern Note!

● *At left:* "SYREN." *This unique shape is typically British—the conventional flowers are in gorgeous colours—the fine earthenware permits a silky finish reminiscent of sunshine.*

● *Below:* "MECCA." *When the public see Doulton "Mecca" they live in hopes of buying it. So fully in shape, so merry in its dashing colours and so modest in cost, that when they learn its price—hope becomes undeferred and satisfied.*

TWO Modern Doulton designs in fine earthenware, with shapes that win by a smiling robustness.

The sunny ground has a cheery effect, and the very quaint designs are vividly coloured.

Ready for hard wear and at prices which sell quantities in the hardest times— Two good lines for to-day's needs.

Doulton Figures continue to expand sales. Have you seen the new models and new miniatures? If not, you have a pleasure in store.

TABLE CLOTHS. One reason why the new, modest-priced Doulton Sets are selling, is the charming new Table Cloths which match the Doulton designs and colourings (guaranteed fast). There are now seven different cloths to choose from, to exactly match the Table Ware at a price unbelievably modest. Table Cloths available matching Syren, "Eden," "Norfolk," "Dubarry," "Rosslyn," "Leeds Spray" and "Arvon." Why not see them?

Royal Doulton

DOULTON & CO. LTD., THE ROYAL DOULTON POTTERIES, BURSLEM, STOKE-ON-TRENT

Left: Advertisement from the *Pottery Gazette*, 1932, showing the *Syren* and *Mecca* tableware designs

Below: Catalogue page, c.1925, showing tea services with rich raised gold decoration

Royal Doulton

This robust design, with quiet colourings will create a new interest and increase sales. Simple modern lines and unusual handling devices give the whole a pleasing effect.

"Casino" offers a choice of three distinctive effects, "Marquis" and "Radiance" (illustrated) being in bands and hair lines; "Envoy," a frieze of blue curves of soft shades. Why not write for full particulars?

DOULTON & CO., LIMITED, THE ROYAL DOULTON POTTERIES, BURSLEM, STOKE-ON-TRENT

Left: Catalogue page, c.1925, showing three popular blue and white designs: *Norfolk*, *Madras*, and *Watteau*

Left: Advertisement from the *Pottery Gazette*, 1934, showing the *Casino* range of tableware designs

Advertisement from the *Pottery Gazette*, 1936, showing the *Rialto* tableware design

Publicity photograph showing the *Congress* pattern on a coffee set, c.1945

Bone china vase printed with an adaptation of the *Gaylee* design, 1935 2¾ in.(7 cm.) high

Right: Publicity photograph showing the *Coppice* pattern on an earthenware body, introduced in 1937

Earthenware cup, saucer and plate in the *Venetian* scenes pattern, introduced in 1956
Plate, 9½ in.(24 cm.) in diam

Publicity photograph showing the *Bamboo* pattern on an earthenware body, introduced in 1956

Publicity photograph showing the *Spindrift* pattern on an earthenware body, introduced in 1958

Above left: Publicity photograph, 1951, showing the *Woodland* pattern designed by C. J. Noke and used on an earthenware body

Right: Publicity photograph showing the *Morning Star* pattern on an English Translucent China body, introduced in 1966

Publicity photograph showing the *English Renaissance* pattern on a bone china body, introduced in 1963

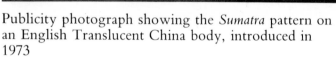

Publicity photograph showing the *Sumatra* pattern on an English Translucent China body, introduced in 1973

Right: Publicity photograph showing a selection of tableware patterns in the English Translucent China *Hot Pot* range, introduced in 1972

Bone china nursery ware printed with scenes from Alice in Wonderland
and Alice through the Looking-Glass, 1907
Plate, 9½ in. (24 cm.) in diam

Catalogue page, c.1903,
showing nursery rhyme
series ware designs by
W. Savage Cooper

Left: Publicity photograph
showing the *Prairie* pattern
from the oven-to-table
Lambeth range, 1979

Bone china breakfast set in gift box, with scenes from the *Bunnykins* series designed by Barbara Vernon, c.1935. Also an earthenware model of *Farmer Bunnykins*, c.1950
7½ in.(19 cm.) high

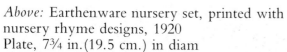

Above: Earthenware nursery set, printed with nursery rhyme designs, 1920
Plate, 7¾ in.(19.5 cm.) in diam

Right: Watercolour drawings for the *Bunnykins* series designed by Barbara Vernon, c.1934, and painted by Hubert Light
6 in.(15 cm.) maximum length

Publicity photograph, 1979, showing the *Bunnykins* range currently in production

Top: Publicity photograph, c.1935, showing part of a *Bunnykins* tea-set

Right: Earthenware jug with printed portrait of Lord Tennyson commemorating his death, 1892. 7 in.(18 cm.) high

Earthenware vase designed by J. Slater and J. Shorter to commemorate the Australian Federation, 1901. 3½ in.(9 cm.) high

Above: Advertisement from the *Pottery Gazette,* 1936, showing examples of Doulton commemorative wares

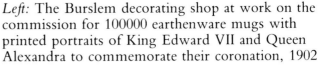

Left: The Burslem decorating shop at work on the commission for 100000 earthenware mugs with printed portraits of King Edward VII and Queen Alexandra to commemorate their coronation, 1902

Earthenware plates made to commemorate: the coronation of George V and Queen Mary, 1911; Victory and Peace, 1919; and the centenary of the Primitive Methodist Movement, 1910. 10½ in.(25.5 cm.) in diam

Left: Bone china loving cup made to commemorate Queen Victoria's Diamond Jubilee, 1897. 7 in.(17.5 cm.) high

Centre left: Bone china tea-set with printed portraits of Queen Victoria, made to commemorate her Diamond Jubilee, 1897. 10 in.(25 cm.) in diam

Above right: Bone china plate commemorating the coronation of King Edward VII and Queen Alexandra, 1902. 8½ in.(21.5 cm.) in diam

Bone china plaques made to commemorate the Silver Jubilee of H.M. King Hussein of Jordan, 1977 10 in.(23.5 cm.) in diam

Below right: Black stoneware loving cups made in limited editions of 500 to commemorate the centenary of Charles Dickens' death, the bicentenary of Captain Cook's landing in Australia, and the 350th anniversary of the sailing of the Mayflower, 1970 9 in.(23 cm.) high

Below: Bone china flagon with printed designs representing aspects of Doulton industries, made to commemorate the 150th anniversary of the Royal Doulton Potteries, 1965 12¼ in.(31 cm.) high

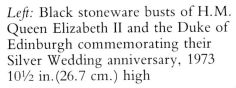

Left: Black stoneware busts of H.M. Queen Elizabeth II and the Duke of Edinburgh commemorating their Silver Wedding anniversary, 1973 10½ in.(26.7 cm.) high

Below: Bone china sweet dish and loving cup commemorating the election of Margaret Thatcher, 1979 4 in.(10 cm.). high

Bone china plaques depicting Queen Victoria, advertising Vinolia soap, 1897, and Edward VII, advertising Moet et Chandon's champagne, 1902 Large plaque, 13 in.(34 cm.) high

Above left: Prince of Wales and *Elizabeth II*, two commemorative figures. The prince was designed by Leslie Harradine in 1926, and the Queen by Margaret Davies, and produced in a limited edition in 1973 to mark the twentieth year of her reign
The Queen, 7¾ in.(19.5 cm.) high

Left: Cecil J. Noke examining a coronation loving cup made to his design, 1953

Right: Earthenware casket and lid in the form of a commode, the cover printed with a nursery rhyme scene from a design by W. Savage Cooper. The casket was used by Huntley & Palmer's as a container for their nursery rhyme biscuits, 1905
6 in.(15 cm.) high

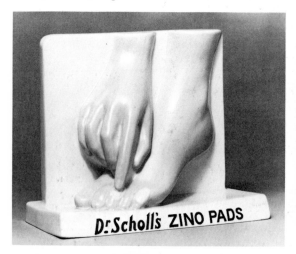

Above: Earthenware jug in the form of the head of an old Scotsman made for McCallum Whisky, c.1930
6¾ in.(17 cm.) high

Top left: A model of a foot on a display stand, one of a range made to advertise Dr Scholl products, c.1935
8 in.(20 cm.) high

Promotional character for the *Sketch* magazine which was interpreted by Doulton as an advertising figure

Left: A group of advertising wares made for Sandeman's Port, Fortnum and Mason, Bell's Whisky, and Younger's Scotch Ale, c.1920–56 Sandeman figure, 10¼ in. (26 cm.) high

Below: Bone china flask in the form of a crow made for Old Crow Bourbon, National Distillers, Kentucky, 1954 13 in. (33 cm.) high

Selection of earthenware ashtrays and cigarette promotional items, c.1925–39 Major bust, 10¾ in. (27 cm.) high

Right: Publicity photograph showing tableware designed for the Savoy Hotel, London, c.1935

Earthenware Toby Jug depicting Cliff Cornell, the owner of the Cleveland Flux Company, made for advertising purposes, 1956
9¼ in. (23.5 cm.) high

Right: Publicity photograph showing bone china tableware designed for use on Concorde, 1978

of His People', and 'So long as the history of the British Empire is written, his reign will be recorded with gratitude 1910–1936'.

1937 *The Coronation that did not take place*

For the intended Coronation of King Edward VIII it had been planned to produce limited editions of 2,000 large-size and 1,000 small-size loving cups. At the time the abdication was announced 1,080 of the large and 454 of the small had been sold through the usual channels and these (though only costing £3 and £2.50 at the time) are today very rare and valuable.

A number of other items featuring a profile portrait of King Edward VIII in Coronation robes and the date 12 May 1937 are also to be found; how many were sold is not recorded but one may assume rather few, for they are not often seen. They include in earthenware: a small two-handled loving cup; cup, saucer and small plate; two sizes of mugs, beakers and handled beakers. In bone china: cup, saucer and small plate; handled beaker; two sizes of mugs, trays and ordinary beakers; three sizes of boxes with lids.

Very rare indeed are some large-size bone china beakers ground-laid in four different colours (green, *Rose du Barry*, ivory and cobalt blue) with a colour portrait of the King on the front in a panel and, on the reverse: 'King Edward VIII God Bless Him. Crowned May 12th 1937.'

Another china mug has been reported with a colour print of the King's head surrounded by flags of Great Britain, Canada, Australia, New Zealand, India and South Africa.

1937 *Coronation of Their Majesties, King George VI and Queen Elizabeth*

A new loving cup (adapted partly from the one featuring Edward VIII) had to be quickly modelled. This was produced in limited editions of 2,000 of the large size and 2,000 of the small.

In earthenware were made: cup, saucer and small plate; beaker, handled beaker and mug. In bone china: cup, saucer and small plate; handled beaker; two sizes of mugs and ordinary beakers. The designs for these in full colour, including conjoined profile portraits of the King and Queen, Coronation regalia and standards, were by the well-known artist, Fortunio Matania, and each piece bore his facsimile signature.

1937 Grand National Coronation Year tankard made for Teofani, the cigarette manufacturers. See page 152.

1937 Mug, gold rim, with sepia portrait of H.R.H. Princess Elizabeth of York, inscribed with her name and date 1937.

Beaker, gold rim, with similar portrait and inscription.

Mug and beaker, similar to the above but with sepia portrait of H.R.H. Princess Margaret Rose of York and inscribed with her name and the date 1937.

1938   Earthenware loving cup to commemorate the laying of the foundation of the Voortrekker Monument. With portraits of those associated with the Voortrekkers and inscriptions in Afrikaans. (Copies of this loving cup were presented to Generals Hertzog and Smuts.)

A rack plate and jug were also issued.

1938   Earthenware jug issued in limited edition of 350 to commemorate the Sesquicentenary of the foundation of the Settlement in New South Wales and the city of Sydney by Captain Arthur Phillip, 26 January 1788.

1941   Earthenware beaker with portrait of Britain's wartime Prime Minister, the Rt Hon. Winston Churchill and a quotation from one of his famous speeches: 'Let us therefore brace ourselves to our duties and so bear ourselves that if the British Empire and its Commonwealth last for a thousand years men will still say: This was their finest hour.'

Other items relating to Churchill issued about this time included cigar box, tray, stein, ashtray, and dessert plate.

1953   *Coronation of Her Majesty, Queen Elizabeth II*

Loving cup, limited edition of 1,000. On one side, sepia portrait of the Queen, view of Windsor Castle, Royal Arms; on the other, portrait of Queen Elizabeth I against background of Tudor Men-of-War. Inscribed on base: 'This Loving Cup is to commemorate the Coronation of Queen Elizabeth II at Westminster Abbey 2nd June 1953.'

Earthenware jug with portrait of the Queen on one side and view of Windsor Castle on the other. Inscribed: 'Commemorating the Coronation of Queen Elizabeth II June 2nd 1953.'

Bone china mug with, on one side, portrait of the Queen circled by wreath of oak leaves and acorns and, on reverse, the Royal Cypher and Crown, and inscription as for jug.

Bone china beaker with similar portrait, Cypher and Crown, with inscription as for jug.

Some variations of decoration on the preceding items have been noted, e.g., omission of inscription or Cypher and Crown.

Commemorative items for the Coronation (flagons, loving cups, mugs and tea caddies) were also produced for Chivas Ltd, Courage and Co., Ltd, Ind Coope and Allsopp Ltd, and Twining Teas. See pages 144, 145, 149 and 153.

1962   Limited edition of 3,000 rack plates for the Women's Voluntary Service with crest of the WVS and the motto: 'Not why we can't but how we can.'

1964   Bone china rack plate with black print portrait of Shakespeare and inscription: 'To commemorate the 400th Anniversary of the birth of William Shakespeare.'

1965 *Sesquicentenary of the Foundation by John Doulton in Lambeth of the Royal Doulton Potteries*

Bust of John Doulton with inscription: 'John Doulton, Founder of the Royal Doulton Potteries, 1793–1873.'

Bone china vase with stopper, shape partly based on that of traditional bottle kiln, deep blue glaze overprinted in gold with portrait of John Doulton, view of Old Lambeth and frieze symbolizing Doulton's contributions to ceramics for home, industry and technology. (200 made.)

Bone china bowl in two sizes; deep blue glaze overprinted in gold with portrait of John Doulton and inscription: 'To commemorate the 150th Anniversary of the Founding of the Royal Doulton Potteries 1815–1965.' (750 of large size and 1,500 of small size made.)

Bone china tray with similar portrait and inscription. (4,000 made.)

Earthenware mug, deep blue with similar portrait and inscription. (4,000 made.)

Similar mug with addition of the badge of St Thomas' Hospital, Lambeth, with which Doulton have had a long association going back to the time of John Doulton. (500 made.)

1969 Bust of H.R.H. Prince Charles made in limited edition of 150 copies to commemorate his Investiture as Prince of Wales. (Copy No. 1 was presented to H.R.H. the Duke of Edinburgh by the Lord Mayor of Stoke-on-Trent.)

1970 Loving cup to commemorate the bicentenary of Captain Cook's landing at Botany Bay, Australia. (Limited edition of 500.)

1970 Loving cup to commemorate the centenary of the death of Charles Dickens. (Limited edition of 500.)

1970 Loving cup to commemorate the 350th anniversary of the sailing of the *Mayflower* from Plymouth, England to Plymouth, Massachusetts in 1620. (Limited edition of 500.)

1972 Busts of H.M. Queen Elizabeth II and H.R.H. the Duke of Edinburgh to commemorate the Silver Wedding of the Royal Couple on 20 November 1972. (Limited to 1,000 pairs.)

1973 Figure of H.M. Queen Elizabeth II to commemorate the twentieth anniversary of her Coronation on June 2nd 1953. (Limited edition of 750.)

1973 Bust of H.R.H. Princess Anne to commemorate her marriage to Captain Mark Phillips. (Limited edition of 750.)

1974 Bust of Sir Winston Churchill to commemorate the centenary of his birth in 1874. (Limited edition of 750.)

1976   *Bicentenary of the United States*

A collection of thirteen military sculptures known as *Soldiers of the Revolution*, representing the regiments of the original thirteen states, was made to commemorate this bicentenary. (See page 77.) (Limited editions of 350 of each figure were made between 1975 and 1978.)

1977   Loving cup designed and modelled by Reginald Johnson to commemorate the Silver Jubilee of H.M. Queen Elizabeth II. On one side, portrait of the Queen in regal dress surrounded by Commonwealth flags and heraldic symbols, the other side emblazoned with the Royal Coat-of-Arms. (Limited edition of 250.)

1977   Two bone china plaques to commemorate the Silver Jubilee of H.M. King Hussein of Jordan 1952–1977. (Each is in limited edition of 750.)

1979   Bone china sweet dish/ash tray and loving cup commemorating the election of Margaret Thatcher, first woman Prime Minister of the United Kingdom.

Besides items made to commemorate specific occasions and anniversaries, the Royal Doulton Potteries have produced a number of presentation jugs, loving cups and other special editions. These include the following:

1930   'M.F.H.' Presentation Jug. (Limited edition of 500.)
1931   Regency Coach Jug. (Limited edition of 500.)
1932   George Washington Jug. (Limited edition of 1,000.)
1933   Sir Francis Drake Jug. (Limited edition of 500.)
1933   John Peel Loving Cup. (Limited edition of 500.)
1933   Shakespeare Jug. (Limited edition of 1,000.)
1933   Captain Cook Jug. (Limited edition of 350.)
1933   Tower of London Jug. (Limited edition of 500.)
1933   William Wordsworth Jug. (Unlimited edition.)
1933   Charles Dickens Jug. (Unlimited edition.)
1934   Apothecary Loving Cup. (Limited edition of 600.)
1934   Guy Fawkes Jug. (Limited edition of 600.)
1934   Pied Piper Jug. (Limited edition of 600.)
1934   Treasure Island Jug. (Limited edition of 600 – sold at £1.00 each wholesale.)
1934   Wandering Minstrel Loving Cup. (Limited edition of 600.)
1935   Admiral Lord Nelson Loving Cup. (Limited edition of 600.)
1936   Three Musketeers Loving Cup. (Limited edition of 600.)
1936   Charles Dickens Jug. (Limited edition of 1,000.)
1936   Village Blacksmith Jug. (Limited edition of 590.)
1938   Robin Hood Loving Cup. (Limited edition of 600 – sold at £1.10 each wholesale.)
1938   Captain Phillip Loving Cup. (Limited edition of 350, made for Prouds, Sydney.) This cup made to commemorate the 150th anniversary of the foundation

of the settlement in New South Wales and the city of Sydney by Captain Arthur Phillip, 26 January 1788.

1952   Jan van Riebeeck Loving Cup. (Limited edition of 300.) This cup was made to commemorate the landing of Jan van Riebeeck at the Cape of Good Hope, 1652.

Commemorative Kingsware whisky flagons produced for John Dewar & Co.

1911   *Sporting Squire*; flagon with black printed medallion incorporating the Royal Cypher, 1911 etc.

1937   *The Crown*; 950 flagons issued in the shape of St Edward's Crown to commemorate the Coronation.

1938   *Captain Phillip*; 100 flagons produced to commemorate the 150th anniversary of the settlement of New South Wales. Inscribed 'Captain Phillip 1788–1938'.

Military Commemoratives

A series of nationalistic bulldogs in military uniform and draped with a Union Jack. These were introduced at the time of the First World War and continued in production for some time.

Bulldog in cream earthenware, draped with the Union Jack, made in three sizes.

'Churchillian' version with top hat and cigar made in three sizes; models occur with or without the cigar.

Bulldog in khaki glaze wearing a tin hat.

Bulldog in khaki glaze wearing a tam o'shanter and kilt.

Bulldog in khaki glaze wearing a sailor's hat.

This last version is known with an additional Union Jack and it is possible that other models exist with variations on the themes above.

XIII

Advertising Wares

The Kingsware flagons, made as an attractive and durable publicity medium for John Dewar and Sons Ltd of Perth, have been dealt with in Chapter VI. In this chapter some of the wares made to publicize the products of other firms will be described. Many of these items, like the Dewar's flagons, served a dual purpose as *container* and *advertisement*; others, such as ashtrays, advertised a host of other products from 'permanent waves' to milk stout.

There is an extraordinary amount of interest nowadays in this fascinating field of pottery and the number of collectors has grown into many thousands. The Doulton Potteries, both at Lambeth and Burslem, have played a major part in the design and supply of such wares. From its foundation, the Lambeth Pottery was making jars, jugs, bottles and other salt-glaze stoneware containers for Warren's of the Strand, manufacturers of boot-blacking; Whitbread of Whitechapel, brewers; Seager Evans and Co. of Millbank, distillers; and Berger of Homerton, paint-makers. A little later on, Stephens Inks and Crosse & Blackwell, the jam-makers, became very important customers. Many of the containers supplied to such firms were printed or indented with their names and/or trade-marks and thus acted also as advertisements. In addition to the pots made for large concerns, Doulton of Lambeth made many thousands of bottles, flasks and flagons for individual taverns, restaurants and public-houses, often inscribed with their names and/or addresses and emblems. These have been described by one collector as the 'prime treasures' of 'Britain's ever-growing army of 16,000-odd bottle diggers'.

Between the turn of the century and the 1950s, advertising pottery of various kinds was also supplied from Burslem to many firms, some of which no longer exist. The minimum quantity for which an order would be accepted was usually 1,000. The following list cannot claim to be complete, for new items are constantly coming to light, but it is the most comprehensive so far published. It is arranged in alphabetical order for convenient reference. Where no particular details are given this is generally because the items concerned bore only the product names, the customers' names and trade-marks or other symbols. Unfortunately the records are not very informative but dates and other details are given when known. (Items about which enquiries are most frequently received are marked with an asterisk.)

Abbot Safety Matches: ashtrays

Abdulla Cigarettes: ashtrays, ashbowls and match-strikers

Ainslie's Scotch: jugs and ashtrays, some inscribed 'Supplied to the Royal Navy'

Allsop's Lager Beer: jugs decorated with child dancers in similar style to those on the Morrisian Wares. (See Chapter VI)

Allsop's: menu-holders in the form of a red hand; similar stands

Apollinaris: jugs and match-strikers inscribed 'The Queen of Table Waters' and 'Natural Mineral Water'

Army Club Cigarettes: busts of the firm's well-known 'Major' on a stand, and also incorporating an ashtray; printed portraits of the 'Major' appear on a variety of ashtrays

Artandia Ltd: models of a cockatoo and an Immortal in various glazes including turquoise, polychrome and Sung made as a wireless loud-speaker for a firm of this name

Atkinson's Ales: jugs

Autoparts Ltd, New Zealand: ashtrays

Barnsley Brewery Mild and Bitter Ales: jugs and ashtrays

Bass and Co.:   match-strikers and jugs inscribed 'Pale Ale and Stout'; trays and match-holders inscribed 'Bottled Bass and Draught Bass'

Beldam's Pilot (Tri-bar) Packing: ashtrays

Bell's of Perth: 2,000 each large and small size whisky flagons in the shape of a bell were supplied in 1957. (Similar flagons in brown stoneware were supplied by the Lambeth Pottery between 1953 and 1956 when the factory closed)

Bellingham Coronation Whisky: jugs

Bentley's Yorkshire Breweries: match-strikers inscribed 'Special Pale Ale'

Birch's 'Black Bottle' Scotch Whisky: jugs

Blundell's Cabinet Whisky: jugs

Bols: see under Erven Lucas Bols

Booth's Gin: ashtrays

Brown and Polson: moulds for their Corn Flour Blancmange, inscribed with a printed recipe; shortbread moulds with an advertisement for Raising Powder; cups and saucers with advertisement for Corn Flour and Paisley Flour

Brown, Corbett and Co.: jugs inscribed 'Special Liqueur Irish Whiskey'

Bull Dog Ale and Stout: ashtrays and jugs

Bull Dog Bottled Beer: ashbowls and jugs

Bull Dog Guinness and Light Ale: bulldog models wearing strapped-on labels 'Guinness' and 'Light Ale'

Burndept Ltd: ashtrays inscribed 'Manufacturers of Wireless Apparatus'

Carlton Hotel, London: ashtrays

Cavender's Navy Cut Cigarettes: ashtrays

Charing Cross Hotel: ashtrays

Charrington's: Toby Jugs in form of seated figure in green coat holding jug and glass; one inscribed on front of base 'One Toby Leads to Another', the other, 'Toby Ale'. (Supplied in 1950s)

Charrington's Toby Ale and Stout: jugs and ashtrays

Chivas: 'Royal Salute' whisky flagons with Royal Coat of Arms. (Supplied in 1953, year of the Coronation of Queen Elizabeth II. Edition of 2,000)

Cinota Tonic Wines: jugs

Civic Pipes: display blocks with model of tobacco-pipe

Claymore Rare Old Scotch Whisky: jugs and ashtrays

Claymore Scotch Whisky: see Greenlees Brothers

Combe's Brown Ale: ashtrays

Cornell: Toby Jugs in the likeness of an American industrialist, Mr Cliff Cornell, were produced in 1956. These were inscribed on the base: 'Greetings . . Cliff Cornell . . Famous Cornell Fluxes . . Cleveland Flux Company.'
500 large size, brown suit
500 large size, blue suit
375 medium size, brown suit
375 medium size, blue suit
The large were 9 in. (23 cm.) high; the medium 5½ in. (14 cm.). A few prototypes of a small size, 2¼ in. (6 cm.), were submitted for inspection but not ordered; some are apparently still in existence. All the Cornell jugs are rare collector's items

Courage's: jugs inscribed 'Courage's Extra Stout'; jugs inscribed 'Courage's Alton Pale Ale'

Courage's: two-handled loving cups, produced in 1953, edition of 1,500, with black print of Queen Elizabeth II on horseback; on reverse the Royal Coat of Arms; inscribed 'Here's a Health unto Her Majesty'. On the base the brewers' cock symbol and wording 'Made for Courage & Company Limited, London'. (Designed by Milner Gray, RDI, FSIA)

Court Bros (BM) Ltd, Canterbury: ashtrays

Craven 'A' Cigarettes: ashtrays

Crittall Metal Windows: ashtrays and match-strikers

Cutler Palmer and Co.:   ashtrays and match-strikers inscribed 'The Wine Merchants of the East'

Daniel Crawford's Scotch Whisky: jugs

De Reske Cigarettes: ashtrays and match-strikers

Dewar's: the first advertising wares made for Dewar's were some rack plates in 1899 which depicted cavaliers and were inscribed with various toasts: 'The Whisky of our Forefathers', 'The King, God Bless Him', 'Our Noble Selves' and 'Sweethearts and Wives'. For over 30 years Kingsware flagons were issued by Dewar's; a list of subjects will be found in Chapter VI. 3 more advertising flagons were issued in earthenware with printed designs; the *Peace Flask* (1919) depicting Britannia (2 versions), *Monarch of the Glen* and *Sydney Harbour* (1914). There are also ashtrays, match-strikers and jugs variously inscribed 'Dewar's Scotch Whisky', 'Dewar's Gold Cup', 'Dewar's White Label Whisky' and 'Dewar's Imperial Institute'

Distillers Agency: ashtrays and match-strikers inscribed 'D.C.L. Scotch Whisky', ashtrays inscribed 'Special Liqueur Whisky', jugs with portrait of King George IV, inscribed 'King George IV Old Scotch Whisky', with Royal Arms and dates of the King's birth and death (edition of probably 2,000, produced in 1930)

Doulton: many items were made to advertise the firm's own products

Dr Scholl: several unusual items were produced in the 1930s for this firm – models of feet on display stands variously inscribed 'Dr. Scholl's Lastik Metatarsal Pads', 'Scholl Instrument Trays', 'Dr. Scholl's Toe Flex', 'Dr. Scholl's Bunion Reducer' and 'Dr. Scholl's Arch Binder'. Some of these stands are inscribed: 'Genuine Doulton Ware. If wiped over occasionally with a damp cloth will preserve its appearance for many years.'

Dunville's Old Irish Whiskey: match-strikers

Dunville's Scotch Whisky: match-strikers

Edward Young and Co.'s Liqueur L.L. Scotch: jugs

Electric 'Diamond' Inhalator: jugs

Embassy Pipes: display blocks

Erven Lucas Bols, Amsterdam (Distillers):   models of bulldog and Pekinese

Eugene Waves: ashtrays inscribed 'Permanently Yours'

146

Evening Sentinel: a limited edition of the figure *Newsboy*, HN2244, was made for Stoke-on-Trent's local newspaper with the word 'Sentinel' printed on his placard

Evercool Pipes: display stands

Falk's Table Salt: salt-cellars

Fellsglen Scotch Whisky: jugs

Flower's Ales and Stout: ashtrays

*Fordham's Ashwell Ales: jugs with print of coach and four, and inscribed 'Best to help you on your way'

Fortnum and Mason: whisky flask simulating early glass bottle found in Fortnum and Mason's crypt

M. B. Foster and Sons Ltd: jugs inscribed 'Bugle Band Bottled Beers'

*Fry's Pure Cocoa: cups and saucers with prints of Coats-of-Arms and Royal Appointments; gold edges

Gaelic B. B. Special Reserve Scotch Whisky: ashtrays and jugs

*Gaelic Old Smugglers Whisky: ashtrays inscribed with name and 'direct from Craigellachie Distillery'

Genders Pipes, Cement, Granite, Bricks: ashtrays

*Gillette: ashtrays inscribed 'Gillette Razor Blades for Clean Shaving'

*Girolamo Luxardo Distillers, Zara: bulldog models

Gordon's: ashtrays and match-holders inscribed 'Gordon's Famous Ivy Leaf Scotch Whisky'

*Greenlees Brothers: jugs and ashtrays inscribed 'Claymore Scotch Whisky'; also Kingsware flasks *Crusader*, *Rob Roy*, *The Governor*, *The Pirates* and a *Tavern Scene* inscribed 'Greenlees Brothers, Claymore Scotch Whisky'

Greer's Distillers: ashtrays inscribed 'Greer's O.V.H. Scotch Whisky'

Grey's Cigarettes: ashtrays and jugs

Grossmiths: *Tibetan girl*, HN582, designed by Leslie Harradine in 1923 to advertise 'Tsang Ihang' Perfume

Grosvenor House, St Leonards: ashtrays

Groves and Whitnall: jugs inscribed 'Grand Old Highland Special Scotch'

Guinness: plates and jugs with printed reproduction of drawing by Phiz of Sam Weller composing his valentine, and showing over the fireplace a contemporary notice of Guinness Dublin Stout

Harvey Macnair: ashtrays and jugs inscribed 'Harvey Macnair's Finest Scotch Whisky. The Whisky that aids digestion'

Heatherdale Distillery: ashbowls and jugs inscribed 'Heatherdale Scotch Whisky Soft and Mellow'

Hoare Brewers: a Toby Jug depicting a seated toper inscribed 'Toby Ale' is recorded as having been produced in the early 1930s

Horonda: see *Moonee Valley*

Hovenden and Orr, Dublin: jugs

Hudson Bay Company: Kingsware flagon, *Micawber* design overprinted for Hudson Bay Company c.1946

Huntley and Palmer: biscuit caskets. These are much sought after by collectors and are most attractive. They were introduced in 1903 and were decorated with illustrations of nursery rhymes by Savage Cooper, a well-known artist of the period. The rhymes illustrated were: *Tom, Tom, the Piper's Son*; *Old Mother Hubbard*; *Hey Diddle Diddle*; *Little Tommy Tucker*; *Ride a Cock Horse*; *There was an Old Woman*; *Where are You going to My Pretty Maid?*; *There was a little Man who had a little Gun*; *Old Mother Goose*; *Simple Simon*; *To Market, to Market*; and *Peter Piper*. There is some doubt as to whether or not there was another featuring *Little Bo-Peep* for which Savage Cooper also did an illustration. These designs were also used on sets of nursery ware marketed by Royal Doulton. The caskets were supplied from time to time until about 1914

Hylus: ashtrays inscribed 'Hylus, New Bond Street, W.1'

Illustrated London News: standing Beefeater figure holding facsimile of the first edition of this periodical (introduced c.1924)

Ind Coope and Allsopp Ltd: Coronation mugs with Royal Arms on front, Royal Cypher on back; bands of ears of barley top and bottom; inscribed on base 'Presented by Ind Coope & Allsopp Ltd.' Edition of 2,000, 1953

Irish Tullamore Dew: jugs and ashtrays

Jacob's Pilsener Lager Beer: ashtrays

Jenner and Sons, South London Brewery: jugs

'Jim Crow': see National Distillers

Johannis Table Waters: ashtrays

Johnnie Walker: jugs with print showing him pouring whisky, with instructions on the right and wrong way to pour

Johnstone's 'Square Bottle' Napier Whisky: ashtrays in shape of a windmill

E. H. Kelsey: jugs inscribed 'Light Bitter Ale, Tunbridge Wells'

Kinahan's L.L. Whisky: jugs

King's Fine Ales: jugs

Links Hotel, Torquay: ashtrays

'Loch Corrie' Scotch Whisky: jugs

Louis Wearden and Guylee Ltd: bulldog models wearing Union Jack, inscribed 'Marvel Drill Chuck'

Macdonald's Liqueur Scotch Whisky: jugs

Mackeson's Milk Stout: match-strikers and ashtrays

MacNair's Distillers: jugs inscribed 'MacNair's Finest Scotch – The Whisky that aids digestion'

MacSymons Stores, Dean Street, Liverpool: ashtrays

D. and J. McCallum: Character Jugs in underglaze slip-painted Kingsware depicting a Scotsman; produced in edition of 1,000–1,500 in the early 1930s

D. and J. McCallum Distillers: jugs inscribed 'McCallum's Scots Whisky'; jugs and ashtrays inscribed 'McCallum's Perfection Whisky'

McMichael Ltd: match-strikers and ashtrays inscribed 'McMichael Ltd., Wireless Apparatus'

McNish Distillers: ashtrays inscribed 'McNish Special Scotch Whisky'

McVitie and Price, Edinburgh and London: biscuit jars with printed Dutch scenes (*Harlem* pattern) in blue, produced in 1904; similar jars in green, 1905–17. (The blue ones are exceedingly rare)

Marston, Thompson and Evershed Ltd, Burton-upon-Trent: jugs and ashtrays made to advertise Marston's Burton Ales

Maryport Brewery: ashbowls

Melachrino Cigarettes: ashtrays

Mellersh and Neale Ltd: jugs inscribed 'Reigate Table Waters'; ashtrays and jugs inscribed 'Ales and Stouts'

Moët et Chandon: Commemorative and advertising plaque depicting Edward VII

Moonee Valley Cordial Company: jugs produced c.1915 inscribed 'Horonda Herb Beer' and with the following doggerel verse:
>   In rising every morn I take
>   For health and strength and comfort's sake
>   The drink that always takes the cake –
>   The grand 'Horonda'

Munich Löwenbraü Lager: ashtrays

National Distillers Products Corporation, Frankfort, Kentucky, USA: 'Old Crow' bourbon flagons in the form of a crow, long a feature of the National Distillers promotion programmes. He wears a formal outfit with white shirt, orange-red vest, pince-nez spectacles and top hat into which the cork was fitted. Some 16,800 were supplied in 1954–5. Very popular with collectors, they are becoming difficult to find, even in America

Old Arden Dew: jugs

Park Lane Hotel, Piccadilly: ashtrays

Peter Dawson's Scotch: Kingsware jugs

Philip Morris 'Bond Street' Cigarettes: ashtrays

Queen's Hotel, Hastings: ashtrays

Rayment's Ales and Stouts, Furneux Pelham, Herts: jugs

Reid's Special Stout: ashtrays and jugs

Revill and Sons: jugs inscribed 'Father's Favourite Scotch'

Robert Porter and Co. Ltd, Kings Cross, London: jugs inscribed 'Bulldog Bottled Beer'

Rosbach Water: ashbowls and ashtrays

Sandeman: flagons in the form of Sandeman's well-known promotional figure, the 'Black Don', were supplied to this famous company of port wine and sherry distributors over a period of many years from the 1920s to 1950s – possibly some 20,000 to 25,000 in all. The dark cloaked figure is holding either a red glass (indicating port) or a yellow one (indicating sherry). In the mid 1930s a few thousand miniatures in the same style were made. There are no records of the exact numbers. Round ashbowls and ashtrays with illustration of the 'Black Don' were also supplied

Sandy Macdonald Scotch Whisky: jugs inscribed 'Stronachie Distillery'

'Satinette' Old Gin: jugs

Schweppes Table Waters: ashtrays and jugs

Scotia Distillers Ltd: ashtrays inscribed 'Old Original Scotch Whisky'

Selfridges, London: ashtrays

Sentinel Waggon Works, Shrewsbury: Sentinel figure, HN523, introduced 1921; a replica of a figure on the factory gate. 17½ in. (44.4 cm.) high. Sentinel became part of Rolls–Royce

Shaw Cockell's Distillery: jugs inscribed 'King's Own Scotch Whisky'

*Sketch Magazine: The Sketch Girl, a figure designed by Leslie Harradine and based on their cover girl, c.1923

Sneyd Collieries and Brickworks Co. Ltd: ashtrays with illustration of a swimmer

Stephens Inks: door plates for shops inscribed 'Stephens' Strongest Mucilage'

Stirling Bonding: jugs inscribed in Spanish with view of Craigellachie, Gleniver Distillery. (Translation: 'Drink Old Smugglers Whisky')

'Sueflakes': soup plates inscribed 'Sueflakes Pure Suet Flakes'

Sunripe Cigarettes: ashtrays

Tanqueray Gordon and Co. Ltd: match-holders and ashtrays inscribed 'London Gin' and 'Ivy Leaf Scotch Whisky'

Taylor (Newport Pagnell) Soda Water: match-strikers and ashtrays

*Teofani Cigarettes: jugs with colour prints of figures in Jacobean dress; ashtrays; and an edition of probably 1,000 to 2,000 mugs with prints of steeple-chaser and Coronation procession inscribed 'Grand National Coronation Year 1937 "Royal Mail" ', also with the names of the horse's owner, trainer and jockey

Threlfall's Salford Brewery: ashtrays, jugs and match-strikers inscribed 'Threlfall's Blue Label Ales'

Tollemache Stout: jugs and ashtrays

Trinidad and Tobago Cocoa Co.: beakers

H. P. Trufitt Ltd, Old Bond Street: beakers

Truman's Brewery: jugs inscribed 'The Sign of a Good House'

Trust Houses Ltd: ashtrays

Tuborg Lager Beer: ashtrays and jugs inscribed 'Very Low Alcoholic Strength'

Tullamore Dew: jugs inscribed 'Ireland's Best'

Turf Cigarettes: ashtrays

Turney's Special Scotch Whisky: jugs

* *Twinings of the Strand:* tea-caddies with decoration of birds, flowers and fruit, inscribed on base 'June 1953 E II R: Twinings of the Strand: Founded in the Reign of Queen Anne'. Edition of 2,000

Usher's Trowbridge Pale Ales and Stouts: jugs and ashtrays

Van Houten's Cocoa: cups and saucers; jugs with print depicting cocoa nuts being gathered

Van Ryn, Cape Town and Johannesburg: jugs inscribed 'Brandies and Colonial Pure Natural Wines'

Verrey's: plaques inscribed 'Luncheons and Dinners in the next room'

* *Vinolia Tooth Paste:* several designs of earthenware boxes, some with on-glaze and others with underglaze prints in various colourings, liquid gold edges; supplied around the turn of the century. It seems that somewhat similar containers were supplied also for Vinolia Shaving Soap. A plaque depicting Queen Victoria was also made to advertise Vinolia Soap, 1897

* *Waechter's Patent Inks:* 14 or possibly more different patterns of containers with on-glaze and overglaze prints in various colourings, liquid gold finish; supplied around the turn of the century

* *W. Walklate Ltd:* small size Character Jugs of *The Poacher, Falstaff* and *Rip Van Winkle* adapted for use as liqueur containers

Watney's Pale Ale: ashtrays

Whittle's Distillery: jugs inscribed 'Whittle's Glenloon Whisky'; others inscribed 'Whittle's O.S.B. Rum'

Wilts United Dairies: jugs

Worthington's Pale Ale: ashbowls

Wrexham Pilsener Lager: ashtrays

Yardley's: a figure model adapted by Leslie Harradine from a Wheatley 'London Cries' engraving, c. 1920

William Younger and Co.: jugs inscribed 'India Pale Ale', 'No. 3 Scotch Ale' and 'Scotch Ale'; some are also inscribed 'Oi be 101 and still going strong'; ashtrays

It is evident from the foregoing list that the opportunities for collectors in this rather 'out-of-the-ordinary' field are extensive. It contains a remarkable number of still famous and once famous names; some of the latter will evoke nostalgic memories for many older readers, even if they are not interested in actually collecting advertising pottery. For those who are collectors of such items there are many unusual and attractive wares worthy of their attention. Even the more prosaic jugs and ashtrays are now being collected in quite a big way; the fact that they bear the Royal Doulton trade-mark gives them added interest and value in the eyes of an increasing number of collectors.

Hotel and associated wares – a note

Since the 1890s the Royal Doulton Potteries have supplied countless millions of pieces of specially designed and badged tableware to hotels, restaurants, taverns, clubs, colleges, air-lines, shipping companies, railways, municipalities and similar concerns throughout the world.

They include such famous names as the House of Lords, the Mansion House, and the Inner Temple in London; the Cunard and Orient Shipping Lines, and British Airways, in particular, Concorde; and renowned hotels such as the Savoy, Ritz, Berkeley, Piccadilly, Hyde Park and Carlton in London; the Park Plaza, New York; the Queen Elizabeth, Vancouver; the Royal York, Toronto; the Mandarin, Hong Kong; and the Trust House Forte organization.

Whether or not badged wares of this kind should be regarded as 'advertising pottery' is a moot point. The china in question is ordinarily seen only by staff and by customers who already know the concern anyway and are probably more interested in what is being served on the plates than in the plates themselves. Frequently, of course, they admire the designs and some may turn a plate or saucer over to see the maker's name; indeed if these wares are 'advertising pottery', they primarily advertise Royal Doulton and the good taste of the concerns who have purchased them.

It must be admitted that in some exceptional (and sometimes questionable!) ways, items of hotel and kindred wares are occasionally acquired by private individuals. If there *are* collectors of these things neither the Doulton Company nor the author ever hear from them.

XIV

What's Past is Prologue

To delve into recent developments at the Royal Doulton Pottery – or to comment in any detail on present-day products and their designers – has not come within the scope of this book as set out in the Foreword. However, at this point, it is worth saying a few words on the subject.

The closure of the Lambeth factory in 1956, brought about by rising transport costs and clean air legislation, meant that North Staffordshire became the centre of Doulton production. Henry Doulton's 'invasion' had succeeded beyond his wildest dreams.

There followed a continuous programme of building and reconstruction, skilfully planned to bring into being, stage by stage, an entirely new factory in Nile Street, without interfering with current production.

By a series of mergers, first with other companies and then in 1968 with Allied English Potteries Group, a new major manufacturer emerged. Doulton and Co. today is the largest manufacturer of ceramic products in the UK, with interests in industrial and sanitary wares, engineering and building materials and glass. Royal Doulton Tableware Limited, the tableware and domestic products section, with its headquarters firmly established in The Potteries, includes many companies whose names tell the history of English ceramics; Minton, Derby, Ridgway, Royal Albert, Paragon and Webb Corbett.

Important developments in the design field have continuously been taking place under the leadership of Jo Ledger, who in 1955 succeeded Jack Noke as Art Director at the Burslem Pottery and is now Design Director of Royal Doulton Tableware Limited. Under his guidance a new generation of designers, artists, engravers and modellers are perpetuating the Royal Doulton traditions and their work is surely destined to become 'heirlooms of tomorrow'.

APPENDIX I

Former Artists, Designers, Engravers, Etchers and Gilders

The following list embraces all those former Doulton Burslem artists and designers of whom it has been possible to discover relevant details. Although engravers, etchers and gilders rarely signed or initialled their work, the names of some of the most important have been included for they contributed greatly to the renown of the Burslem Wares.

More information has survived about some individuals than others; the amount of space devoted to each is, therefore, not necessarily an indication of his relative importance. If any readers can supply further particulars concerning any former members of the Doulton Burslem design staff (including any not mentioned in the following list) such information will be greatly appreciated.

The dates given relate to the periods of service; where shown in *italics* they are approximate within a year or two.

Those Burslem artists who signed their work usually did so in full; on comparatively few pots (and those usually small ones) initials only are found. Both signatures and initials are almost always easy to decipher and ascribe to the artist concerned. Monograms are very rare and are found mostly on *flambé* and kindred wares. The two Nokes usually signed their surname only in a somewhat similar style but Charles's may be distinguished by the two dots underneath. It should be noted, however, that a facsimile of Charles's signature is sometimes found on *flambé*, Sung and Chang pots originated by him but produced after his retirement.

Several typical signatures of Burslem artists are given below; those of others are equally clear.

157

Alphabetical list

ALLEN, F.:
An artist who worked with Charles J. Noke in the 1930s on Sung and other wares.

ALLEN, Harry: 1900–1950, Artist
Son of Robert Allen (see below), Harry was apprenticed to Doulton at the age of 14. His training was supervised by his father and by Harry Piper (q.v.). He also studied at the Burslem School of Art for ten years, becoming already in his early twenties one of Doulton's most versatile artists, excelling equally in painting landscapes, birds and flowers. Among his many subjects were Arab villages, Moorish mosques and palaces, Nile views, desert scenes, Breton fairs, strolling players, figures in woodland and river landscapes, moonlight scenes. His paintings of birds were among the finest in the industry, and are seen particularly well in the Titanian Wares featuring kingfishers, owls, toucans, nightingales, thrushes and other species. His skill with the brush led to his becoming one of the first of the small band of painters of early Royal Doulton figures and from about 1924 onwards this became his main activity.

Harry Allen occasionally used the pseudonym 'Richmond' on items mainly lithoprinted with additional hand-painting.

ALLEN, Robert: 1870–1929, Designer
After a brief period as a boy worker at Minton's, Robert Allen came to the Nile Street factory while it was still owned by Pinder, Bourne. He studied under the supervision of their art director, John Slater, becoming one of his most gifted artists and designers. He was also an outstanding student for many years at the Burslem School of Art. His paintings of birds, insects, flowers and seascapes were of a high order.

Allen became head of a department, controlling a group of outstanding artists and craftsmen to whom the finest and most expensive types of decoration were entrusted. It became Allen's special *forte*, from the time of the Chicago Exhibition of 1893 onwards, to design raised gold and acid gold patterns in Florentine and other Renaissance styles to harmonize with the work of floral, landscape and other artists in his department. Examples of his own signed work are fairly rare but the initials RA followed by a number are found on a great variety of items produced under his aegis. He was involved in the development of the early Titanian wares, as was his son, Harry. He also designed some of the Lactolian Wares.

ALLEN, William: 1883–1935, Engraver
After serving an apprenticeship with a freelance engraver in Burslem, Allen joined Doulton in 1883. He and Charles Vyse (q.v.) formed the backbone of what became one of the finest teams of engravers in Staffordshire. He was particularly adept in grasping and interpreting the ideas a designer had in mind.

ARROWSMITH, Samuel: 1907–1955, Gilder
Trained at Minton's as a gilder, Arrowsmith came to Doulton in 1907 and worked under Robert Allen. He was a raised gold specialist whose work was of the highest quality and many special pieces for exhibitions and famous customers were entrusted to his care.

ASH, A.: Artist
Ash's signature is found on items made at Burslem in the late nineteenth century.

BAILEY, Arthur: 1912–1932 and 1939–1957, Slip-painter
Bailey was a specialist in painting with slips and was responsible for painting the prototypes of many of the Kingsware patterns. He also translated into slip-painting treatment, designs submitted by Frank Brangwyn. He was largely responsible for the

production of a series of underglaze floral designs – e.g. *Wild Rose, Magnella, Nasturtium, Chrysanthemum* – which were especially popular in the Australasian and South African markets. His initials AB are sometimes found blended into the patterns.

BAKER, Alfred: 1888–1928, Modeller
After an early training at the Cauldon Place Pottery, Baker became a close assistant of Charles J. Noke who entrusted many of the most intricate and skilled tasks to his care.

He was responsible for modelling some of the elaborate vases and other items displayed at famous exhibitions.

BENINSON, Joseph: Artist
This artist is said to have specialized in floral painting and to have spent some eight years at the Burslem Pottery early this century.

BENTLEY, Leonard: 1889–1926 (intermittently), Artist
Bentley was a clever painter of flowers in many different styles. It is said of him that his speed in freehand painting of flowers, butterflies and *Dresden birds* had to be seen to be believed. He executed many of the floral designs initiated by John Slater in the so-called 'Spanish' style.

Cecil J. Noke, when he first joined Doulton in 1920, studied under Bentley for a period.

BETTELEY, Herbert: 1886–1930, Designer
Herbert Betteley, familiarly known as 'Harry', came to Doulton at the age of 26, having studied for many years at the Burslem School of Art and worked as an artist for other local potteries as a 'free-lance'. His ability, especially in carefully executed line drawing and intricate gold patterns, was quickly appreciated by John Slater and the designs of many beautiful service plates and other items for the Chicago Exhibition of 1893 were his handiwork. Like Robert Allen (q.v.) he was entrusted by Slater with the control of a select group of gifted artists and craftsmen and, in a sense, he and Allen ran,

in friendly competition, two rival schools. The initials HB, usually followed by a number, identify many of the designs produced under Betteley's supervision. He trained many young artists.

BILTON, Louis: 1892–*1912*, Artist
Bilton was trained at Minton's under the former Sèvres artist, William Mussill, a gifted painter of flowers and birds and a keen student of nature. After leaving Stoke, Bilton spent a few years in Australia painting watercolours of Australian flora for a publication known as *The Picturesque Atlas*. He came to Doulton in 1892, bringing with him a splendid portfolio of Australian flowers – wattle, waratah, wild fuchsia, desert pea, flannel flower, bottle-brush, etc. His painting of some of these on vases and other pots displayed at the 1893 Chicago Exhibition won world-wide acclaim. Examples of his original work are in many private collections and in Australian and New Zealand museums. Some of his floral drawings were lithographed for reproduction on tableware services and were popular for many years.

Bilton was a versatile artist; he was responsible also for some of the designs in Spanish and Luscian styles and for drawings of children and Japanese girls reproduced from prints in underglaze blue.

BIRCHALL, F.: Artist
Examples of landscape painting on dessert plates and other items made in the 1920s and signed by this artist have been noted.

BIRBECK, Joseph: 1900–1926, Artist
A member of a distinguished family of ceramic artists, Birbeck had been at the Cauldon Pottery for many years before joining Doulton in 1900 at the age of 38. He was a versatile artist whose work included flower painting in the eighteenth century Bow and Chelsea styles, exotic birds, Alpine and Highland scenery, landscapes after Turner and other artists. His special *forte*, however, was the painting of fish and game and his brilliant technique in portraying underwater

effects, distant woods and hazy moors has probably never been excelled. He painted many outstanding sets of dessert and service plates for the North American and other markets. Apart from watercolour painting, his hobbies included the collecting of birds, eggs, butterflies and fossils.

BIRKS, Edward: 1875–1890, Artist
Birks joined Pinder, Bourne in 1875. He was regarded by John Slater as a flower painter of exceptional ability who executed many fine pieces in traditional styles. His death at the early age of 33 cut short what had promised to be a brilliant career. Signed pieces by him are rare.

BOTT, Thomas D.: 1889–1900, Artist
Bott, a member of a well-known Worcester family of ceramic artists, came to Doulton in the same year as Charles J. Noke, whose friend he had been at Worcester. He was an accomplished artist who specialized in flower painting. Examples of his signed work are rare; they include some dessert and service plates executed for the Chicago Exhibition, 1893.

BOULLEMIER, Henri: *1901–1904*, Artist (extramural)
Henri's father, Anton or Antonin, was born in Lorraine in 1840. He studied under a descendant of Fragonard and subsequently worked as a ceramic artist for Sèvres. He came to England about 1870 and in 1872 joined Solon and other French artists at Minton, where he produced work of the highest quality, his figures and portrait subjects being particularly famous.

Henri and his brother, Lucien, also worked for Minton; their style is generally much influenced by their father's work. Early this century, Henri – presumably as a free-lance – did some work for Doulton; service and dessert plates with his signature, depicting children, cherubs, portrait heads and female figures, have been noted bearing dates from 1901 to 1904. These are very rare.

BOULTON, James: 1880–1917, Artist
Apprenticed to Pinder, Bourne at the age of thirteen, Boulton became a fine painter, especially of flowers. He was responsible for attractive dessert sets shown at the Chicago and other exhibitions. Some of the rack plates and other items – depicting children at play and in rural scenes, in underglaze blue – are attributed to him.

BOWDEN, R.
This artist's signature has been noted on rack plates and tea-wares, decorated with poppies and other flowers, produced c. 1919–1922.

BROUGH, Charles: 1903–1911, Artist
Brough came to Doulton from Copeland in 1903. Some vases decorated by him in Sèvres style were shown at the St Louis Exhibition the following year. During the eight years he was at Burslem he decorated many of the richest types of dessert sets and service plates, including some for King Edward VII and several Indian rulers. His lovely flowers – often in Sèvres and Meissen styles as well as English – are particularly noteworthy but he was a versatile artist and his painting of game birds, cattle and landscapes is also of a high order. His work is rare and much sought after.

BROWN, Reginald: 1925–1962, Artist
Apprenticed to Doulton at the age of sixteen, Reginald Brown was trained under Herbert Betteley as a china painter specializing in flowers and landscapes. In or around 1930 he was transferred to the then still fairly small department where the Royal Doulton Figures and Animal Models were painted, later becoming foreman and manager. In the expansion of this section he played a most important part. In 1951 he took charge of all on-glaze china decoration. He died in service in June 1962.

BROWN, Wilmot: 1879–1930, Artist
This artist was apprenticed to Pinder, Bourne at the age of fourteen and was trained under John Slater. He also studied at

local Schools of Art. During his long career at Doulton he first became widely known for his landscapes, views of English cathedrals and other historic buildings. A great nature-lover, he also painted flowers in Spanish and Luscian styles, his treatment of chrysanthemums, roses and peonies being characteristic of his original style and breadth of expression. He could also paint sheep and cattle very effectively.

In later years he played an important part in the decoration of the *flambé* and other reduction glaze wares, and many fine pieces bear either his signature or initials. Apart from his own landscape painting he also designed many scenes for printing from copper engravings.

BUTTLE, George: 1905–1911, Artist
Buttle was thirty-eight when he came to Doulton, having previously worked for Wedgwood, Bishop and Stonier, and Moore Brothers. He left in 1911 to return to Bishop and Stonier as Art Director.

He was a gifted figure painter and executed many fine vases decorated with classical themes such as *Venus rising from the Sea*. Other works include ceramic cameos, miniatures painted on china, dessert sets and service plates decorated with cupids, portrait heads of children, female figures in both romantic and classical dress.

A large vase by Buttle was shown at the Brussels Exhibition of 1910.

CALLOWHILL: Artist and Gilder
Some vases in the John Slater Collection in the Museum of Applied Arts and Sciences, Sydney, N.S.W. are attributed to Callowhill, of whom the catalogue remarks: 'Callowhill was a product of the Worcester factory, and some of the richest and most daring raised gold work issued from Nile Street was the product of his skill and patient industry. He never signed his works but in nearly every case an insect will be found which was looked on as Callowhill's sign manual.'

There were two brothers, James and Thomas Scott Callowhill at Worcester c. 1855–1885 who both specialized in figure subjects, heads, chased gilding and raised enamels in Limoges style. One of them – which is not clear – worked at Nile Street later in the century. The vases in Sydney have raised gold and enamel decorations of ferns, barley, butterflies, dragonflies and snakes.

CHALLINOR, William: 1900–1939, Engraver.
Challinor was a fine engraver who was responsible for much of Doulton Burslem's highest-class work in this important sphere. He retired before his time because of failing health but continued to do some work at home for the department up to the time of his death in 1943.

CURNOCK, Percy: 1885–1954, Artist
Percy Curnock's name is no doubt particularly associated with his exquisite paintings of roses but during his well-nigh seventy years at the Nile Street studios there were few branches of ceramic art in which he did not equally excel.

He began his apprenticeship under John Slater and Robert Allen in 1885 when he was just thirteen. For many years he studied at the Burslem School of Art. In the course of time he came under the influence of such distinguished artists as Edward Raby, Fred Hancock and David Dewsberry, but by the early twentieth century he had evolved his own distinctive style of painstaking flower-painting. His note-books are filled with beautiful detailed water-colour sketches not just of roses but of many other flowers both from the fields, hedgerows and cottage gardens and from the gardens and conservatories of Trentham, Chatsworth and other stately homes. These sketches provided the inspiration for a great deal of his work but his paintings after Corot, his Italian lake scenes, his castles and other landscape subjects are equally fine examples of his artistry.

Several of his designs provided the material for lithographed tableware patterns which became widely popular in all markets. Among the best-known of these were *Glamis Thistle*, *Passion Flower*, *Clovelly* and *Arcadia*.

DEWSBERRY, David: 1889–1919, Artist
Dewsberry trained at the Hill Pottery in Burslem and subsequently worked at other factories before joining Doulton in 1889 at the age of thirty-seven. Examples of his work featuring views of Scotland and other landscapes are known but it is particularly for his paintings of orchids that he is famous, being regarded by many connoisseurs as the finest ceramic painter of orchids the trade has ever known.

He made many studies of a great variety of orchids in the conservatories of the Duke of Sutherland, Mr Joseph Chamberlain and other well-known orchid-growers. His work is characterized by the fidelity and delicacy of its tints and the masterly grouping of the flowers on various shapes. Apart from orchids, other examples of his floral painting include begonias, roses, daffodils, crab-apple blossom and leaves. Paintings of humming birds are also recorded.

Dewsberry's signature is found too on a number of pieces of Luscian and Lactolian Wares.

DONCASTER, R.
This signature is found on some wares decorated with raised enamels in the 1890s.

EATON, Arthur Charles: 1889–1932, Artist
Eaton was fourteen when he first came to Nile Street in 1889 to learn the art of ceramic painting under Slater and Allen. He studied part-time for many years at the Burslem School of Art and later taught there and at Tunstall in the evenings. Meanwhile he had become one of Doulton's most versatile decorative artists, equally at home with both underglaze and on-glaze painting of pastoral scenes and other landscapes, figures, portrait heads, animals and flowers.

He developed a special flair for painting in coloured slips and played a leading part in helping Noke to evolve the Rembrandt and Holbein Wares. His delicate line drawing and masterly use of pastel colours were other characteristics seen especially in the Hyperion Wares.

In the second half of his career, Eaton became closely associated with Noke and Nixon in the decoration of *flambé* and Sung Wares. He delighted in the intricate colour palette of these wares and decorated them with his swirling dragons and soaring birds of paradise.

EVANS, George: *1929–1931*, Artist
Evans came of a Worcester family of artists. After serving an apprenticeship and several years as a painter there, he left during a business slump to work for Doulton for a short period, after which he returned to Worcester where he was one of the first painters of the well-known Doughty birds.

While at Doulton he painted among other wares a number of the less expensive types of dessert sets and service plates – some with landscapes after Corot.

FENTON, Harry: 1903–1911 and 1928–1953, Modeller
During his first period of service at Nile Street Fenton assisted Noke mainly with the modelling of tablewares and other domestic pottery. After about eight years' experience he, like a number of other potters in that period, was attracted to try his fortunes in the United States. He remained there for nearly seventeen years, working mostly in pottery factories in Trenton, New Jersey, where he gained further experience which stood him in good stead on his return to Staffordshire. (While in Trenton he took out American citizenship.)

During the second period with Doulton, Fenton became Noke's most accomplished and able assistant. He was responsible for many of the early Doulton Character and Toby Jugs. In the Character Jugs especially he showed a rare sense of subtle humour

162

and observation of country types. He collaborated with Noke in developing the now much sought after limited edition loving cups and presentation jugs, also with Noke and Harradine in some of the figures.

FERNYHOUGH, Frederick: Gilder
A gilder of this name was apparently at Burslem for some years in the latter part of the last century.

FERNYHOUGH, George: *1887*–1905, Artist
Fernyhough's signature or his initials GF will be found on many earthenware and china items produced during the years he was at Nile Street. He was particularly associated with dog and horse subjects, hunting scenes, and animals in different types of landscapes. Engravings from copper plates were made of several of his designs for reproduction in underglaze flow blue on dinnerware, rack plates and early Series Ware. He taught in the evenings at the Newcastle School of Art.

GEORGE, A.
This signature or the initials AG was used by George White (q.v.) on wares which were mainly litho-print decorated with only a small amount of hand-painting.

GLEAVES, Victor: *1930–1938* (intermittently), Modeller
Gleaves was a modeller with a fine sense of form and line. He worked for several factories, including Minton, besides two periods at Nile Street. He later set up on his own account at Hanley.

GRACE, William E.: 1902–1959, Artist
Grace was apprenticed under Slater when he was thirteen, going to Robert Allen's department where he was tutored by Harry Piper (q.v.). He also studied under Stanley Thorogood at the Burslem School of Art

where he won many prizes including the King's Prize.

At Doulton he first became a pictorial draughtsman, producing designs for reproduction by litho-prints or engraving. Then, under Noke, he became associated with underglaze Series Ware, in the evolution of which he played a leading part both in interpreting Noke's ideas and in developing his own. Many of the designs for rack plates also came from his studio. As well as being an outstandingly good draughtsman he was also a fine underglaze painter and many of the prototypes of the limited edition jugs and loving cups were painted by him, as were some of those of the early fine earthenware Royal Doulton Figures. He was an accomplished painter in oils and his pictures appeared in many local exhibitions.

GRIFFITHS, George: 1939–1948, Engraver
Griffiths was already well into his sixties when he came to Nile Street, where he rendered invaluable assistance during the difficult Second World War period. A first-class engraver and draughtsman, he was apprenticed at Wedgwood in 1886, later joining Steele and Wood. After serving in the First World War from 1914–1919 he then worked for a long period for Minton. He taught for many years at the Newcastle School of Art, held the South Kensington Art Class Teacher's Certificate, and was a member of several art guilds and ceramic societies to which he often gave papers on various aspects of pottery decoration.

HALL, Sidney: 1891–1952, Artist
Apprenticed under Slater at the age of fourteen, Hall remained with Doulton for sixty-one years. A versatile painter, he is perhaps known especially for his floral subjects but many fine dessert services, service plates, vases etc. with paintings of landscapes, fish and game also bear his signature. In his later years he was in charge of hand-painted Series Wares and had a school of young painters under his guidance.

HANCOCK, Fred: 1879–1913, Artist
After a short-lived career as a clerk Hancock joined Pinder, Bourne under Slater and became one of his most versatile pupils.

As a painter of fish and game in their natural surroundings he was considered without an equal in the trade. His signature is found also on vases, dessert sets, service plates, plaques and dinner, tea and coffee services painted with a wide variety of other subjects – among them chrysanthemums, carnations, roses and other flowers, groups of fruit, birds among marshes with wild flowers and grasses in the foreground, highland cattle and moorland sheep, leopards and other wild animals, a girl with geese, Eastern mosques, Egyptian desert scenes, rural English landscapes and misty Scottish moors.

Despite the remarkable speed at which he painted the most exacting subjects, his technique was always superb. Examples of his work, especially large vases embellished with raised and acid gold ornament designed by Robert Allen, featured prominently in all important International Exhibitions. It was well said of him on his retirement that, as Samuel Johnson said of Oliver Goldsmith, he touched nothing 'that he did not adorn'.

Although he left Doulton in 1913 he carried out various commissions for the firm for several years, so that his signature is found on pieces with later dates than 1913. He died in 1931.

HANCOCK, Joseph: 1890–1926 and 1942–1945, Artist
Hancock came to Nile Street as a boy of fourteen. He was trained by Piper and Noke and studied at local art schools in the evenings. He is especially well-known for his painting of fish, game birds and animals in their natural surroundings but his signature is also found on some of the Luscian Wares painted with floral subjects, and on vases and other items depicting landscapes after Corot and subjects such as *The Woodman*, *The Ploughboy* and *Boy cutting bracken* after La Thangue. A painting of his of highland cattle was greatly admired by King George V. Many fine vases modelled by Noke were painted by him and gilded by William Skinner with decoration designed by Robert Allen. He would sometimes work for fourteen days on a vase which had to be painted and fired several times to achieve the delicate tones and beautiful backgrounds which are notable features of his work.

HARPER, Frank: *1925–1928*, Artist
Formerly with Worcester, this artist's signature is found on tablewares and other items hand-painted with fruit and flowers. He was apparently with Doulton for only about three years.

HARRADINE, A. Leslie:
See pages 71–75, 79, 86, 147, 152, 154

HARRISON, C.: Artist
No details are known about this artist whose signature has been noted on wares dated between 1906 and 1908, richly hand-painted with a wide range of roses and other flowers.

HART, Charles H., Senior: 1880–1927, Artist
This artist, a native of Burslem, came to Pinder, Bourne when he was thirteen to study under Slater; he also attended the local School of Art for many years. Although he first became known as a painter of flowers (and continued to paint them from time to time) it was as a painter of fish and game that he really made his name. His style was distinctively different from that of Birbeck and the Hancocks but had a great appeal at home and overseas, especially in the North American market.

His signature is also found on paintings of castles and romantic lakes.

HART, Charles, Junior: 1922–1950, Artist
Joining Doulton when he was fourteen, this artist's training was undertaken by his father. He produced some original paintings

of fish and game in the 1930s and 1940s before transferring to the underglaze figure painting department in the development of which he played a notable part.

HENK, Max: Designer and modeller
See page 86

HENRI, F.: Artist
No details are known about this artist whose signature has been noted on Titanian, *flambé* and other wares bearing dates between 1915 and 1922. His range of subjects included herons, flamingos, storks, cranes, seagulls and other birds, bamboo groves, cottages and landscapes.

HEWITT, Jack: *1885–1893*, Artist
During the few years he was with Doulton, Hewitt, a talented painter of figure subjects, executed many fine pieces. He received his early training at the Minton studio in London under W. S. Coleman and was later associated in turn with Copeland and Wedgwood before joining Doulton c.1885. The *Pottery Gazette*, recording his death at an advanced age in 1930, described him as 'not only a distinguished ceramic artist but a man of great personal charm. . . . In the course of time he earned the reputation of being the best figure painter on pottery that the district has ever produced.'

Some of his subjects were also reproduced, during and after his period of service, in underglaze flow blue from prints made from engraved copper plates. Examples of these dated in the late 1890s and early 1900s have been noted.

HINDLEY, J.: Artist
Examples of fine quality *pâte-sur-pâte* painting signed by this artist have been noted. He was apparently at Nile Street around the turn of the century but no details are recorded.

HODKINSON, Fred: 1895–1949, Gilder
The son of William G. Hodkinson (see below), Fred was thirteen when he was apprenticed to Doulton under Herbert Betteley. He became a raised paste gilder of considerable ability but it was for his work in acid gold that he was most noted. He eventually became manager of the acid gold department and many fine services for Royalty and for notabilities all over the world passed through his hands.

HODKINSON, James: Gilder
The only information recorded about this member of the Hodkinson family, possibly a brother of William, is that he was employed as a gilder between c. 1888–1894.

HODKINSON, William G.: 1880–1920, Artist and Gilder
William Hodkinson, a native of Derby, was apprenticed at Minton under Léon Arnoux, coming to Doulton in his twentieth year. He attended the Hanley and Stoke Schools of Art, winning distinction at both, and during his many years with Doulton won honours at the Chicago, St Louis, Paris and other Exhibitions.

A talented all-round decorative artist, equally versed in on-glaze enamel painting and gilding, he could turn his hand to *pâte-sur-pâte* decoration, floral painting in old Bristol and other earlier styles as well as new, and landscape painting – especially with cattle and sheep in evidence. He created several best-selling *Art Nouveau* tableware designs in the early 1900s and collaborated with Noke in developing the Holbein Wares and *flambé* wares; many of the early *flambé* effects owed much to his inspiration.

Hodkinson also worked closely with Noke on many enamelled panels, featuring classical and romantic themes, in which rich enamel work is combined with raised gold work and moulded effects. The majority of these panels are believed to have been sold in Australia and New Zealand. His delicate painting in gold depicting birds, lily ponds, fish swimming among weeds and starfish on a red *flambé* ground, also exemplifies the fine decorative quality of his work.

HOLDCROFT, George: 1884–1951, Etcher
Apprenticed to Doulton at the age of thirteen, Holdcroft studied the art of etching under Wright and Swettenham (q.v.), two fine craftsmen, and in course of time gained the reputation of being the finest ceramic etcher in the Five Towns. He spent 67 happy years with Doulton, refused absolutely to retire, and was still working eight hours a day in his Nile Street studio until a month before his death in his eighty-first year.

He was one of some seventeen members of the Holdcroft family to work for Doulton in various capacities, their combined years of service being nearly 500. It was through the services of families such as this that the Royal Doulton tradition was built up.

HOLDCROFT, Rowland: 1925–1973, Artist
Holdcroft began his apprenticeship under Harry Tittensor. He became a skilled painter of figure subjects and landscapes, executing many large and expensive vases depicting winding country lanes, trees, meadows and other rural scenes. Some of the designs for Series Wares and rack plates were also his work. In later years he transferred to the Royal Doulton Figure Department where he excelled in the painting of the faces and the more intricate details.

HOLLINSHEAD, Enoch: 1920–1965, Artist
In his earlier years, Hollinshead was engaged mainly in painting floral subjects and birds. Later on he became a painter of Royal Doulton Figures.

HOLLINSHEAD, J.: Artist
No records have so far come to light concerning this artist whose signature is found on some of the Holbein Wares.

HOPKINS, Charles B.: *1893–1922* (intermittently), Artist
Hopkins came to Doulton in the early 1890s and studied under Noke as well as at local art schools. He was painting floral subjects in 1893, dated specimens of his work in that year having been noted. He was, in his later years, known as 'the McWhirter of the Potteries' because his landscape painting was thought to be similar to that artist's. He specialized in mountains and pastoral scenes with cattle and sheep. Many large vases by him are now in Australia where his work was very popular.

JOHNSON, Leslie: *1900–1937* (intermittently), Artist
Johnson is probably best known for his delicate, skilful paintings on vases, comports, service plates, dessert services, etc., in the styles of Fragonard, Watteau and Wheatley. He was also a clever miniaturist who executed many historical portraits – among them Charles I, Charles II, Lord Nelson and Lady Hamilton, the young Queen Victoria, Queen Elizabeth I and Mary Queen of Scots. He decorated later versions of *Dante* vases in the early 1900s and his portraits are also found on vases with landscapes by Hancock, roses by Curnock and gilding by Skinner.

His work was frequently asked for specifically by American and Australian customers.

JOHNSON, Reginald: 1923–1930, Artist
Although only fourteen when he came to Doulton and twenty-one when he left, Reginald Johnson, who studied under Tittensor, developed a marked gift for landscape painting. Some of his earlier work is reminiscent of his teacher's style but later he developed his own lighter style, examples of which are found on large vases and other pieces painted with British landscape scenes.

JOHNSON, William: Designer
It is recorded that William Johnson was with Doulton for some twenty-six years but the precise dates are not known. He is thought, however, to have come in the early 1890s after having been apprenticed with William Slater at Longton and having studied at the Stoke School of Art. He was mainly con-

cerned with the design and production of less expensive but none the less well-finished tablewares, Series Wares, rack plates and 'fancies'.

KEATES, Norman W.: 1907–1917 and 1919–1960, Artist
Keates was apprenticed under David Dewsberry in 1907 at the age of fourteen. He was one of the last 'bound apprentices' to be engaged by Doulton. He studied for ten years at the Burslem School of Art under Thorogood and other artists and obtained the Art Teacher's Certificate. Although he sometimes painted landscapes and figure subjects it is mostly on paintings of roses, orchids and other flowers that his signature is found. After the death of David Dewsberry in 1929 he carried on the tradition of orchid painting for many years. After his retirement in 1960 he worked for a while at Coalport.

KELSALL, J. or T.: Artist
Little is known about this artist, examples of whose floral painting and *pâte sur pâte* are found on vases dated in the 1890s and early 1900s.

One record gives the initial T and another J but whether these were actually two different artists has not been established. There was apparently also a Robert Kelsall or Kelshall at Burslem in the late 1880s who worked with Slater on the development of the *chiné* wares. (There was a fruit and floral artist named Kelshall at Coalport around the 1850s.)

KITTERIDGE, J.: Artist
A floral painter, some examples of whose work in the late 1880s and early 1890s have been noted, mainly chrysanthemums and roses in the so-called Spanish style.

LABARRE, Charles: Artist
One of the few foreign artists employed by Doulton, Labarre was specially brought over by Slater from Paris for about a year to work on some of the large vases for the 1893 Chicago Exhibition. He was particularly known for his painting of cupids and classical figures in Sèvres style. He collaborated with George White in painting the original *Dante* vase; he also painted the *Columbus* vase, the *Love* vases and one of the four *Diana* vases.

LANGLEY, Leonard: c.1868–1916, Designer
Langley was John Slater's first apprentice, taken on shortly after Slater himself had joined Pinder, Bourne as Art Director. He eventually became the head of a department which was responsible for the design of a great deal of the less expensive wares, decorated with engraved prints, block prints and lithographs. He also played a big part in the design of several of the early Series Wares. Wares produced under his supervision sometimes bear numbers preceded by the initials LL.

LEACH, A.: Artist
This signature has been noted on some Titanian Wares with paintings of birds, c. 1915–1920.

LEWIS, J.: Artist
This artist's signature is found on some vases and plates with floral decoration in Spanish style, late 19th century.

LIGHT, Ernest W.: 1912–1918, Modeller
Light was a well known local sculptor and modeller who produced a number of figure designs for Doulton. He lived in Hanley and was master in charge at Stoke School of Art from 1920–1932.

LIGHT, Hubert: 1916–1948
Hubert was the son of the sculptor Ernest Light. He worked specifically on the *Bunnykins* range, adapting Barbara Vernon's ideas for production.

MASSEY, William: 1928–1956, Gilder
Trained at Minton, Massey was a craftsman-gilder, specializing in raised gold treatments. He was responsible for the gilding of many

notable pieces including *The Queen's Vase* produced by members of the Fine China Association to commemorate the Coronation of Queen Elizabeth II in 1953. Much of the very delicate gilding on the more expensive Titanian Wares was also his work. He did the intricate gold tracing and raised gold work on many examples of the large figure *Princess Badoura*.

MILWARD, Harry C.: 1898–1918, Gilder
Having served his apprenticeship at Derby, Milward came to Burslem at the age of twenty-eight. This was at a time when Charles Noke was modelling elaborate and expensive vases, service plates, centre-pieces and the like and Milward was entrusted with the raised paste designs on many of these. One of the most important commissions with which he was associated was a £30,000 order (a great deal of money in those days!) for dinner sets, vases and other pieces for an Indian Maharajah; work on this took three years to complete.

MITCHELL, Henry: *1891–1908*, Artist
Mitchell was a gifted animal, bird and landscape painter who had already won a name for himself at Minton and other factories before joining Doulton in the 1890s when he was then over forty. Some of his earlier work had been shown in the Vienna Exhibition of 1873. On the Doulton Stand at the Chicago Exhibition of 1893 service plates and dessert sets painted by him were shown and he was also responsible for the painting of one of the *Diana* vases.

A versatile artist, his signature is found on many items depicting animals, birds, fish, mermaids, seaweeds and shells and pastoral, mountain and moorland landscapes. It was said of him that his atmospheric values were rarely equalled and never bettered. Noke wrote of his work: 'There are few more beautiful sights in ceramic painting than the silver grey tones of the middle distances in Mitchell's landscapes.' A masterly stylist, his delicate touch is particularly well exemplified in his beautifully drawn animal studies with their framing of trees and landscapes.

MOORE, Frederick: 1927–1957, Artist
Fred Moore was one of the chief artists responsible for the striking *flambé* and Sung glaze effects.

MOORE, Warwick: Artist
Son of Fred Moore, Warwick also specialized in *flambé* ware but left to work for a lithographic printer.

MORREY, Harry: 1884–1944, Artist
Apprenticed to Doulton when he was fourteen, Morrey became primarily known as a landscape painter although his signature is occasionally found on pieces decorated with floral and figure subjects. He was particularly adept in depicting rural scenes and farming subjects – ploughing, harvesting, sheep-shearing, milking cows, etc. During his period with Doulton he spent several months sketching in Australia, which provided subjects for some rack plates and other wares depicting Australian scenes.

Morrey was associated also with the production of some of the Holbein Wares.

MORTON, Thomas: 1905–1925, Gilder
Morton was already in his late fifties when he joined Doulton. With many years of experience at Copeland and Minton behind him, he came with a very high reputation, especially for his raised paste work. His gilding is found on vases, plates, etc. by Allen, Curnock, Tittensor, Eaton and others. His service plates were described by Noke as being 'as fine as anything ever done on china'.

MOUNTFORD, Harry: Artist
Some pieces produced in the 1890s bear this artist's signature. Among those noted are vases and jugs, including a Royle's Patent Self-Pouring Water Jug, painted with azaleas in Spanish style.

NIXON, Harry, N. R. D.: 1900–1950, Artist

Apprenticed to Doulton at the age of fourteen, Nixon studied for over ten years in the evenings at the Burslem School of Art and later became a part-time teacher there for many years. He won numerous awards in National Competitions including medals for plant drawing and pottery designs. A versatile artist himself, he trained several young artists, including one of Doulton's present Art Directors, Walter Hayward.

An accomplished draughtsman and floral painter, he was responsible for many of the most successful tableware and decorative ware patterns of the first half of this century. He was very much involved in the early development of the Royal Doulton Figures – a fact which is reflected in the letters HN preceding the numbers given to these from 1913 onwards to the present day. In collaboration with Charles Noke he evolved many of the finest effects in the *flambé*, Sung, Chang and Chinese Jade Wares. Yet another development in which he played an important role was the Titanian Ware.

In 1946 Nixon, who was an active church worker in the Stoke area, had the honour of designing a beautiful *rouge flambé* vase and cover, 21 inches high, for Staffordshire's famous cathedral in Lichfield.

NOKE, Charles John: 1889–1941, Art Director
See pages 24, 28–65, 69–73, 83–92, 100–121

NOKE, Cecil Jack, N.R.D.: 1920–1954, Art Director
See pages 34, 35, 48, 63, 73–86, 91, 119, 155

NUNN, Walter: *1897*–1910, Artist
Nunn came to the Potteries from London where he had studied at the South Kensington School of Art. William Owen wrote of him: 'Walter Nunn was an artist of a most unconventional type but of rare ability. In illustrating on pottery scenes and characters from Shakespeare's immortal plays, he brought a mind and hand in absolute sympathy with his work. He was a keen and capable student and could be depended on to make his subjects as historically correct as they undoubtedly were artistically satisfying. A bright and cheery optimist; many a year shall roll before we look upon his like again.'

Apart from vases, rack plates, dessert sets and other wares decorated with Shakespearean scenes and characters, Nunn was also the designer of several other series. He also designed some of the Holbein and Rembrandt Wares.

PARRY, Edward E.: 1887–1893, Artist
Parry worked for several different pottery firms in the Stoke area, including Cauldon and Grimwade. During the six years he spent with Doulton he was known primarily for his clever flower painting in a style somewhat similar to that of John Slater.

PERCY, E.
There was no artist of this name. It was a *nom de plume* used on less expensive tablewares and other items which were largely lithodecorated with additional hand-painted touches by either Edwin Wood or Percy Curnock or both – the E standing for Edwin and the Percy of course for Curnock. This 'signature' is found on wares produced in the 1920s and early 1930s.

PERRY, Arthur: 1926–1947, Artist
Perry had worked for a few years for Coalport and many years for Copeland before joining Doulton at the age of fifty-five. He retired when he was seventy-six but continued for some years to do occasional work. A great walker, swimmer and gardener, he also became a 'Grand Old Man of the Potteries', reaching the age of 102. He was an accomplished painter of fish and game, having his own distinctive style but equally capable of working in a similar style to that of Birbeck to meet continued demands from American agents and customers. At Doulton he was regarded as the foremost fish and game painter of his day.

His signature is also found on paintings of cottages and trees, castles and cathedrals, and rural landscapes.

PHILLIPS, Thomas: 1888–1930, Artist
After serving an apprenticeship at Worcester, Phillips came to Burslem just a year before Charles Noke. He was particularly associated with the so-called Spanish onglaze decorations so popular in the 1890s and early 1900s and examples of his work were shown at the Chicago, Paris and other exhibitions. In his later years he turned to underglaze painting and was in charge of a large group of decorators.

PIPER, Enoch: 1892–1914, Artist
Piper was already fifty when he joined Doulton from Coalport in 1892. He made his name primarily as a heraldic artist and painted arms and crests on many expensive services for British and Foreign Royalty, nobility, landed gentry, etc. His signature is found occasionally on paintings of game birds, flowers, Luscian Ware and landscapes.

PIPER, Harry: 1892–1912, Artist
The son of Enoch Piper, Harry - then twenty-seven – joined Doulton from Coalport in the same year as his father. A flower painter of outstanding ability, he decorated many fine pieces, including vases, service plates and dessert sets for the Chicago, Paris, St Louis and other exhibitions. Roses were considered his speciality but paintings of many kinds of flowers, fruits and birds also bear his signature. There was a great demand for his work from Tiffany and other American stores.

Apart from his own artistic work, Harry Piper rendered sterling service by training a group of boy apprentices. His death at the early age of forty-seven was a great loss to the industry.

PLANT, John Hugh: 1902–1920, Artist
After studying at the Hanley School of Art and serving an apprenticeship at the Brown-Westhead, Moore Pottery in that town, Plant spent many years with Coalport and Wedgwood as a painter of landscapes and animals before joining Doulton in 1902. A versatile artist, his signature is found on many fine pieces depicting views of Venice, Rome and other Italian cities, rustic scenes, old castles, palaces, cathedrals and cottages. His architectural sketches and drawings were of a high order. Other examples of his work include paintings of ships after Turner, fishing boats, barges, yachts, deer and other animals, game birds and fish.

PRICE, Jack: 1894–1932, Artist
Apprenticed to Doulton when he was about fourteen, Price became an invaluable member of Slater's and Noke's staff. His special *forte* was floral painting but, when needed, he could turn his hand to almost any type of ceramic painting – woodland and rustic scenes, Italian and Swiss lakes, castles, animals, birds.

He left in 1932 to go to Grimwades; later, after a period with Copeland, he joined Crown Derby where he became decorating manager at Osmaston Road.

PROUDLOVE, Albert and Alfred: Artists
These two artists were apparently at the Burslem Pottery in the late nineteenth and early twentiety century. Their signatures are found on floral painting. Unfortunately, so far no other record of their activities has been discovered.

RABY, Edward John: *1892*–1919, Artist
Born in Worcester, where he attended art school and was trained in the famous porcelain works, Raby is believed to have come to Doulton soon after Charles Noke. There is some doubt about the date as examples of Worcester porcelain bearing his monogram have been reported with dates as late as 1896; these, however, could have been derived from engraved prints, incorporating the monogram, made before he left Worcester but tinted after that.

Raby was the son of a flower modeller at Worcester and grandson of Sam Raby, a

Bristol flower modeller. One of the pre-eminent ceramic flower painters of all time, he went straight to nature for his inspiration. His sketchbooks of water-colour paintings were treasure-stores of beauty and delicacy; his rich blendings of colours, including what was said to be a secret Raby mauve, and the exquisite grouping of his forms made his paintings live and glow. Examples of his work range from small miniatures to vases over five feet high depicting peonies, roses, delphiniums, wistaria and thistles, Italian gardens, birds and other subjects. A feature of many pieces is their unusually bright and sparkling surface, said to have been achieved by enamel firing at a higher than normal temperature. It was said of his work that it was 'a perfect rendering of flower forms' and that it showed 'a quality of broad expression and a depth of colour, especially in the reds, that is quite uncommon in floral painting'.

Raby painted early examples of the Titanian Wares and his monogram or name is found also on some *Art Nouveau* designs and landscapes. An unusual subject for him is a painting of Milton's house at Chalfont St Giles, Bucks.

After retirement he spent many happy hours in a boat on the River Severn at Worcester, making studies for pictures. He was a religious man and a member of the Salvation Army. He used to go quite often down the Staffordshire coal-pits near Burslem at four in the morning to talk to the miners about Christianity, before going on to the studio in Nile Street.

'RICHMOND': see ALLEN, H.

RIDGWAY, Richard: 1888–1930, Gilder
Ridgway studied at the Stoke School of Art and served an apprenticeship with Minton. He worked for several years with William Skinner after joining Doulton when he was twenty-one. He was entrusted with much of the high-class gilding for which Royal Doulton was renowned, including a tea-set for Queen Mary. In later years he became Jack Noke's lieutenant and was responsible for inspecting all gilded ware as it came from the kilns, to ensure the quality was kept up to standard.

RODEN, Jack: 1904–1955, Artist
One of Doulton's most experienced and versatile underglaze painters, Roden eventually was put in charge of one of the largest departments, producing underglaze decorated dinnerware. When the more complicated large figure models such as *Saint George, King Charles* and *Princess Badoura* were produced the whole of the painting of the prototypes was executed by his brush.

ROWLEY, C.: Artist
This signature is found on vases and dinnerware made in the early 1900s, painted with floral panels and also broad floral treatments.

SCOTT, Arthur: 1896–1907, Artist
Trained personally by Robert Allen during his apprenticeship at Burslem, and a gifted student of the Stoke Art School, Scott's *forte* was floral painting, especially of roses. He left to become a teacher at South Kensington School of Art. Between 1919 and 1948 he was Principal of the Watford School of Art.

SEEDON, R.: Artist
Signed pieces (vases and plates) painted with floral designs in raised gold and enamels, dating to the late 1880s and early 1890s, have been reported.

SIMPSON, William: 1893–1917, Gilder
William Simpson and Harry Milward worked together during their period with Doulton and both were associated especially with raised gilding on vases and dinner services for distinguished customers. Simpson left in 1917 to work in Trenton, USA.

SKINNER, William: 1886–1916, Gilder
Skinner recalled that as a boy apprentice at Davenports, while still only eleven, he saw children being 'belted' if they were late. He

came to Doulton from Davenports in his twenty-second year and became a gifted gilder – one of the team to whom the finest and most elaborate work was entrusted. He worked in close collaboration with Raby, Hancock, Dewsberry, Curnock, Tushingham and other artists.

SLATER, George:
There is a ewer in the Sydney Museum of Arts and Sciences, with incrusted gold decoration on a Doulton-Slater *chiné* background. This is described in the museum catalogue as 'a unique piece by George Slater, a brother of John Slater', but no other records have been discovered.

SLATER, John: 1867–1914, Art Director
See pages 17–37, 45–53, 58, 119

SLATER, Walter: *1885–1905*, Artist
Son of Albert Slater, a Minton floral artist, and nephew of John Slater, Walter was apprenticed to Doulton after an initial period at Minton. He became one of the foremost flower painters at Burslem and, among other subjects, was closely associated with the development of the Luscian and Lactolian Wares. Charles Noke said of his work that 'it was of the highest quality, and the beautiful arrangements and delicate tones of his floral groups showed the love he had for his subjects'.

Slater left in 1905 to become a designer at Wileman & Co., The Foley Pottery, Fenton – predecessor of Shelley Potteries Ltd., of which firm he became Art Director, remaining there until his death.

SWETTENHAM, Louis: 1886–1915, Etcher
Swettenham had his early training at Minton and was twenty-six when he came to Doulton. Noke recorded: 'Etching for some effects is far more pleasing than engraving, and many of his plates were full of fine details, yet bold, clear and sympathetic in execution. His clever work was always first-class.'

SUTTON, Fred: *1898*–1913, Artist
Sutton came to Doulton from Worcester where he had been a painter specializing in figure subjects. He was a talented portrait painter and miniaturist. His portraits after Romney, Reynolds, Hopper and other painters are outstanding examples of the miniaturist's art. His signature has been noted also on cameos and medallions.

TAYLOR, Harry: Artist
It is strange that no record has been found in the Doulton archives of the work of this artist who is described in the catalogue of the John Slater collection in Sydney as 'one of the geniuses of the Nile Street Works. Some of the richest productions came from his versatile pencil, though like many other artists his works were not always utilitarian or practical.'

There are several pieces in the collection bearing his signature, e.g. a dessert plate, moon shape, modelled in high relief, painted with fruit blossoms on moonlit ground with gold scroll clouds; another dessert plate, scalloped edge, painted with autumn leaves richly overlaid and outlined in gold, with red seeded border. A Sèvres shape dessert plate is described as having 'water lilies in Harry Taylor's unique and inimitable gold and colour style. A flowing river is shown in gold outline, flecked with turquoises and leaves. A unique specimen.' Another dessert plate is of shell shape; 'yellow water lilies in natural colours outlined in gold on enamel diaper background; border of shells and crustacea in raised gold on four shell panels . . . gold work by William Skinner.'

THEAKER, Harry J.: *1893–1900*, Artist
The son of George Theaker, teacher at the Burslem School of Art, Harry was a fine figure painter, especially of classical subjects. Examples of his signed work are rare. He left to take up teaching.

(George Theaker designed a large Doulton vase for the Chicago Exhibition, 1893.)

TIPPING, Edward: 1882–1906, Gilder

Tipping was a gilder of high repute who came to Doulton from Worcester. He was one of a fine team which did work of the highest class for the many large exhibitions held in the late 1800s and early 1900s.

TITTENSOR, Harry, R.I.: 1900–1925, Artist

Apprenticed to Doulton at the age of fourteen, Tittensor rapidly developed into a first-class artist. He studied at the Burslem School of Art and there also quickly showed great promise. An artist who could master any technique, his versatility and speed made him outstanding even among the many gifted artists at Nile Street.

From the most delicate figure painting to the most rugged type of Rembrandt Ware, he displayed his unique qualities. He played an important part in the development of early Royal Doulton figures, Holbein Ware and Titanian Ware.

He painted many vases, large and small, with subjects such as *Aphrodite, the laughter-loving Goddess, Circe, Omar Khayyam, Harvest Time, Dolce far Niente, The Wayfarer, Bringing Home the Stags, Ploughing, The Geisha.*

Tittensor left in 1925 to take up commercial art and to teach at the Burslem and other Schools of Art. He was a member of many art societies and adjudication committees. He painted in both oils and watercolours and much of his work was exhibited and sold by The Fine Art Society in London. His death at the relatively early age of fifty-six robbed North Staffordshire of one of its most talented artists.

TUSHINGHAM, S.: Artist

This artist was working at the Pinder, Bourne factory when Doulton took it over. His signature is found on vases decorated with figure subjects and plates with portrait heads. He taught in local art schools and is thought to have left Doulton about 1922. In later life he apparently became a successful society portrait painter.

VYSE, Charles: 1877–1927, Engraver

Vyse was apprenticed to Heath and Baddaley of Burslem, leading engravers in North Staffordshire. He studied also at the Burslem School of Art where he won many prizes.

He worked at the Cauldon factory for a short period before joining Pinder, Bourne in 1877. One of the old school, he was responsible for many of Doulton's finest engravings and his sympathetic interpretation of the designer's work was of the highest order.

WALKLATE, Fred: *1888–1927* (intermittently), Artist

Very little is recorded about this artist who came to Doulton as a boy but was continually moving camps. After many earlier changes, he appears to have left finally in 1927.

Judging from signed pieces which occasionally appear in the salerooms, Walklate was a talented artist, his special subjects being flowers and landscapes. He worked on Hyperion and Lactolian Wares, and there are dated examples in the 1890s and early 1900s of his raised paste decoration

WEBSTER, Eric A.: 1910–1962, Artist

Apprenticed to Doulton at the age of fifteen, Webster was trained under Herbert Betteley and painted landscapes, floral and bird subjects. He was one of the first artists to paint early Royal Doulton figures and in 1925 took charge of a special section for painting animal models. He was also responsible for training a group of young artists.

Webster painted *Monaveen* for the then Princess Elizabeth, now HM The Queen. He also painted the first Championship Dog model, *Lucky Star of Ware.*

WHITE, George: 1885–1912, Artist

A product of the Lambeth and South Kensington Art Schools, George White soon became Doulton's chief painter of figure subjects. It was said of him by Charles Noke that 'not only did he depict "the human

173

form divine" with beauty, grace and delicacy but he had the unusual power of fixing the personality of his subject. As a portrait painter "he caught the likeness" which is more than could be said of many who profess to paint portraits.'

White painted one of the *Diana* vases for the 1893 Chicago Exhibition, also a *Dante* vase in collaboration with Labarre. A large vase entitled *Titania* was made specially for Prince Ranjitsingh. He painted portraits on china of Sir Henry Doulton and his brother and partner, James; also of several of his Burslem colleagues. These are very rare indeed.

Among his many subjects on vases large and small, of many different shapes, were: *Zephyr wooing Flora, Cupid and Psyche, Spring Frolic, The Love Philtre, Youth and Pleasure at the Prow, Midsummer Night's Dream, Spirit of the Morning, The Vintage, Autumnal Frolic, The Dance, Homer, King of the Night* (owl), *Orpheus and Eurydice, Bacchanalian Festival, Feeding the Swans, Romeo and Juliet,* and *Sleeping Beauty.* Examples are found also of vases with paintings after D. G. Rossetti, Millais and Holman Hunt, also with Watteau-type figures.

WILSON, Samuel: 1880–1909, Artist
An artist of great ability, Wilson contributed a great deal to the artistic traditions of Doulton of Burslem. His delightful paintings, depicting wide expanses of landscape, hill and dale, with deer or cattle browsing in their natural environments, are superb examples of their genre. His studies of fish and game, his sporting and hunting scenes are of the highest rank. He painted one of the *Diana* vases for Chicago; also a dessert service in 1894 to the order of Princess Louise for her to present to Queen Victoria for the Diamond Jubilee. Many private collections and museums have examples of his work.

WILSON, Tom: Artist
Examples of plates painted with game, birds and fish, dated between 1911 and 1920, and signed by this artist, have been reported but no further information has been found.

WOOD, Edwin: 1898–1938, Artist
Wood began his training at the Crown Derby China Works and then spent some time at Wedgwoods in Etruria. He was twenty-nine when he joined Doulton. He specialized in painting small groups of flowers somewhat after the Chelsea style but his signature is found on a variety of floral designs and sometimes on fish and game plates. (See also E. Percy.)

WOODINGS, Norman: 1916–1967, Artist
Apprenticed at fourteen to Doulton and trained under Robert Allen, Woodings for several years painted flowers, fruit and birds and occasional seascapes. In 1923 he joined Harry Nixon, Charles Nixon and Harry Allen in the then still small figure-painting department and later became responsible to the Art Director for painting and creating the style of colouring for each new Royal Doulton figure.

WOODMAN, Stanley, ARCA, NRD: 1938–1957, Designer
As a young man, Woodman studied design for four years at the Royal College of Art where he won scholarships and diplomas. He later taught at the Macclesfield School of Art where he had once been a student. After a period as a commercial artist, he joined Minton as a designer and became, for some fifteen years, their Art Director. He brought with him to Doulton a wide knowledge of ceramic design and techniques, especially perhaps of period styles in tableware for which he had a great flair. Many of the patterns he designed for Doulton, both traditional and modern, proved great successes in several different markets.

174

WRIGHT, Albert: 1870–1906, Designer and Etcher

Wright was with Pinder, Bourne when Doulton took that firm over. Many early Doulton artists owed much to his tuition. George Holdcroft studied etching under him in the 1880s.

YEOMANS, Charles: 1883–1936 and 1939–1951, Artist

Yeomans, whose father had worked for Pinder, Bourne, was apprenticed to Doulton under Slater when he was thirteen. He worked in several decorating departments and became adept in both underglaze and on-glaze painting, especially of landscapes, fruit and flowers. He first retired in 1936 but came back on the outbreak of war (he was then sixty-nine) and stayed on, giving valuable service, for another twelve years.

Yeomans was one of four veteran artists presented to Princess Elizabeth, now HM The Queen, when she visited the Burslem Pottery in November 1949, the others being Percy Curnock, Sidney Hall and George Holdcroft. The total service of the four amounted to 253 years! Long service and distinguished family service records abound in the Royal Doulton annals. At the time of the Royal visit the Princess was told that eleven families between them accounted for 2271 years.

APPENDIX II

Trade Marks, Backstamps and Other Guides to Dating

The reference numbers for the Doulton Burslem marks have been prefixed by the letter 'B' to distinguish them from those also numbered 1 and up in the list of Lambeth marks given in *The Doulton Lambeth Wares*.

Between 1878 (when Henry and James Doulton acquired the major interest in the Pinder, Bourne factory in Nile Street, Burslem) and 1882 (when the name of the firm was changed to Doulton & Company, Burslem) existing Pinder, Bourne marks continued in use, such as the name in full: PINDER BOURNE & CO.; and the initials P.B. & CO. or P.B.

B.1 	Other devices occur incorporating the name of the pattern. Several of these were adopted after 1882 by Doulton and remained in use for about twenty years. The following are two typical examples found on the patterns *Rouen* and *Kew*. Various other pattern names will be found. (The coronet on B.1 was added c.1886.)
B.2	

B.3

This mark, adapted from a similar Lambeth mark incorporating a device of four interlocking D's was introduced c.1882 (not 1879 as was once thought). After 1891 the word ENGLAND was added underneath. The mark continued in use until 1902.

B.4

The coronet was probably added to the earlier mark c.1886 to mark the appointment of Henry Doulton as 'Potter to H.R.H. The Prince of Wales' (later King Edward VII). ENGLAND was added underneath after 1891. This mark continued in use until 1902. It appears to have been used instead of B.3 especially on bone china products and on the more expensive earthenwares. A simplified version showing only the coronet on a flat base and the word DOULTON was also used.

B.5

An adaptation of B.4 used on the Holbein Wares mainly between 1895 and 1903. Occasionally found also between 1903 and 1915 along with B.7 but the later Holbein Wares were not always specifically marked. The printed or impressed word HOLBEIN is also found on some examples of this particular ware.

B.6
DOULTON & SLATERS
PATENT

Several variants of this mark (with or without the words CHINE WARE) are found on *Chiné* and *Chiné-gilt* Wares together with marks B.3, B.4 or B.7 for relevant periods between 1885 and 1939.

B.7

Introduced in the latter part of 1901 to mark the grant of the Royal Warrant by King Edward VII together with the specific right to use the word ROYAL to designate Doulton products. This mark was in general use at Burslem between 1902 and 1922. On smaller wares, only the bottom half of this mark (i.e. omitting the lion and crown) is found. Although B.8 was generally used between 1923 and 1927 B.7 is occasionally found on wares made during these years.

B.8

This mark which differs from B.7 by the omission of the crown was in use between 1923 and 1927. The reason for the variation is not known. The bottom part only of this mark is found on smaller wares up to the present day and by itself is not a useful indication of date.

B.9

Differing from B.7 by the addition of the words MADE IN ENGLAND, this mark was commonly in use after 1932. However, the exact date of introduction is not known. Many dated examples between 1928 and 1931 exist, and occasional examples dated between 1923 and 1927 have also been noted although B.8 was more generally used in those years (with the words MADE IN ENGLAND at the *bottom* of the mark in place of the single word ENGLAND). This mark is still used on fine earthenware products such as Character Jugs.

B.10

This is the same as B.9 except for the addition of the words BONE CHINA. It was in use for all Fine Bone China products between 1928 and 1959 and is still used today on figures, animal models and other non-tableware Bone China products.

B.11

Introduced in 1959 to replace B.10 for use on Fine Bone China Tableware. Still in use today.

B.12

Introduced in 1960 for the then newly launched English Translucent China Tableware. In use until 1973–4 when the name was changed to Fine English China and the new trade-mark B.13 was introduced.

B.13

FINE CHINA

Introduced during the period 1973–4 for the newly named Fine English China and still in use today.

Various special marks will be found on figures, Character Jugs, animal models, Series Wares, Titanian, Morrisian, *Flambé*, Sung and Chang Wares, etc. These, by themselves, are not of much help for the purpose of dating but fortunately they are usually in addition to the standard trade-mark in use at the time, e.g. B.7 to B.10. A *Flambé* piece with B.7, for example, will have been made before 1927 and probably before 1922. Pattern numbers, Registration numbers and artists' signatures can also help to indicate the period of production. A few examples of special marks are given below:

B.14

A special mark often found in conjunction with B.7 on Morrisian Wares, 1901–1924.

B.15

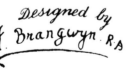

A special mark found on Titanian Wares, especially small items 1916–c.1933. On larger pieces B.7 to B.9 are found with the word TITANIAN printed underneath.

B.16

Designed by
F. Brangwyn R.A

This mark, either by itself, or together with B.9, appears on Brangwyn Wares made between 1930 and c.1942.

B.17

ROYAL DOULTON FLAMBÉ

This mark appears on early *Flambé* Wares especially small pieces. Several variations of the standard trade-mark are found with the word *FLAMBÉ* printed underneath.

B.18  Sung script mark used in conjunction with *Flambé* trademark c.1920–c.1940. Also in this example are C. J. Noke's signature and Fred Moore's monogram.

B.19  Chang script mark used in conjunction with standard trademark 1925–c.1940. Also in this example are C. J. Noke's signature and Harry Nixon's monogram.

B.20  Chinese Jade script mark uses in conjunction with standard trademark 1920–c.1940. Also in this example are C. J. Noke's signature and Harry Nixon's monogram.

B.21  Many Series Ware patterns also have their own special back-stamps. Two typical designs are illustrated:

Under the Greenwood Tree

B.22

The Gallant Fishers

B.23

There are numerous special marks referring to glaze effects, specific patterns and commissioned pieces.

This mark is found on a simulated Chinese glaze effect bowl. Also marked with impressed word DOULTON.

B.24

This mark is found on biscuit barrels produced for McVitie and Price.

B.25

This mark was used on a loving cup made for Courage & Co. to celebrate Queen Elizabeth II Coronation, 1953.

B.26

This mark is used on *Bunnykins* nursery ware.

B.27 Some marks found on Doulton figures:

A Highwayman.

Beggar's Opera.

H.N.527

Potted by. Doulton. & Co

B.28

Dainty May
RdNº 793086

B.29

"Market Day"
COPR.1946
DOULTON & CO. LIMITED
RdNº 846731
RdNº 23896
RdNº 122/46

B.30

Soiree
HN 2312
COPR 1966
DOULTON & CO LIMITED
Rd No 926655
Rd No 10721
Rd No 492/66
Rd No 49854

Some of the marks found on Doulton Character Jugs:

B.31

RdNº 787515

B.32

B.33

"Lord Nelson"
D 6336
(COPR 1951
DOULTON & CO LIMITED
RdNº 864844
RdNº 29157
RdNº 6405
RdNº 113/51

B.34

HENRY VIII
D 6642
© ROYAL DOULTON
TABLEWARE LTD 1975

Detailed descriptions of figures, Character Jugs and Toby Jugs, with dates of introduction and (where applicable) of withdrawal, will be found in the publications *Royal Doulton Figures* and *Royal Doulton Character and Toby Jugs*, both published by Royal Doulton Tableware Limited, Stoke-on-Trent, Staffs.

Pattern and code numbers

The following numbers indicate the approximate periods during which the patterns so marked were *first introduced*. It must be kept in mind that some patterns remained in production and usually kept the same number for many years. The trade-marks were, however, changed several times between the 1880s and now, and these can help to establish the period of production.

There was sometimes an overlap in numbering between the end of one year and the beginning of another, so that some of the dates of introduction given below may be a year out. Because of missing records it has not always been possible to give the numbers year by year.

Many pieces fortunately carry in addition to trade-mark and pattern number an impressed or printed indication of when they were made. The impressed date may give the year only, e.g. 1900; the month and year, e.g. 12 – 06 for December 1906; or, occasionally, the full date, e.g. 10 – 6 – 09 for 10th June 1909. The impressed dates are not always easy to see and may be overlooked if one is not careful.

The printed dates are usually indicated by Code Numbers beginning with 1 for 1928 and up to 30 for 1957. A simple way of calculating the date is to add the number in question to 1927. Thus 14 indicates the year 1941 and 23 indicates 1950. On some patterns, particularly on china, the date has been written in special ink.

A– NUMBERS (FINE EARTHENWARE)

1 –	6882	c.1881 – 1892
6883 –	7467	1893
7468 –	8084	1894
8085 –	8592	1895
8593 –	9144	1896
9145 –	9617	1897
9618 –	10000	1898

C– NUMBERS (CHINA)

1 –	1705	1884 – 1888
1706 –	4240	1889 – 1891
4241 –	4945	1892
4946 –	5930	1893
5931 –	7070	1894 – 1895
7071 –	8085	1896 – 1897
8086 –	9065	1898 – 1899
9066 –	10000	1900 – 1901

D– NUMBERS (FINE EARTHENWARE)

1 –	339	1899
340 –	769	1900
770 –	1137	1901
1138 –	1495	1902
1496 –	1869	1903
1870 –	2161	1904
2162 –	2442	1905
2443 –	2723	1906
2724 –	2914	1907
2915 –	3079	1908
3080 –	3229	1909
3230 –	3374	1910
3375 –	3519	1911
3520 –	3635	1912
3636 –	3714	1913
3715 –	3821	1914
3822 –	3939	1915
3940 –	4074	1916 – 1918
4075 –	4143	1919 – 1920
4144 –	4230	1921 – 1922
4231 –	4360	1923

H– NUMBERS (CHINA)

4361 – 4470	1924	
4471 – 4559	1925	
4560 – 4659	1926	
4660 – 4737	1927	
4738 – 4822	1928	
4823 – 4969	1929	
4970 – 5069	1930	
5070 – 5169	1931	
5170 – 5230	1932	
5231 – 5429	1933	
5430 – 5520	1934	
5521 – 5612	1935	
5613 – 5749	1936	
5750 – 5875	1937	
5876 – 6009	1938	
6010 – 6110	1939	
6111 – 6285	1940 – 1948	
6286 – 6390	1949 – 1952	
6391 – 6408	1953	
6409 – 6438	1954	
6439 – 6454	1955	
6455 – 6464	1956	
6465 – 6492	1957	
6493 – 6507	1958	
6508 – 6547	1959	
6548 – 6558	1960	
6559 – 6567	1961	
6568 – 6587	1962	
6588 – 6596	1963	
6597 – 6606	1964	

H– NUMBERS (CHINA)

1 – 359	1916	
360 – 709	1917	
710 – 759	1918	
760 – 906	1919	
907 – 1049	1920	
1050 – 1179	1921	
1180 – 1443	1922	
1444 – 1812	1923	
1813 – 2268	1924	
2269 – 2649	1925	
2650 – 3180	1926	
3181 – 3599	1927	
3600 – 3770	1928	
3771 – 3909	1929	
3910 – 4010	1930	
4011 – 4099	1931	
4100 – 4189	1932	
4190 – 4240	1933	
4241 – 4329	1934	
4330 – 4425	1935	
4426 – 4519	1936	
4520 – 4609	1937	
4610 – 4710	1938	
4711 – 4821	1939 – 1942	
4822 – 4849	1943 – 1946	
4850 – 4906	1947 – 1952	
4907 – 4930	1953	
4931 – 4935	1954	
4936 – 4941	1955	
4942 – 4950	1956 – 1957	
4951 – 4956	1958	
4957 – 4959	1959	
4960 – 4961	1960	
4962 – 4964	1961	
4965 – 4968	1962	
4969 – 4975	1963	

E– NUMBERS (CHINA)

1 – 940	1901 – 1902
941 – 1950	1903
1951 – 3040	1904
3041 – 4054	1905 – 1906
4055 – 6015	1907 – 1910
6016 – 7683	1911
7684 – 8277	1912
8278 – 8933	1913
8934 – 9527	1914
9528 – 10000	1915

V– NUMBERS (CHINA)

The V– numbers were almost always used after 1927 for patterns on an ivory-tinted china body. Before 1927 some H– numbers were also used for this body.

1	–	376	1927	–	1928
377	–	820	1929		
821	–	1000	1930		
1001	–	1190	1931		
1191	–	1320	1932		
1321	–	1490	1933		
1491	–	1619	1934		
1620	–	1710	1935		
1711	–	1800	1936		
1801	–	1909	1937		
1910	–	2069	1938		
2070	–	2170	1939		
2171	–	2250	1940		
2251	–	2295	1941	–	1942
2296	–	2365	1943	–	1948
2366	–	2384	1949	–	1950
2385	–	2400	1951	–	1954

RA– NUMBERS

Hand-painted, and largely hand-painted, wares designed and decorated by Robert Allen and artists in his studios, were often given RA– numbers, written by hand, in addition to the usual trade-mark and any other number. Unfortunately many of the record books giving details are missing, but despite this what is available is interesting as giving some idea when pieces so numbered were designed. These hand-painted wares were not reproduced in great quantities and some items bearing RA– numbers would probably never have been repeated.

The dates below are when the books containing the designs recorded in each were purchased. They give a fairly close idea of the dates of the designs. It will be noted that in the book numbered 26, the pattern numbers begin again with RA–1. By this time, of course, the lion and crown badge was in use so there need be no confusion. The RA– numbering was continued for several years after Allen had retired.

Books 1–6	RA	1 – 763	These books purchased before Nov. 1892 are missing.
7	RA 764 – 1323	Book purchased	18 Nov. 1892
8–9	RA 1324 – 2234	,, missing	
10	RA 2235 – 2763	,, purchased	10 Nov. 1897
11	RA 2764 – 3254	,, ,,	14 Jan. 1899
12	RA 3255 – 3705	,, ,,	17 Dec. 1900
13	RA 3706 – 5000	,, ,,	21 Apr. 1902
14	RA 5001 – 5404	,, ,,	27 Apr. 1903
15	RA 5405 – 5805	,, ,,	11 May 1904
16	RA 5806 – 6202	,, ,,	11 Oct. 1905
17	RA 6203 – 6602	,, ,,	1 Feb. 1907
18	RA 6603 – 7002	,, ,,	22 May 1908
19	RA 7003 – 7402	,, ,,	10 Dec. 1909
20	RA 7403 – 7806	,, ,,	28 Apr. 1911
21	RA 7807 – 8204	,, ,,	18 Nov. 1912
22	RA 8205 – 8606	Date missing. Probably early 1914.
23	RA 8607 – 9004	Missing. (First World War period.)
24	RA 9005 – 9402	Book purchased	9 Apr. 1919
25	RA 9403 – 9802	,, ,,	27 Aug. 1921
26	RA 9803 – 9999	,, ,,	Nov. 1923
	RA 1 – 199		
27	RA 200 – 509	c. Dec. 1925 – Nov. 1928
28	RA 510 – 709	c. Nov. 1928 – Dec. 1930
29	RA 710 – 906	c. Dec. 1930 – June 1932
30	RA 907 – 1112	c. June 1932 – Nov. 1933
31	RA 1113 – 1333	c. Nov. 1933 – June 1934
32	RA 1334 – 1538	c. June 1934 – Mar. 1937
33	RA 1539 – 1741	c. Mar. 1937 – ? 1943
34	RA 1742 – 1774	During the Second World War

The RA– numbers were discontinued about 1943 or 1944 and not resumed.

187

Index

Art directors, designers and artists are already listed in alphabetical order in Appendix I, as are advertising wares in Chapter XIII. Commemorative wares, loving cups and other special editions are listed in chronological order in Chapter XIII.